MAX WEBER IN A THEOLOGICAL PERSPECTIVE

STUDIES IN PHILOSOPHICAL THEOLOGY, 21

1   H. de Vries, *Theologie in Pianissimo & zwischen Rationalität und Dekonstruktion*, Kampen, 1989
2   S. Breton, *La pensée du rien*, Kampen, 1992
3   Ch. Schwöbel, *God: Action and Revelation*, Kampen, 1992
4   V. Brümmer (ed.), *Interpreting the Universe as Creation*, Kampen, 1991
5   L.J. van den Brom, *Divine Presence in the World*, Kampen, 1993
6   M. Sarot, *God, Possibility and Corporeality*, Kampen, 1992
7   G. van den Brink, *Almighty God*, Kampen, 1993
8   P.-C. Lai, *Towards a Trinitarian Theology of Religions: A study of Paul Tillich's Thought*, Kampen, 1994
9   L. Velecky, *Aquinas' Five Arguments in the* Summa Theologiae *Ia 2, 3*, Kampen, 1994
10 W. Dupré, *Patterns in Meaning, Reflections on meaning and truth in cultural reality, religious traditions, and dialogical encounters*, Kampen, 1994
11 P.T. Erne, *Lebenskunst. Aneignung ästhetischer Erfahrung*, Kampen, 1994
12 U. Perone, *Trotzidem Subjekt*, Leuven, 1998
13 H.J. Adriaanse, *Vom Christentum aus: Aufsätze und Vorträge zur Religionsphilosophie*, Kampen, 1995
14 D.A. Pailin, *Probing the Foudations: A Study in Theistic Reconstruction*, Kampen, 1994
15 M. Potepa, *Schleiermachers hermeneutichse Dialektik*, Kampen, 1996
16 E. Herrmann, *Scientific Theory and Religious Belief, An Essay on the Rationality of Views of Life*, Kampen, 1995
17 V. Brümmer & M. Sarot, *Happiness, Well-Being and the Meaning of Life, a Dialogue of Social Science and Religion*, Kampen, 1996
18 T.L. Hettema, *Reading for Good. Narrative Theology and Ethics in the Joseph Story from the Perspective of Ricœur's Hermeneutics*, Kampen, 1996
19 H. Düringer, *Universale Vernunft und partikularer Glaube. Eine theologische Auswertung des Werkes von Jürgen Habermas*, Leuven, 1999
20 E. Dekker, *Middle Knowledge*, Leuven, 2000
21 T. Ekstrand, *Max Weber in a Theological Perspective*, 2000

MAX WEBER IN A
THEOLOGICAL PERSPECTIVE

THOMAS EKSTRAND

PEETERS
LEUVEN – PARIS – STERLING, VIRGINIA
2000

Library of Congress Cataloging-in-Publication Data

Ekstrand, Thomas
  Max Weber in a theological perspective / Thomas Ekstrand.
    p. cm -- (Studies in philosophical theology; 21)
  Includes bibliographical references.
  ISBN 9042909447 (alk. paper)
    1. Weber, Max, 1864-1920. 2. Philosophical theology. 3. Religion and sociology.   I.
Title. II. Series.

BT40 E53 2000
230'.092--dc21
                                                                        00-063714

© 2000 – Peeters – Bondgenotenlaan 153 – 3000 Leuven – Belgium.

ISBN 90-429-0944-7
D. 2000/0602/149

Ich erlaube mir gewisse Leser darauf aufmerksam zu machen, daß ich auch Geheimnisse im religiösen Leben anerkenne, daß ich aber eben darüber, was Geheimniß ist und bleibt, schweige.

ALBRECHT RITSCHL

CONTENTS

ABBREVIATIONS

AJ   Weber, Max: *Ancient Judaism.* London: Allen & Unwin, 1952.

FMW   *From Max Weber. Essays in Sociology* (2nd ed.), eds. Gerth, Hans H. & Mills, C. Wright. London: Routledge, 1991.

GARS   Weber, Max: *Gesammelte Aufsätze zur Religionssoziologie.* Tübingen: J.C.B. Mohr (Paul Siebeck),1920/21/22.

GAW   Weber, Max: *Gesammelte Aufsätze zur Wissenschaftslehre* (7. Aufl). Tübingen, J.C.B. Mohr (Paul Siebeck), 1988.

GPS   Weber, Max: *Gesammelte politische Schriften.* München: Drei Masken Verlag, 1921.

MSS   Weber, Max: *The Methodology of The Social Sciences*, eds. Shils, Edward A. & Finch, Henry A. New York: The Free Press, 1949.

MWG   *Max Weber Gesamtausgabe.* Tübingen: J.C.B. Mohr (Paul Siebeck), 1984 (continuing).

PW   Weber, Max: *Political Writings*, eds. Lassman, Peter & Speirs, Ronald. Cambridge, Cambridge University Press, 1994.

R&K   Weber, Max: *Roscher and Knies: The Logical Problems of Historical Economics.* New York: The Free Press, 1975.

ACKNOWLEDGEMENTS

As I have experienced with this book, it can be very lonely working on a doctoral dissertation. But at the same time I would have been unable to complete this investigation if I had not been surrounded by colleagues, friends and family who in various ways have given me both professional and personal help and support. Of course, I alone bear the responsibility for deficiencies which remain.

My supervisor, professor Anders Jeffner, has been a source of great inspiration and encouragement. He unites in his person characteristics which, in my experience, seldom are found together in academic life: generosity, brilliance, humility and patience. Without his criticisms and suggestions I would have given up a long time ago. Docent Cristina Grenholm and professor Carl Reinhold Bråkenhielm have both commented upon various versions of the text and contributed with valuable criticisms. Cristina has also been a source of great personal support. Professor Anders Bäckström kindly commented upon a very early version of chapter six, and Dr. Ola Agevall, Dr. Lars Andersson and Docent Björn Skogar have commented upon an earlier version of the whole manuscript. Professor Pål Repstad, Oslo, functioned as faculty opponent when I presented this thesis before the Faculty of Theology in Uppsala. His comments have been very valuable.

Professor Eberhard Herrmann has been of great importance in two ways. His academic production has provided me with philosophical tools necessary for my constructive interpretation of Weber's texts. He has also read and commented upon several drafts of the manuscript and encouraged me to develop my thinking on Weber's relevance for theology, even if we prefer to use the term 'theology' in different ways.

My colleagues and friends at the Theology Department of Uppsala University have provided me with an academic milieu in which we have shared the joy and trouble of academic life. Teol. lic. Mattias Martinson has been a major discussion partner, and Dr. Per Sundman and fil. mag. Maria Essunger have read and commented upon various parts of the manuscript. Fil. kand. Maria Södling commented upon an earlier version of chapter two. I also want to express my gratitude to Dr. Craig Graham McKay, who has done his best to improve my English, and to my editor at Peeters Publishers, Liesbeth Verloove. Many others, whose names would take too much space to list, have also been of great help to me.

My family has contributed to this book in more ways than I am able to express. My wife, Britt-Karin, cannot be properly thanked in words. Her love and her practical support has been a source of strength and happiness. My parents-in-law, Anna-Britta and Ingemar, have generously opened their home for me whenever I have been in need of a refuge, and my nephew Christopher has been a good playmate when I have needed distraction.

But perhaps the most important person of all has been my friend the Rev. Mikael Alm. Our long discussions about the rationality of Christian theology and about the tribulations of human existence have encouraged me in many ways. And, most important of all, it was Mikael who made me forego my plans to study political science and made me venture upon theology. Therefore this book is dedicated to him.

Uppsala, in June 2000

Thomas Ekstrand

1. INTRODUCTION

When I was about ten years old, I was the catalyst for a heated argument between my father and my maternal grandfather. I had just told my grandfather about what we had been doing in school lately, namely learning about Darwin and his theory of evolution. My grandfather, who was a conservative-minded Pentecostal Christian, was infuriated and tried to persuade me that what I had just learnt in school was nothing but an expression of secular disbelief in the infallible Word of God, and nothing to take seriously.

Later on, I told my father, who was a typical Western intellectual agnostic, about the conversation. My father was infuriated too; not with my schoolteacher, but with my grandfather, who, in my father's eyes, had tried to talk me into a superstitious Christian belief and remove me from the light of Enlightenment. My father claimed that it was irrational to believe in anything which could not be made probable on conventional scientific grounds, and my grandfather accused my father of reductionism and disbelief. Their dispute was never settled.

However, it made a deep impact on me. Both my grandfather and my father were important figures in my life, and I have picked up many things from both. My grandfather taught me to love the stories of the Bible, he took me to church and he made me understand that religious faith can be an important resource in human life. My father brought me up in the tradition of Enlightenment reason, taught me to distrust all claims to authority, and imputed in me a strong sense of intellectual honesty. Kant's famous dictum *Sapere aude!*, is perhaps the most important inheritance my father left me.

I am a child of both Western Enlightenment culture and Christian religious tradition. As a person with such dual citizenship, I have to come to grips with both Christianity and secular reason, and try to integrate them into a coherent whole.[1] By the term *integration* I want to express a basic principle of mine. I am unable to live with a split mind. My religious life, political convictions and theoretical beliefs must not contradict each other. There is something strange, I believe, with people

---

[1] cf. Milbank, John: *Theology and Social Theory,* p. 380. Note that in the footnotes the references are in abbreviated form. Full information is given in the bibliography.

who make religious truth-claims which conflict with well-established scientific knowledge, especially since almost no one can live in modern society without relying on science. This basic principle does not, however, imply that I automatically presuppose that Christian faith and theology have to contain truth-claims on the same logical level as scientific statements. The demand for integration in this context should rather be understood as the moral demand that one should not tolerate contradictions among one's beliefs or values, but strive towards coherence in one's system of beliefs and among one's ideals.[2]

But just as Christianity is a very many-faceted phenomenon, so is modern scholarship. Our intellectual situation is characterised by plurality. There are different views on science and its methods, and as a result, different interpretations of life and world. This must be recognised even by someone, like myself, who does not want to fall prey to a total perspectivism and relativism when it comes to the understanding of science. Therefore any effort to integrate Christian faith with modern science must choose which kind of scientific effort it wants to converse with.

In my opinion, Western intellectual culture has not abandoned its classics, at least not in the humanities and social sciences. Machiavelli is not dead to political scientists, nor Kant and Marx to philosophers and sociologists. Within the humanities, there is an ongoing conversation with the founders of Western thought in a way that would be inconceivable within the natural sciences: Ptolemaeus is not of any particular interest to astronomers, for example.[3] Max Weber, as one of the classical theoreticians of modern rationalised culture, belongs to the living heritage of Western culture and scholarship. The bibliography in almost any book in sociology or religious studies contains at least some reference to his works. Many scholars take great pains to understand his thinking and use it in their own works, others mention him more as an act of courtesy. But almost nobody within the humanities and social sciences can avoid to get into contact with Max Weber.

---

[2] On the principle of integration, see Jeffner, Anders: *Kriterien christlicher Glaubenslehre*, pp. 139-143. However, Jeffner is more ready than I am to view integration as taking place between religious and scientific truth-claims. Eberhard Herrmann's non-integrative approach to the relation between science and religion in regard to statements – Herrmann proposes a division of labour between science and views of life, where science provides us with knowledge and our views of life provide us with values – can thus be contained within my understanding of integration. See Herrmann, Eberhard: "A Pragmatic Approach to Religion and Science".

[3] This argument is based on a comment in David Martin's book *Reflections on Sociology and Theology*, p. 22.

Challenged by the claim by many experts on Weber's thinking that Weber's philosophical and sociological thought excludes the possibility of living fully in modernity as a Christian,[4] I have examined his texts regarding the possibility of formulating an integrated Christian theological position in modernity as understood by him. It is important to remember, however, that I choose Weber as *one* viable option among many, since I do not believe that there is only one legitimate scholarly standpoint with which Christian faith should be integrated. Rather, I conceive of the integrative effort as a never-ending conversation, in which my investigation is just a small sample.

One central tenet in Weber's thought is his theory about the rationalisation process. According to this theory, human culture has undergone a development towards an instrumentalisation of reason and a systematisation of thought patterns, which in modernity has lead to a scientific culture directed at means-end calculation and fragmentation. This puts traditional Christianity in jeopardy, since many of its dogmas are in conflict with secular reason, its morality hostile to means-end rationality and its conception of the world makes it hard for it to positively embrace fragmentation and pluralism. Weber puts us, it might seem, in front of an either-or: either we have to live in modernity with its secular reason, or we have to make a *sacrificium intellectus* and live in an *altera civitas*, the church.[5] For someone like myself, who finds her- or himself standing with one foot in the Enlightenment tradition and one foot in the Christian tradition, this seems to be problematic.

Weber's analysis of the modern condition is still highly relevant, even if it is not without its problems. Just a quick glance at the secondary literature shows that his thinking is still regarded as central when we try to come to grips with our own cultural situation.[6] The fact that Weber is still seen as an acute analyst of modernity has inspired me to find a third way between the two options that Weber seems to offer in regard to

---

[4] e.g. Turner, Bryan: *Max Weber*, p. 241; Schluchter, Wolfgang: *Paradoxes of Modernity*, p. 77 and Tyrell, Hartmann: "'Das Religiöse' in Max Webers Religionssoziologie", p. 223.

[5] Weber, Max: "Wissenschaft als Beruf", *MWG I/17*, pp. 108-110.

[6] See e.g. Owen, David: *Maturity and Modernity;* Turner, Bryan: *Max Weber,* p. vii: "To understand modernity is to understand Weber". Weber's scientific production is still used as starting point for many specialised analyses of modern problems. In political science, for example, his concept of bureaucracy is still highly relevant. See Page, Edward: *Political Authority and Bureaucratic Power*, p. 3. Many more examples of Weber's importance in the contemporary scholarly discussions could be given. Some of them will appear later in this book.

Christian faith and modernity. In my opinion, Weber's position is much more complicated than the standard interpretation seems to imply and in this book I shall argue for another interpretation of his texts.

As I see it, the question about the place of religion and theology in modernity as Weber understands it depends on what *kind of* Christian theology is taken into account. Therefore I want to investigate what would be required of a Christian theology if it should be able to be integrated with Weber's thought in such a way that it is possible both to live fully in modern, rationalised culture, as Weber understands it, and still be a Christian. This means that I have a *revisionary* purpose.[7] I do not claim to describe what Christians believe, and as a scholar, I do not accept any religious authorities as criteria in my work. Rather, I intend to show in what way Christian theology has to be revised *if* it should be viable in modern culture as interpreted by Weber. Whether or not it is desirable to strive towards such an integration is a matter of faith.

Purpose and Method

This investigation aims at 1) providing an interpretation of Max Weber's texts in regard to the function of views of life in modern society and 2) suggesting *one* possible way of revising Christian theology so that it becomes possible to integrate with Weber's view on views of life, science and modernity.

Weber cannot be interpreted otherwise than as pointing to a clear divide between modernity and Christian faith. When it comes to the possibility of overcoming the divide, however, he can be read in different ways, which are equally reasonable. Which one that is chosen is of course dependent on the interpretative aims of the interpreter. In this investigation, I focus on such interpretations that make his texts maximally relevant for my integrative purpose. I shall show that there are ideas in Weber's thought which make it possible to accept certain forms of revisionary theologies without opting out of the cultural conditions of modernity.

Inspired by a terminology developed by Cristina Grenholm, I shall call my way of interpreting Weber *constructive*. I do not aim at historically explaining Weber's texts, but at relating his thinking to and making it relevant for Christian theological reflection.[8] By labelling my

---

[7] See Sutherland, Stewart: *God, Jesus and Belief,* p. 6.
[8] Grenholm, Cristina: *Romans Interpreted,* pp. 72-74. See also Grenholm, Cristina: *The Old Testament, Christianity and Pluralism,* pp. 5-7.

interpretation 'constructive' I want to underline that the main aim of this investigation is to choose among the possible interpretations the one that is most fruitful from a contemporary theological perspective.

My interpretation of Weber thus has certain distinctive features. First, it is oriented towards the contemporary situation rather than towards history. This is not an investigation within the academic field of the history of ideas. Rather it tries to show Weber's relevance for modern theology. This also accounts for the systematising tendency in my treatment of Weber. There is a never ending debate about the thematic unity of Weber's texts, some arguing that the theme of rationalisation is the unitive element in the Weberian corpus,[9] and others questioning this.[10] My own position is that there are some questions that permeate Weber's texts from different epochs, and they have to do with the fate of humankind in rationalised culture. Already at his inaugural lecture in Freiburg 1895 Weber stated that it is important to breed "those characteristics which we think of as constituting the human greatness and nobility of our nature" in people.[11] This theme of the true human personality and its future fate in face of rationalisation recurs in Weber's texts several times.[12]

Basically, I agree with Dirk Käsler's view that it is most fruitful to regard Weber as an essayist, and not as a writer of monographs. Käsler argues that Weber presents his ideas as hypothetical and tentative attempts to understand the relationship between the individual and the social reality in which the individual lives. If, for example, the *Wirtschaft und Gesellschaft* is regarded as a collection of essays trying to come to grips with the fate of the individual in modernity, much of the discussion on the unity or fragmentation of Weber's *œuvre* becomes less important.[13] But there is enough unity, historically speaking, for a more constructive approach to the totality of the Weberian corpus to be justified. However, I recognise that the degree of systematisation of

[9] e.g. Bendix, Reinhard: *Max Weber: An Intellectual Portrait,* p. 9; Brubaker, Rogers: *The Limits of Rationality,* p. 1 and Turner, Bryan: *Max Weber,* p. 115.

[10] e.g. Tenbruck, Friedrich: "The Problem of Thematic Unity in the Works of Max Weber". Wilhelm Hennis has suggested that Weber's theme – permeating his entire production – is the question of the relation between personality and life order. Se e.g. his article "Personality and Life Orders", p. 71.

[11] PW p. 15. Weber, Max: "Der Nationalstaat und die Volkswirtschaftspolitik" *MWG I/4,* p. 559: *"diejenige Eigenschaften...mit welchen wir die Empfindung verbinden, daß sie menschliche Größe und den Adel unsrer Natur ausmachen".*

[12] e.g. in Weber Max: "Roscher und Knies", *GAW,* p. 132; "Die protestantische Ethik", *GARS I,* pp. 203-204; "Parlament und Regierung", *MWG I/15,* pp. 465-466.

[13] Käsler, Dirk: *Max Weber: An Introduction to His Life and Work,* p. 215.

Weber's texts in my investigation is a bit higher than what a strictly historical method would have allowed for. This is justified in the light of my interpretative purpose to make Weber relevant for modern theology.

Second, in order to achieve this relevance, I shall engage in a variant of what the Swedish philosopher Anders Wedberg has called the *extension of theories* (*teoriutbyggnad*).[14] A philosophical investigation of a theory can show that the theory has implications which its author might not have conceived of. In my view, this is the case with Weber's philosophy of values. If Weber's texts are read from the theoretical perspective of Anders Jeffner's notion *view of life*, some interesting conclusions for modern theology can be drawn, which of course Weber himself could not conceive of, but which are perfectly reasonable given a responsible constructive interpretation.[15]

Such an interpretation is not – and this deserves to be mentioned – arbitrary. Weber's texts are the basis of my interpretation. However, the full consequences of Weber's reasoning have not been – and of course could not have been – spelled out in his writings. When I try to extend his thinking, I purport to show what the full consequences of his thinking are, given that it is interpreted in the light of more recent philosophical and theological thought. Without claiming any other similarities, I would say that I follow the path of Wolfgang Schluchter to the extent that I attend to "matters left unfinished by Weber".[16]

In a few cases, where Weber's thinking seems impossible to accept for any Christian theology, I shall suggest some very modest improvements to his approach. This procedure, however, is only followed with great hesitation and restriction, since my purpose is not to criticise Weber from a Christian perspective, but Christian theology from Weber's point of view. Basically, my argument has the following structure: if you have found Max Weber's interpretation of modern culture convincing, and if you in addition to that are a Christian who wants to integrate your faith with this Weberian interpretation of modernity, you

---

[14] Wedberg, Anders: *Filosofins historia. Antiken och medeltiden,* p. 203.

[15] The concept 'view of life' will be clarified in chapter three. The definition, however, runs as follows: "A view of life is the theoretical and evaluative assumptions which constitute or have central impact on an encompassing view of humanity and the world and that constitute a central system of values and expresses a basic mood." See Jeffner, Anders: "Att studera livsåskådningar", p. 13: *"En livsåskådning är de teoretiska och värderingsmässiga antaganden som utgör eller har avgörande betydelse för en övergripande bild av människan och världen och som bildar ett centralt värderingssystem och som ger uttryck åt en grundhållning."*

[16] Schluchter, Wolfgang: *Paradoxes of Modernity,* p. 2.

might plausibly think of your faith in the revised way which I propose. If you, on the contrary, hold that Weber is wrong in major respects, you cannot be rationally obliged to accept the conclusions of this investigation.

Third, I shall sometimes make what I call *unguarded choices* of interpretation. The meaning of this concept can be clarified with an analogy which I have adopted from Eberhard Herrmann's article *A Pragmatic Approach to Religion and Science*. Herrmann uses the analogy in a different context than I, though.[17] Imagine a donkey in front of two equally desirable stacks of hay. As far as he can see, there is no difference in the inherent quality of the hay in the two stacks. However, he cannot eat from both stacks at the same time. He has to choose one of them, lest he wants to starve to death in front of the hay. When he chooses, he makes a rationally unguarded choice. Both alternatives are equally plausible in regard to the quality of the hay. Perhaps he chooses on the basis of chance (since he is an extraordinary donkey, he might throw a dice to decide from which stack he should eat) or on some aesthetic criteria.

When reflecting on theological matters, or interpreting texts, we are often put in situations where we do not have compelling reasons to choose just one interpretation and exclude others. But if we wish to get anywhere in our reflection, we have to choose one possible option from which we then can proceed. Sometimes it is possible to exclude some alternatives by rational argument, and often we can give good, albeit not compelling, reasons for our choice. When I on certain points in this investigation make such choices, it is because I find myself in a similar position as the donkey in front of the two stacks of hay. I have to get on with my reflection, but I cannot find any absolutely compelling reasons for choosing one way rather than another. On such points, I shall try to be as clear as possible about the grounds of my choice, but since they are not compelling, it might happen that the reader makes a choice different from mine.

Two Elusive Concepts

In his little book *What is Theology?*, Maurice Wiles concludes that the subject-matter of Christian theology is elusive, since it is about God, and God is not really something which it is easy to pin down as an

---

[17] Herrmann, Eberhard: "A Pragmatic Approach to Religion and Science", p. 127.

object of study.[18] But not only the subject-matter of theology is elusive; even the concept of theology is hard to define, and how one defines it is central to how it is regarded within the academic community. In this investigation I use 'theology' in two distinct senses, and I only ascribe scientific status in a strict sense to the second of them.[19]

First, 'theology' can mean the intellectual systematisation of religious belief, as done within religious communities. On this definition, Christian theology is the systematisation of Christian belief done by Christians. This does not imply that there is only one *substantive* Christian theology. Within Christianity, both historically and today, there are many rival versions of Christian theology. For example, some conflicts are about to what extent Christian theology should be integrated with scientific knowledge.

Second, I use 'theology' as a term denoting the kind of philosophical investigations of Christian theology that has developed at the University of Uppsala during the last 20 years, under the name *Studies in Faiths and Ideologies*. Basically this study has two features. On the one hand it tries to analyse and systematise different Christian theologies, both historical and contemporary, so as to make them as clear and understandable as possible. But this descriptive and analytic task is often accompanied by a more normative effort, which tries to investigate the intellectual problems Christian theology has to confront if it is to be reasonable in the modern intellectual context. Scholars often regard the intrusion of norms as something that should be avoided at all costs in their writings. There is something good in this. If we do not uphold the idea that scholarly work can be intersubjectively valid, it would be quite pointless to invest so much resources in science. If normative elements are to be acceptable, it has to be in the form of such judgements which are open to public criticism. Any theological activity purporting to the status of science thus has to stay absolutely clear of any reference to religious authority in its argument.

Academic, scientific theology, as I understand it, is thus primarily a critical discipline which tries to point out weaknesses in Christian teachings. But just as a physician does not only make a diagnosis but also proposes a cure, academic theology can suggest, albeit in a very tentative and humble way, improvements in Christian theology which would

---

[18] Wiles, Maurice: *What is Theology?*, p. 2.
[19] In this I am inspired by – albeit not a strict follower of – Ragnar Holte's little book *Människa, livstolkning, gudstro*, pp. 38-41.

make it more acceptable in the light of reason. That such an amelioration is religiously plausible is of course nothing that can be decided scientifically. This book is written for those who, like myself, *believe* that it is. My investigation tries, *in that respect*, to be a service to religion. But, and this has to be stressed, its *religious* value can only be decided on religious grounds. Intellectually, however, it should be open to criticism from everyone. I agree with the Danish theologian Jens Glebe-Møller that theology, if it should be able to claim scientific status, must be conceived as *organised scepticism*. Academic theology can never tell what the characteristics of true Christianity are. Its normative task must be limited to the constructive criticism of Christian theology, based on the methods and values accepted within the scientific community.[20] From this perspective, academic theology programatically stands in the service of secular society.

Another elusive notion in this book is the concept of *science*. In my mother tongue, as well as in Weber's German, the closest equivalent (Swedish: *vetenskap*; German: *Wissenschaft*) contains both the humanities and the natural sciences. In the literature on Weber, *Wissenschaft* is translated in various ways. Either one tries to specify exactly what kind of intellectual activity he has in mind in each case, and translates with the closest English equivalent, or one stipulates a definition of *science* so that it covers the same areas as the German *Wissenschaft*. Since it is often difficult to decide the precise extension of Weber's use of *Wissenschaft* in each context, unless when he explicitly says otherwise, I shall follow the second option. The word 'science' should, thus, be understood as including both the natural sciences, the humanities and the social sciences. 'Natural science' will be the concept used for what often is only called 'science' in English.

Material

Many of Weber's texts have become available in a critical edition called the *Max Weber Gesamtausgabe (MWG)*. I have referred to this edition whenever it has been possible. However, since the edition is not yet completed, I often have had to use older editions.

Weber's famous study *Die protestantische Ethik und der Geist des Kapitalismus* exists in different versions. The original version was

---

[20] Glebe-Møller, Jens: *Den teologiske ellipse,* pp. 135-141.

published in the *Archiv für Sozialwissenschaft und Sozialpolitik* in two
parts 1904-1905, while the second version, which Weber had revised,
was published after Weber's death in the first volume of his *Gesammelte Aufsätze zur Religionssoziologie* (*GARS*). I have used this later
version because it is the one which is most used in the secondary literature, and also it is this version which was translated into English by
Talcott Parsons as far back as in 1930.[21] Since my purpose is constructive, I do not pay much attention to the historical problems that arise in
the analyses of the different versions of Weber's texts, especially since
the differences are not of a kind that seems to have any bearing upon
the aspects of Weber's thinking that are relevant for my investigation.
For the same reasons, I refer to the edition of *Das Antike Judentum* in
the *GARS*, and not to the articles in *Archiv*.

Weber's production is enormous, and I have not made any effort to
cover it all.[22] I have only used the letters published in the *MWG* and in
Jugendbriefe on a few occasions, where they throw light on important
aspects of Weber's thinking. On one occasion I refer to a letter which is
only reprinted in the first edition of Weber's *Gesammelte politische
Schriften* (*GPS*). Weber's central methodological writings, which are the
basic source for his philosophy of values, are available in the *Gesammelte Aufsätze zur Wissenschaftslehre* (*GAW*), and have yet not been
published in the *MWG*. Originally, *Roscher und Knies* was published
during the period 1903-1906 as three separate articles in Schmoller's
*Jahrbuch für Gesetzgebung, Verwaltung und Volkswirtschaft im
Deutschen Reich* and collected and published together in the *GAW* by
Weber's wife Marianne after his death. *Die 'Objektivität' sozialwissenschaftlicher und sozialpolitischer Erkenntnis* was originally published in the *Archiv* in 1904, *Kritische Studien auf dem Gebiet der kulturwissenschaftlichen Logik* was published in *Archiv* in 1906, *Rudolf
Stammler's Überwindung der materialistischen Geschichtsauffassung*
was originally published in *Archiv* in 1907, and *Der Sinn der 'Wertfreiheit' der soziologischen und ökonomischen Wissenschaften* was originally published in *Logos* in 1917.[23] The essay on objectivity has a central place in my investigation, since it is written as a positive statement
of Weber's position on methodological and philosophical questions and

---

[21] Parsons's translation is easily available in reprint with an introduction by Anthony
Giddens. See Weber, Max: *The Protestant Ethic and the Spirit of Capitalism*.
[22] A good overview both of original works, collections and English translations is provided in Käsler, *op.cit.*, pp. 235-274.
[23] The bibliographical information is based on Käsler, *op.cit.*

not as polemics against other positions, as for example the Roscher and Knies-essays.

Two texts which are contained in Weber's great project *Die Wirtschaftsethik der Weltreligionen*, namely the *Einleitung* and the *Zwischenbetrachtung*, are published in *MWG I/19*, which has the title *Die Wirtschaftsethik der Weltreligionen Konfuzianismus und Taoismus*. In referring to them, and also to other writings published in the *MWG*, I do not use the title of the actual volume of *MWG*, since Weber's writings are most widely known and referred to under their original names.

Besides Weber's work on the Protestant ethic, the *Wirtschaft und Gesellschaft* is perhaps the most famous of his writings, and by many regarded as his *magnum opus*, still widely read, and one of the real successes of the Mohr/Siebeck publishing house.[24] *Wirtschaft und Gesellschaft* too was published posthumously. Originally it was intended to be part of a series with the title *Grundriß der Sozialökonomik*, which Weber edited. *Wirtschaft und Gesellschaft* consists, as hitherto published, of two parts, the *Soziologische Kategorienlehre* and *Die Wirtschaft und die gesellschaftlichen Ordnungen und Mächte*. The second part is the older of the two, written within the period 1910-1914. The first part was written in 1918-1919.[25] I do not, however, take sides in the conflict about whether Weber intended *Wirtschaft und Gesellschaft* to have the form in which it has appeared, or if he had other intentions.[26] The text in *Wirtschaft und Gesellschaft* is the one available, and for my constructive interpretative effort, I do not think it matters very much if the text ought to be arranged in a somewhat different way, since I engage in more of a synchronic than a diachronic reading of Weber.

Another matter which cannot be neglected is the relationship between Weber's scientific texts and his political writings. In this investigation, I make use of both kinds of material without always distinguishing between them. In my opinion this procedure is justified for the following reasons. 1) According to Weber's own methodological standpoint, the values of the scholar are crucial in the process of forming the research object. Even if facts and values are logically distinct, this implies that an analysis of Weber's scientific production has to acknowledge the importance of his

[24] Swedberg, Richard: *Max Weber's Handbook in Economics: Grundriss der Sozialökonomik*, p. 13.
[25] A brief overview of how *Wirtschaft und Gesellschaft* came into being can be found in Käsler, *op.cit.*, pp. 142-143.
[26] See e.g. Schluchter, Wolfgang: *Rationalism, Religion and Domination*, pp. 433-463, esp. pp. 461-463.

political writings, and *vice versa*. 2) There is, because of the fact that Weber's political standpoints to a large extent set the agenda for his scholarly work, a basic substantive continuity between the more scholarly and the more political writings. Furthermore, his political texts are full of analyses of the most profound scholarly character.[27] Weber's political views cannot be separated from his interpretation of the cultural condition of modernity, for example. On the one hand, his view on politics was conditioned by his scholarly perception of the cultural situation, but, on the other hand, his preoccupation with the fate of humanity in modernity was driven by his high evaluation of the autonomous personality.

I refer to Weber's German text. However, for the sake of readability, quotations in the text are in English, but given in the original German in the footnote. Whenever it is possible, I quote from available translations of Weber's texts. In certain cases, though, it has been necessary to provide own translations, since the published translation is misleading. The same principle is followed in regard to most quotes from other German texts. In a few cases, when the quote is of minor importance, I have only quoted the English translation. In referring to secondary literature, I have chosen English translations whenever they have been available to me. When no reference is given, the translation is my own. The reason for this procedure is simply that this investigation is oriented towards the English-speaking world, and it seems inconvenient to refer English-speaking readers to German or Scandinavian languages when this can be avoided.

Previous Research

The number of books on Weber is very large, and new ones are published all the time. I thus have neither intention nor possibility to survey all, or not even a large part of, the secondary literature. The amount of articles on Weber published in scholarly journals is not smaller than the amount of monographs.[28] To survey all literature on Weber is a worthy

[27] The close relation between the political and the scientific texts have been pointed out by e.g. Mommsen, Wolfgang: *The Political and Social Theory of Max Weber,* pp. 3, 10 and Turner, Bryan: *Max Weber,* p. 198. However, cf. Bendix, Reinhard & Roth, Günther: *Scholarship and Partisanship,* pp. 55-56.

[28] As a curiosity it might be mentioned that only in Japan over 2 000 articles and books on Weber have been published. See Schwentger, Wolfgang: "Western Impact and Asian Values in Japan's Modernization", p. 171.

research project in itself (probably it would have to be a joint project of several scholars). Accordingly, I have had to limit my discussion with the secondary literature to such works that are outstanding within Weber research, and to such books and articles which specifically relate to my field of study.

When it comes to the more narrow topic on the theological relevance of Weber, the number of titles is much smaller. However, I have not been able to find any book with the same integrative theological approach as the one I pursue. The most extensive systematic theological treatment of Weber published in the English-speaking world is John Milbank's *Theology and Social Theory,* which is a theological critique of secular social theory. Milbank's book contains a large section on Weber. Milbank's perspective is totally different from mine, however. He sets out to "isolate and refuse" modern secular reason, under which label he for example counts such various phenomena as social science and the philosophy of Paul Ricoeur.[29] The sociology of religion, as exemplified by, among others, Weber, is, in Milbank's eyes, an expression of the secular ambition of "policing the sublime".[30]

In some sense, however, I agree with Milbank. Milbank has correctly observed that social theory, if accepted, demands a revision of Christian theology.[31] Milbank also claims that Weber's thinking is biased towards liberal Protestantism.[32] There is, however, a point of agreement between Milbank and Weber, which Milbank does not observe. Weber claims that for those who cannot live within or accept secular modernity, the open arms of the Christian churches are the only viable option.[33] This does not seem to be wholly different from Milbank's own position. However, even if his analysis of Weber is valuable, I am unable to follow him. I fully acknowledge the traditioned character of human life. However, in modern society no one is shaped by just one tradition, but by many, as the American theologian Sheila Greeve Davaney points out in her critique of post-liberal theology.[34] I cannot choose between secular reason and Christianity, since I am shaped by, and want to be loyal to, both. For me personally, the only way forward is to try to integrate them into a coherent whole.

---

[29] Milbank, *op.cit.,* p. 263.
[30] Milbank, *op.cit.,* p. 106.
[31] Milbank, *op.cit.,* p. 2.
[32] Milbank, *op.cit.,* p. 76-77.
[33] Weber, Max: "Wissenschaft als Beruf", *MWG I/17,* p. 110.
[34] Davaney, Sheila Greeve: "Mapping Theologies", p. 30.

Among German scholars, an interest in Weber's relations to theology has developed. This interest, though, is mainly historically oriented, as is clear from two articles by the theologian Friedrich Wilhelm Graf. In *Max Weber und die Protestantische Theologie seiner Zeit*, Graf investigates the contacts between Weber and his contemporary theologians, and in *Die "kompetentesten" Gesprächspartner?* he points to Weber's theological biases.[35] I have made use of both.

Hartmann Tyrell has pointed to the tragedy of religion in Weber, namely that the value-rationalisation brought about by religion in the long run has led to the rise of secular modernity, in which religious truth-claims cannot be reasonably held.[36] I have referred to Tyrell and similar investigations when I have found it helpful. However, Tyrell and others have not discussed if the same conclusion on the place of religion in modernity in Weber should be drawn if a revisionist version of Christianity is taken into account. This revisionist program enables me to claim a *tertium datur*.[37]

I should also mention Rogers Brubaker's book *The Limits of Rationality*, to which I am highly indebted for my understanding of Weber's very complex theory on rationalisation. Furthermore, Brubaker's analysis of Weber's moral thought is, in my opinion, the most lucid and brilliant hitherto published. Brubaker also shares my conviction on Weber's continuing relevance for the interpretation of modernity. However, he has no outspoken constructive interpretative purposes. Rather he explicitly states that he only wants to reconstruct Weber's moral thought.[38]

Weber's personal position in religious matters is quite elusive. One effort to describe him as a kind of liberal Protestant Christian was done by Paul Honigsheim, who in his youth frequently visited Weber's intellectual salon in Heidelberg. Honigsheim, as well as another of Weber's *protégés* who has tried to describe Weber as a philosopher, Karl Jaspers, writes about Weber in an extremely panegyric style, which makes it impossible to fully rely on the portrait.[39] In one sense I think Honigsheim has caught something essential, though. Honigsheim claims that for

---

[35] Graaf, Friedrich Wilhelm: "Max Weber und die protestantische Theologie seiner Zeit", "Die 'kompetentesten' Gesprächspartner?".

[36] Tyrell, Hartmann: "Religion und 'intellektuelle' Redlichkeit".

[37] cf. Krech, Volkhart & Wagner, Gerhard: "Wissenschaft als Dämon im Pantheon der Moderne", p. 764.

[38] Brubaker, *op.cit.*, p. 91.

[39] Honigsheim, Paul: "Max Weber: His Religious and Ethical Background And Development", and Jaspers, Karl: *Max Weber: Politiker, Forscher, Philosoph.*

Weber the divine element in the human spiritual life is the capacity for moral choices.[40] As my investigation will show, I follow Honigsheim to the extent that I try to establish a point of contact with Weber's demand for responsible value-choices and theology. However, I do not claim, as does Honigsheim, to thereby have described Weber's own religious position.

Not only the literature on Weber is impossible to overview in the brief space available here. The same holds for the literature on the topic of theological integration, if 'integration' is understood in the wide sense which I employ. Three scholars have been especially important for my understanding of the problem and its possible solutions, though. Anders Jeffner's book *Theology and Integration* states the problem and the principle of integration in a clear way, as does his *Kriterien christlicher Glaubenslehre*.[41] However, I am not as optimistic as Jeffner about the cognitive capacities of an integrated theological position. Following Eberhard Herrmann, I have more of a pragmatic view on religion, even if I am diverging from him on some points too. Herrmann's philosophical position has been stated in his *Scientific Theory and Religious Belief*. Herrmann's suggestion that sciences and views of life should be regarded as having two different, albeit both necessary, functions, in that science provides us with knowledge and views of life with values, opened my eyes to this trait in Weber's thinking.[42] A great deal of my constructive interpretation of Weber is dependent on Herrmann's work.

I also draw upon Gordon Kaufman's theological thinking, especially his claim that God-language is a good and superior way to orient ourselves in the world and his critique of classical theism. I do not make much use of his view on evolution, though. Kaufman's position is most clearly stated in *In Face of Mystery*.[43]

A Biographical Sketch

The most extensive biography over Weber is the one written by his wife Marianne Weber under the title *Max Weber: Ein Lebensbild*. Her book has been translated into English in 1975. Despite its panegyric

[40] Honigsheim, *op.cit.*, p. 231.
[41] Jeffner, Anders: *Theology and Integration*, pp. 7-8, *Kriterien christlicher Glaubenslehre*, pp. 139-143.
[42] Herrmann, Eberhard: *Scientific Theory and Religious Belief*, pp. 23-24.
[43] Kaufman, Gordon: *In Face of Mystery*.

character, Marianne Weber's biography is still the best overview over Weber's personal life.[44] Since I am not trying to interpret Weber historically, I shall not dwell upon his biography at any length, but restrict myself to give some very basic facts and hint to one theologically interesting passage in Marianne Weber's text and to a letter written by Weber to Ferdinand Tönnies.

Weber was born in Erfurt in 1864, but grew up in Berlin where his father Max Weber Sr. made a parliamentary career for the National-liberal party. In 1889 Weber was awarded a doctorate at the university of Berlin for his dissertation on the history of trading companies in the Middle Ages, and in 1891 he presented his *Habilitation* thesis in front of the Faculty of Law at the Berlin University.[45] In 1895 Weber held his famous – and infamous – inaugural lecture as a professor of economics at the University of Freiburg, in which he argued for an aggressive germanisation of the Eastern parts of Prussia. In 1896 he was appointed to a professorship in Heidelberg, which he had to leave for reasons of health in 1903. The same year he was appointed honorary professor at the University of Heidelberg.

During the First World War Weber warned against a chauvinistic German policy and argued for the introduction of parliamentary democracy. After the fall of the monarchy he – unofficially – took part in the elaboration of the Weimar constitution and argued for a strong presidency. He also was an advisor to the German delegation to the peace conference at Versailles. In 1919 he was appointed to a professorship of social science at the university of Munich and succeeded Lujo Brentano on that chair. Weber died on June 14 1920 of pneumonia.

In her biography, Marianne Weber claims that her husband always had a deep respect for Christian religion and the biblical texts, even if he felt himself unable to embrace Christianity as his personal faith.[46] The same impression is given by Weber himself in a letter to Ferdinand Tönnies, which deserves to be quoted quite extensively. Just before the quote, Weber has discussed what makes ethics into a science, and he concludes that for him an intellectual activity must either be a demonstration of facts or a discipline of the critical study of concepts (*Begriffskritik*) if it should deserve to be called science. He also states that

---

[44] Weber, Marianne: *Max Weber: A Biography*. The 1988 edition has been supplemented by an introduction by Günther Roth which is very valuable.

[45] Weber, Max: *Die römische Agrargeschichte in ihrer Bedeutung für das Staats- und Privatrecht*, reprinted in *MWG I/2*.

[46] Weber, Marianne: *op.cit.*, p. 337.

respectable intellectual activity does not stop at the borders of science.[47] Weber writes:

> I am religiously absolutely 'unmusical' and have neither need nor capacity to construct any spiritual 'building' of religious character in myself – it is impossible and I abstain from it. But, and I have reflected seriously upon the matter, I am neither anti-religious nor *irreligious*. I find myself, also in this respect, to be a handicapped, mangled man, whose fate it is to have to confess this to himself (...) This attitude has *several* consequences: For you a liberal theologian (Catholic or Protestant) must, consequently, as a typical representative of half-heartedness, be something very despicable – for me he is...as a *human being* endlessly more valuable and interesting than the intellectual (basically: cheap) Pharisaism of naturalism...[48]

From this passage it is clear that Weber cannot in any simple manner be described as a liberal Protestant Christian, as Honigsheim does. But on the other hand, it must also be acknowledged that he had great sympathy for Christian liberal theology, and lamented the fact that he could not be a religious man himself. In making a constructive theological interpretation of Weber, I go beyond his intentions for his own texts. However I do not think that I betray Weber's fundamental values when I interpret him theologically, provided that the interpretation is true to his scientific ideals. I believe that mine is.

Outline

Anticipating the conclusion, I would say that a Christian theology which purports to be relevant and acceptable in modernity as understood by Weber has to be a radical revision of traditional theological thinking. If theology should be possible to integrate with Weber's thinking it has to be praxis-oriented rather than concerned with the

---

[47] Weber, Max: "Letter to Ferdinand Tönnies 19/2 1909", *MWG II/6*, p. 64.
[48] Weber, Max: "Letter to Ferdinand Tönnies 19/2 1909", *MWG II/6*, pp. 65-66: "*Denn ich bin zwar religiös absolut 'unmusikalisch' und habe weder Bedürfnis noch Fähigkeit irgendwelche seelischen 'Bauwerke' religiösen Charakters in mir zu errichten – das geht einfach nicht, resp. ich lehne es ab. Aber ich bin, nach genauer Prüfung, weder antireligiös noch irreligiös. Ich empfinde mich auch in dieser Hinsicht als einen Krüppel, als einen verstümmelten Menschen, dessen inneres Schicksal es ist, sich dies ehrlich eingestehen zu müssen (...) Aus dieser Attitüde folgt* viel: *Ihnen muß zum Beispiel konsequenter Weise ein 'liberaler' (katholischer oder protestantischer) Theologe als typischer Represäntant einer Halbheit das Verhaßteste von allen sein – mir ist er...* menschlich *unendlich wertvoller und interessanter als der intellektuelle (im Grunde: billige) Pharisäismus des Naturalismus...*"

metaphysical interpretation of reality. This means that theology must be about how we ought to live our lives. Stated in another way, Christian theology would have to be about values rather than beliefs. Since Weber points out that we need values if we should be able to act rationally in the world, a point of contact between a revised Christian theology and modernity in Weber's interpretation can be established. The path along which I have walked to arrive at such a conclusion can be described as follows.

The second chapter has two purposes. On the one hand I provide a picture of Weber's intellectual context, in order to facilitate a reasonable understanding of his texts. Weber's political writings cannot be properly understood if the political life of Wilhelmine Germany is not taken into account, and his methodological ideas have to be seen against the background of both neo-Kantian philosophy and Marxism. On the other hand, I point to some affinities between Weber's thinking and the theology of his time. This is not primarily done in order to establish any causal relation between Weber and theology, even if it, for example, is probable that Hermann Gunkel deeply influenced his understanding of Old Testament prophetism. Rather I point to these affinities in order to gain resources for my constructive interpretation *of Weber*.

The second chapter is structured in the following way. First I describe the political and social context of the Empire. Second, I give an overview over some themes in neo-Kantian philosophy which are especially relevant for the understanding of Weber. I also provide an interpretation of Wilhelm Windelband's philosophy of religion. This is done in order to provide resources for a constructive extension of Weber's thinking in chapter six. Third, I discuss the relation between Weber and Marxism, and claim that the main difference is Weber's stress on the basic multicausality in history. I also point out that Weber and Marx share the interest in the fate of humanity in modern capitalism; they both have an *emancipatory* interest. Fourth, I try to establish some points of contact between Weber and his contemporary theologians.

In the third chapter I construct a reasonable understanding of Weber's view on the role of values in scientific work. It is claimed that for Weber values are crucial in all scientific efforts, since they a) establish the research object, and b) show us how to employ scientific knowledge in our lives. This is done with the neo-Kantian epistemology of Heinrich Rickert as background. I also discuss what should be understood by the demand for objectivity and value freedom in science. For Weber, objectivity does not rest in correspondence with noumenal reality, but in the procedures employed in scientific work. By interpreting Weber's concept of value-systems in the light of Anders Jeffner's understanding of *views of life*, I am able to show that the Weberian understanding of science cannot do without religion or various forms of secular value-systems. I also discuss the role of science when it comes to forming views of life which can be integrated with a scientific worldview.

In chapter four I provide an interpretation of Weber's view on the fate of humanity in modern Western culture. It is claimed that Weber's understanding of the risks of modernity can be understood as a threat of *alienation*, defined according to Lars Andersson's model of alienation. Following Wolfgang Mommsen, I claim that Weber's solution to the threat of alienation is that charisma and rationality have to join forces to combat the negative consequences of the process of rationalisation. This requires values which are viable enough to resist the juggernaut of modernity. I also analyse Weber's understanding of the escape from modernity, and in a modest way I propose another understanding of the secularisation thesis. On my interpretation, Weber cannot be understood as a simple advocate of such a thesis.

In chapter five, Weber's challenges to Christian theology are stated in a unified manner and I propose criteria for an integrated theological position in regard to Weber's thought. Basically I claim that any integrated position has to accept Eberhard Herrmann's proposal of a division of labour between views of life and science. However, I also claim that views of life can contain what I call *heuristic assumptions*, that is assumptions which are necessary for establishing a discourse, even if they do not have status of being theoretical statements. One such assumption is that human beings are free agents. In my view, this cannot be proven. However, it is still necessary that we assume that we are free, if for example any ethical discourse should be meaningful. In a final paragraph, I discuss the possibility of a religious critique of science.

In chapter six, I develop a model of revelation which is compatible with Weber's thinking. I do this by providing a constructive interpretation of Weber's theory of *charisma*. By taking Weber's ideas of routinised charisma seriously, a one-sided accentuation of the solitary ecstatic prophet as the fountain of revelation can be avoided, and the relation between the historical basis in Jesus' ministry and the importance of the church for the development of Christianity can be maintained.

In the final chapter, I draw up the contours of *one* possible way to intellectually systematise Christian faith in a way that can be integrated with Weber's thinking. In doing this, I balance between what I regard as scientific theology and Christian theology. However, it must be kept in mind that I do not regard my effort as an expression of authentic Christian belief, since I hold it to be impossible to scientifically establish criteria of authenticity, and I do not claim that it is the only plausible way to integrate Christian theology with Weber. Rather, I put forward a suggestion which can be tested by asking if it really is true that such a position would be acceptable in front of my constructive interpretation of Weber.

Chapter seven is organised in four parts. First I try to develop an understanding of the idea of God as a kind of *focus imaginarius* in the Christian view of life. In that way, God can be seen as a kind of heuristic assumption necessary for Christian theology and Christian life. Second, I discuss the importance of Christology in theology. This can, due to the limited space, only be done in a very fragmentary way. Basically it is centred around the question what reasonably can be understood by the claim that Jesus is God's Son. Third, a view of humanity is sketched, in which the assumption that humans are free, rational and responsible agents plays a central role. Finally I analyse the concept of the *kingdom of God* as a way to understand basic Christian values.

2. THE SETTING

Wilhelmine Germany

Max Weber's life roughly coincides with the second German Empire. Since Weber was deeply engaged in the political problems of his time, it is necessary to have some understanding of the structure and political milieu of the Empire in order to understand his thinking. His theory of charismatic authority, for example, cannot be fully understood if the German political context is not taken into account.[1]

Germany was later industrialised than Western Europe, and the agrarian elements in the economy continued to be important during the 19th century. In the beginning of the 1870s Germany's economy had become more like the industrialised capitalist countries of Western Europe, but industrialisation was concentrated to regions like Ruhr, Saar and Upper Silesia. Other areas, like East Prussia, continued to be characterised by an agrarian, feudal economy.[2] This remarkable economical development did not correspond to a political development. The political élite of the Empire continued to be dominated by the agrarian nobility, which desperately defended its economic and political privileges.[3]

The German Empire was a semi-feudal confederation of twenty-two principalities and three Hansa-cities. The Empire was governed by the Chancellor, appointed by and responsible to the Emperor, who also was king of Prussia, the most influential member-state. There was also a Parliament (the *Reichstag*), elected by all male citizens of the Empire. The Parliament had influence over the budget and over civil legislation, but it had no control over foreign policy or the army and it could not exert any direct influence over the Government. The suffrage in the member-states was not as 'democratic' as in the Empire. Suffrage to the Prussian *Landestag*, for example, was strictly limited, so that only the wealthy had any real influence. This enabled the privileged classes to exert a decisive influence, since the individual member-states had control over vital parts of domestic policy.

---

[1] Giddens, Anthony: *Politics and Sociology in the Thought of Max Weber,* p. 38; Turner, Bryan: *Max Weber,* pp. 217-221.

[2] Wehler, Hans-Ulrich: *The German Empire,* p. 32.

[3] Wehler, *op.cit.,* pp. 37-38, 45-46.

During the period 1870-1890 Otto von Bismarck was Chancellor. He completely dominated the political scene. When Wilhelm II ascended to the throne in 1888, Bismarck could no longer control the Emperor, and in 1890 he was forced to resign. One problem that Weber thought more serious than anything else in the German political situation was that Bismarck's domination had been so total, that no capacity for leadership and political vision had been able to develop in other politicians.[4] After Bismarck's resignation, Germany was governed by bureaucrats who were incapable of providing Germany with political leadership. Wehler has characterised the period after Bismarck as a time of polycracy and a constant crisis of government.[5] Despite his victory over Bismarck, Wilhelm II lacked the ability to fill out the power vacuum which occurred after the Chancellor's resignation.

This chaotic situation continued until the fall of the monarchy in November 1918 and, tragically, during most of the Weimar Republic. The parliamentary institutions had relatively low status; if anyone had called the Chancellor a politician, he would have taken it as an insult. The members of the Government considered themselves as the Emperor's servants, not as politicians striving towards a political goal. The low status of the Parliament and the political parties was partly caused by the widespread idea that in a good society there were no conflicts. The Government was seen as a neutral organiser of the common good, elevated above the party squabble.[6] When the monarchy fell, one of the main problems was how to prevent the same political chaos in the republican constitution. This should be remembered when Weber's argumentation for a strong charismatic leadership and a powerful President is in focus.[7]

The universities of Wilhelmine Germany had a good international reputation and in many areas they were world-leading. But, and especially in the humanities, they were also centres for political indoctrination. The ideal of value-neutrality in academic teaching was not common; many teachers thought that the university should not just prepare the students for their professional career, it should also cultivate their

---

[4] Weber, Max: "Politik als Beruf", *MWG I/17,* pp. 218-222. On the importance of the 'leadership question' in Weber's thought, see e.g. Giddens, Anthony: *Politics and Sociology in the Thought of Max Weber,* p. 54 and Mommsen, Wolfgang: *Max Weber and German Politics,* pp. 163-172.

[5] Wehler, *op.cit.,* p. 62.

[6] Wehler, *op.cit.,* p. 130.

[7] Weber, Max: "Reichspräsident", *MWG I/16,* pp. 220-224.

characters – or, in the German idiom, the universities should promote *Bildung*.[8]

Most of the academic teachers represented a social-conservative ideology which they made to an integrated part in their teaching. These social-conservative academics – the '*Kathedersozialisten*' (the pulpit socialists) – had great respect for the imperial state and were concerned to preserve the existing political order. Their social engagement was often – as was also the case with Bismarck's social reforms – caused by a strive to conserve the political order. Social reforms were primarily needed as a means to avoid political instability and revolution. This made the universities to an excellent instrument for the training of a bureaucracy loyal to the Emperor.[9]

Imperial Germany was a religiously divided country. Prussia and the Emperor were Protestant, as well as a majority of the population. A large minority were Roman Catholics. In the 1870s Bismarck had tried to weaken the influence of the Roman Catholic Church by anti-church legislation, for example by introducing obligatory civil marriage. This so called '*Kulturkampf*' made a deep impact on the German society. Wehler even claims that it made the Catholics *more* (sic!) loyal to the Empire, because they were anxious not to become a pariah people in the German state.[10]

The Protestant churches were effective legitimators of the existing political system, and often closely related to the ruling king or prince. In Prussia the king was the *summus episcopus* of the church. This close alliance with the ruling classes contributed to the fact that the workers distanced themselves from the church. In the end of the 19th century secularisation had gone relatively far. For example, in 1874 only 62 per cent of the children born in Berlin were baptised.[11]

Within the Protestant church there was an ongoing conflict between conservative and liberal theology.[12] This conflict was both a conflict over church politics and over the methods and aims of academic theology.[13] The term liberal theology was, and is, vague – liberal theology

---

[8] Ringer, Fritz: *The Decline of the German Mandarins,* p. 104.
[9] Wehler, *op.cit.*, pp. 124-125.
[10] Wehler, *op.cit.*, p. 117.
[11] Wehler, *op.cit.*, p. 115.
[12] Graf, Friedrich Wilhelm: "Einleitung", pp. 10-13.
[13] In some sense the conflict also had political overtones. Within the Evangelical Social Congress conservative and liberal theologians met and discussed Christian social action. In this discussion, the liberals tended to be more 'leftist' than the theologically conservative. But there were also exceptions to this, as for example the liberal Julius Kaftan,

consisted of different directions which competed with each other. Graf defines the common trait in liberal theology as the conviction "that religion must not be reduced to ecclesiastical matters, and that the liberty-promoting difference between piety and theology must be essential to Protestantism".[14] Many liberal theologians wanted to change the theological education at the universities and transform the confessional theological faculties into faculties for religious studies.[15] In academic conflicts over appointments, Weber always took sides with the liberal theologians.[16]

Neo-Kantianism

As a reaction to Hegelianism, a revival of Kant's philosophy started in the middle of the nineteenth century. This neo-Kantian movement was not a direct return to Kant, but an elaboration of themes in Kant's philosophy. Neo-Kantianism consisted of different schools and was never a unified movement within German philosophy.[17]

For most neo-Kantians the question of scientific methodology was a burning issue deserving philosophical attention, due to the tremendous development of the natural sciences in the later part of the nineteenth century. Neo-Kantian thought was characterised by the idea that reality could not be known directly, but only through concepts constructed by human beings. At the same time the neo-Kantian philosophers were eager to preserve the objectivity of science. This interest in concepts and concept-formation is closely related to their value theory, since, as Willey has shown, practical reason is in focus in neo-Kantian thought.[18] The form of neo-Kantianism that influenced Weber was the Baden or South-western School, whose main representatives were Wilhelm Windelband and Heinrich Rickert, and therefore I shall limit my discussion of neo-Kantianism to certain aspects of their thinking.

---

who distanced himself from any Christian social engagement. See Liebersohn, Harry: *Religion and Industrial Society,* pp. 25-29.

[14] Graf, Friedrich Wilhelm: "Einleitung", p. 13: *"daß Religion nicht auf Kirchlichkeit reduziert werden dürfe und für den Protestantismus die freiheitsdienliche Unterscheidung von Frömmigkeit und Theologie konstitutiv sei".*

[15] Graf, Friedrich Wilhelm: "Einleitung", p. 10.

[16] Honigsheim, *op.cit.,* p. 234.

[17] Willey, Thomas: *Back to Kant,* pp. 24-39.

[18] Willey identifies five common tenets in neo-Kantian philosophy, of which the primacy of practical reason perhaps is the most important. See his *Back to Kant,* p. 37. On the primacy of practical reason in Rickert, see e.g. p. 144.

Windelband gave his answer to the discussion about scientific method in the natural sciences and the humanities that went on between German scholars in the end of the 19th century and in the beginning of the 20th century with his distinction between *ideographic* and *nomothetic* sciences.[19] Nomothetic sciences, according to Windelband, try to establish general laws, while ideographic sciences describe and explain single events, sometimes with the help of laws established by nomothetic sciences. Natural sciences are nomothetic, because for them the individual object is of no value in itself, but is only important as a way to establish lawlike generalities. History is for Windelband an example of an ideographic science, since the task of the historian is to describe and explain single events.[20]

Windelband was not especially fond of Dilthey's distinction between the *'Geisteswissenschaften'* and *'Naturwissenschaften'*. According to him, this distinction causes confusion because sciences like psychology cannot be categorised by it. For Windelband it is clear that psychology is a nomothetic science because it tries to understand the human mind by establishing psychological laws.[21] Windelband views the division between "Naturwissenschaften" and "Geisteswissenschaften" as problematic, because it presupposes a qualitative difference between the objects studied.[22] The only relevant distinction is a methodological one, since the same object often can be studied both from an ideographic and a nomothetic perspective.

The epistemology of Windelband's disciple Heinrich Rickert influenced Weber, who developed its significance for history and sociology in his methodological writings. The question of exactly how deep Rickert's influence on Weber really was, has been widely debated. My opinion, for which reasons are given in the next chapter, is that Weber was impressed by Rickert, and built his own methodology on Rickert's works, but that he also departed from Rickert on crucial matters, such as what constitutes scientific objectivity.[23]

---

[19] Windelband, Wilhelm: *Präludien*, pp. 136-160.
[20] Windelband, Wilhelm: *Präludien*, p. 150.
[21] Windelband, Wilhelm: *Präludien*, pp. 142-143.
[22] Schnädelbach, Herbert: *Philosophy in Germany*, pp. 57, 129.
[23] My own position on the question of Rickert's influence is largely consonant with Bruun, Hans Henrik: *Science, Values and Politics in Max Weber's Methodology*, pp. 95-98. cf. Thomas Burger who has argued that Weber is almost totally dependent on Rickert. See his *Max Weber's Theory of Concept Formation*, p. 8.

The starting-point for Rickert's philosophy is his view of reality as an infinite multiplicity.[24] Reality, according to Rickert, is in principle infinite, and therefore it is impossible for science to represent it fully. Any scientific study has to produce concepts that order the flux of reality. In doing this, many aspects of reality get lost, but concept-formation is necessary if we are to have any knowledge at all. In connection with Windelband's distinction between nomothetical (or nomological) and ideographical sciences, Rickert holds that there are two types of knowledge of reality: either a knowledge which tries to grasp reality in its totality by establishing generalities, or a knowledge which tries to understand *individual* phenomena. Both types of knowledge are problematic in face of the assumed ideal to gain total knowledge. Nomothetic knowledge grasps reality because it establishes generally valid laws, but in this process individuality gets lost, and since reality consists of an infinite flux of individual phenomena, nomothetic knowledge in another way falls short of its purpose: in establishing generalities, it can only know what is common to phenomena. Ideographical knowledge, on the other hand, understands individuality, but since the world consists of an infinite number of individual phenomena, it cannot understand reality in its totality.

According to Rickert, the necessary concept-formation in the humanities are closely related to values. Because reality is infinite, we have to choose which individual phenomena should be studied. Therefore our concept-formation has to pay attention to the value-relevance (*Wertbeziehung*) of phenomena. To say that a certain phenomenon has value-relevance is the same as saying that it is worth to know according to a certain value.

Since reality is infinite, and the objects of research are constituted by their value-relevance, Rickert thinks that the objectivity of ideographic sciences cannot rest in the degree of correspondence with reality. What constitues objectivity is rather the relation which those values that constitute the value relevance have to objective, transcendent values.[25] It is important to note that cultural values, which establish value-relevancies, do not have to be ethical, they can just as well be aesthetical or theoretical. One example could be the value 'politics'. Two persons who have very different views on political matters, still have to define *the political*

---

[24] Rickert, Heinrich: *Die Grenzen der naturwissenschaftlichen Begriffsbildung* (hereafter: *Grenzen*), p. 33. Weber shared this view. See e.g. his "'Objektivität'", *GAW,* p. 171.
[25] Rickert, Heinrich: *Grenzen,* pp. 640, 701-704.

in the same way, lest there would be no disagreement. They thus establish the concept of the political domain in human life with relevance to the same cultural value, according to Rickert.[26]

The epistemological views of Windelband and Rickert deeply influenced Weber. Their influence seems basically to have been restricted to this area of philosophy. The philosophy of religion of the neo-Kantians is not discussed at any length by Weber. This does not mean that there are no affinities between Weber's thought and neo-Kantian philosophy of religion. This will be analysed more fully in the chapter on revelation. At this stage, I shall be content to give a brief outline of Windelband's philosophy of religion.[27]

Windelband's philosophy of religion is grounded on the assumption that the human consciousness is organised in four spheres of experience, namely the logical sphere, the ethical sphere, the aesthetical sphere and the religious sphere.[28] Windelband's argument for this division of the human consciousness runs – as far as I can understand – as follows.

It is evident that the human mind has three psychological functions: cognition, volition and feeling.[29] This leads us to assume that there are three distinct areas in the human consciousness: the logical, the aesthetical and the ethical spheres. The logical sphere answers questions about what is true, the ethical sphere is about what is right and the aesthetical sphere is about what is beautiful. But when we try to understand what religion is, we see that it cannot be understood entirely within this scheme. It is, according to Windelband, true that we can see religion from a logical, an ethical and an aesthetical perspective. But in Windelband's eyes this does not cover what religion is – a description of religion within any of these spheres will be one-sided.[30] Therefore it is necessary to assume that religion is an independent sphere in the human consciousness. The religious sphere is about what is *holy*.[31]

---

[26] Rickert, Heinrich: *Grenzen*, p. 364.

[27] An overview of neo-Kantian philosophy of religion is provided in Hans-Ludwig Ollig's article "Die Religionsphilosophie der Südwestdeutschen Schule".

[28] Windelband, Wilhelm: *Präludien*, p. 297. Since the religious sphere constitutes the norm consciousness of the other spheres, it is, as Windelband points out, of a different logical order than the three others. It should be noted that "logic" and "logical" in the neo-Kantian tradition signifies more than formal logic. See Burger, *op.cit.*, p. 19. Ola Agevall has pointed out that 'logic' denotes something like the philosophy of science in Rickert's works. See his *A Science of Unique Events*, pp. 110-113.

[29] Windelband, Wilhelm: *Präludien*, p. 299.

[30] Windelband, Wilhelm: *Präludien*, pp. 298-299.

[31] Windelband, Wilhelm: *Präludien*, p. 297.

According to Windelband, a philosophical analysis shows that in the three spheres of logic, ethics and aesthetics we can observe the antinomy of conscience, which means that the real and the ideal by necessity never can be united. This experience of imperfection gives us bad conscience. This bad conscience is partly a product of our social context, partly a product of what Windelband calls a "deeper life-context".[32] The conscience is built on what Windelband calls the "metaphysical reality of the norm consciousness".[33] This reality is not equivalent to empirical reality, but is nevertheless absolutely valid because it is grounded in the transcendent, and therefore we call it "the holy". The *holy* is the normative consciousness of the logical, ethical and aesthetical life, and according to Windelband it is neither to be explained as a product of our psyche nor as a product of the social context.[34] Windelband writes:

> The holy, then, is the consciousness of norms of the true, the good and the beautiful, experienced as transcendent reality.
> So far as a human being in his conscience knows himself to be bound by something overarching Transcendent he is religious. He lives in reason and reason in him. *Religion is transcendent life*; the essence of it is to transcend experience, to know that one belongs to a world of spiritual values, to not be content with the empirically real.[35]

To be religious, then, is for Windelband basically to feel oneself to be bound by norms, the source of which is transcendent. The feeling of transcendence is void of cognitive elements, but it is necessary for the human mind to give this indefinite feeling concretion. The dogmatic content is a product of the historical context, but has its ground in the experience of the holy.[36] For example, the theistic concept of God is a way to express belief in ultimate values: In his/her person, God represents the highest values and ideals.[37] Religion is more a way of life than

---

[32] Windelband, Wilhelm: *Präludien*, p. 304: "*tiefere Lebenszusammenhang*".

[33] Windelband, Wilhelm: *Präludien*, p. 304: "*metaphysische Realität des Normalbewußtseins*". Windelband uses the somewhat strange word "*Normalbewußtsein*" as equivalent to "*Normbewußtsein*", which is obvious from e.g. p. 304.

[34] Windelband, Wilhelm: *Präludien*, p. 305.

[35] Windelband, Wilhelm: *Präludien*, p. 305: "*Das Heilige ist also das Normalbewußtsein des Wahren, Guten und Schönen*, erlebt als transszendente Wirklichkeit.//Insofern der Mensch in seinem Gewissen sich so durch ein übergreifendes, Transszendentes bestimmt weiß, ist er religiös. Er lebt in der Vernunft und sie in ihm. Religion ist transszendentes Leben; das Wesentliche an ihr ist das Hinausleben über die Erfahrung, das Bewußtsein der Zugehörigkeit zu einer Welt geistiger Werte, das Sichnichtgenügenlassen am empirisch Wirklichen.*"

[36] Windelband, Wilhelm: *Präludien*, pp. 308-310.

[37] Windelband, Wilhelm: *Präludien*, pp. 313-314.

something cognitive, it is related to the conscience rather than to the cognitive faculties of the human mind: "The light of eternity does not shine in my knowing, but in my conscience".[38]

Weber shared Rickert's view of reality as an infinite multiplicity. The world consists, according to Weber, of an infinite number of phenomena, and the only way to gain knowledge of them is to select certain aspects which we choose to study because we find them "worthy of being known".[39] Just as Rickert, Weber makes theoretical reason secondary to practical reason.

Connected to this is Weber's theory of the importance of values in scientific work. Weber agrees with Rickert that it is the value-relevance of phenomena that decides if they are worth studying or not.[40] What Weber cannot accept, however, is that it is the relation to objectively given cultural values that justifies claims to objectivity. Objectivity is, according to him, a formal attribute of scientific explanations and arguments, implying that no value premise may be part of the argument.[41] Weber illustrates this idea by saying that our scientific analyses of reality should be valid also for the Chinese, even if he does not accept the values which are the starting-point for our study.[42]

The importance of Windelband's philosophy of religion for this investigation will be discussed in the chapter on revelation. Here only two points should be clarified. First, there is a crucial difference between Weber's view of values and Windelband's. For Windelband the consciousness of norms has an objective character: there are eternal, objective values of which we can be aware.[43] Such a view is hardly compatible with Weber's strong sense of the plurality and fragmentation of the modern world. But a common trait is the view that a religiosity relevant for the modern world is more of a way of life than a set of beliefs about a transcendent reality.

Second, Weber and Windelband share the view that religious phenomena has to be seen as caused by several factors. Religion is a social phenomenon and as such necessarily influenced by social factors. But at the same time religion cannot be reduced to social and economic factors.

[38] Windelband, Wilhelm, *Präludien*, p. 342: "*Das Licht der Ewigkeit leuchtet mir nicht im Wissen, sondern im Gewissen.*"
[39] MSS p. 72. Weber, Max: "'Objektivität'", *GAW*, p. 171: "*wissenswert*".
[40] Weber, Max: "'Wertfreiheit'", *GAW*, p. 511.
[41] Weber's view on objectivity and his dependence on Rickert is discussed at length in chapter 3.
[42] Weber, Max "'Objektivität'", *GAW*, p. 155.
[43] Windelband, Wilhelm: *Präludien*, p. 342.

They have in common the conviction that religion, although shaped by and conceptualised through culture and language, cannot be reduced to social phenomena, but in some respect must be seen as a basic human response to life, grounded in an autonomous experience.[44]

Weber and Marxism

Max Weber has often been understood as strongly opposed to a Marxist view on social change; Weber is thought to have proposed an idealistic conception of history instead of the materialistic conception of Marx.[45] This must not be understood as if Weber sees no value at all in Marx's thinking. On the contrary, he often repeats that he thinks that Marx's work provides the social sciences and history with many valuable insights, and especially Marx has helped historians and social scientists to see the importance of economic factors in explanations of social phenomena.[46]

What Weber criticises is what Anthony Giddens has called "reflective materialism", which he understands as the idea that ideologies, religious ideas etc. are a direct reflection of material circumstances.[47] Weber strongly opposes materialistic dogmatism; economic factors are important as one aspect of explanations of social phenomena but one cannot say that they are the only relevant factors. When all social phenomena are understood as economically conditioned, dogmatism has replaced science. Weber points out that every phenomenon has many relevant causes, and therefore there is no ground for giving economic factors principally more weight than any others. What are the most adequate explanations of a phenomenon have to be discovered in each single case, and cannot be decided in advance.[48] Weber's view about historical causation could be described as an advocacy of the acceptance of historical multicausality. There is, according to Weber, no primary force in history, to which causality can be reduced.[49]

---

[44] Weber, Max: *Das antike Judentum*, pp. 322, 326-327.
[45] See e.g. Schroeder, Ralph: *Max Weber and the Sociology of Culture*, pp. 155-157.
[46] See for example Weber, Max: *"Die protestantische Ethik"*, *GARS I*, p. 192, n. 1.
[47] Giddens, Anthony: *Capitalism and Modern Social Theory*, p. 211. Weber formulated his critique of the materialistic conception of history in his "R. Stammlers 'Überwindung' der materialistischen Geschichtsauffassung".
[48] Weber, Max: *"'Objektivität'"*, *GAW*, pp. 169-170.
[49] Ringer, Fritz: *Max Weber's Methodology*, p. 152.

Those features of Marx's thinking which Weber most strongly opposes, are those which come close to reflective materialism. Marx writes in *A Contribution to the Critique of Political Economy* that

> Just as one does not judge an individual by what he thinks about himself, so one cannot judge such a period of transformation by its consciousness, but, on the contrary, this consciousness must be explained from the contradictions of material life, from the conflict existing between the social forces of production and the relations of production.[50]

One possible interpretation of this passage is that it prescribes that historical change shall be explained with reference to the conflict between productive forces and the modes of production. As opposed to this, Weber constantly stresses that it is impossible to say beforehand what have caused historical phenomena. In some cases, the explanation has to be done with reference to 'spiritual' forces, sometimes with reference to material factors, and most of the time by reference to several factors which have worked the effect together.[51]

As Karl Löwith has pointed out, Weber did not clearly distinguish Marx from his followers. Therefore much of his critique of Marxism often only hits "vulgar economistic 'Marxism'".[52] Anthony Giddens comes to a similar conclusion when he argues that Weber's methodology should rather be seen as a vindicator of Marx against the distortions brought into Marx's teachings by his followers.[53] Weber's critique of reflective materialism and stress on the multicausality in history should be read as expressions of his fundamentally anti-metaphysical position, which of course also makes him fundamentally opposed to idealistic conceptions of history. In his view, since reality is an infinite manifold which we only can grasp partially through our concept-formation, we cannot have any access to those principles which govern the development of world and history, if indeed there are such principles. In science,

---

[50] Marx, Karl: *A Contribution to the Critique of Political Economy*, p. 21. MEGA II:2 s. 101: "*So wenig man das, was ein Individuum ist, nach dem beurtheilt, was es sich selbst dünkt* [sic!, my comment], *eben so wenig kann man eine solche Umwälzungsepoche aus ihrem Bewußtsein beurtheilen, sondern muß vielmehr dies Bewußtsein aus den Widersprüchen des materiellen Lebens, aus dem vorhandenen Konflikt zwischen gesellschaftlichen Produktivkräften und Produktionsverhältnissen erklären.*"

[51] With biting irony, Weber criticises monocausal theories by showing what absurdities a theory claiming monocausal status for religious factors would lead to. See his "R. Stammlers 'Überwindung' der materialistischen Geschichtsauffassung", *GAW*, pp. 294-296.

[52] Löwith, Karl: *Max Weber and Karl Marx*, p. 100.

[53] Giddens, Anthony: *Capitalism and Modern Social Theory*, p. 211.

we should not base any research effort on any a priori assumptions of what should be regarded as proper causes in history.

Weber does not only criticise Marxism for its "monistic" way of explaining social or historical facts as products of economical circumstances. He also holds that the idea of a "scientific socialism" is impossible. The problem with Marxism is not that it is grounded on values, but that it presents its value premises as scientific facts.[54] According to Weber's understanding of science, this is illegitimate – values and facts are logically distinct, and therefore no value judgement can be part of a scientific explanation.[55] This is not to say, however, that socialistic ideals or values are illegitimate from a scientific point of view. For Weber, values are indispensable for concept-formation and they can motivate a scientific study because they decide the goal of scientific work, but they cannot be premises in scientific explanations.

Connected to this is Weber's critique of Marxist determinism. In so far as Marxism implies the belief that it can be scientifically established that history is led by unchangeable laws towards an utopian happy future, it is dangerous and unscientific.[56] To dream about a happy future is possible and can be desirable, but such a dream can never have scientific status. In addition to this, Weber remarks that the communist utopia is utterly unrealistic. The most serious problem that confronts modern society is for Weber the growing bureaucratisation, which kills human freedom, creativity and spontaneity. A socialist or communist economy would require an enormous bureaucracy for organising production and distribution, and so it would counteract its own goals: the promoting of true humanity.[57]

According to Löwith, there is a basic similarity between Weber and Marx, despite all differences and despite Weber's ardent critique of Marxism, namely the passionate interest in human emancipation.[58] According to Löwith, the underlying interest of both Weber's and Marx's analysis of capitalism is to understand what is "the fate of man in the human world".[59] Both Weber and Marx thought that modern

---

[54] Löwith, op.cit., p. 31.

[55] Giddens has pointed out that this epistemological view of Weber is what most typically separates him from Marx. See his Capitalism and Modern Social Theory, p. 195.

[56] Weber, Max: "'Objektivität'", GAW, p. 205.

[57] See for example: Weber, Max: "Parlament und Regierung", MWG I/15, pp. 451, 464. Bryan Turner pertinently remarks that for Weber socialism implies a reification of human relationships not hitherto seen in history. See his op.cit., pp. 179-180.

[58] Löwith, op.cit., p. 22.

[59] Löwith, op.cit., pp. 19-20.

industrial capitalism threatened true humanity, even if they understood this threat differently. Marx wanted to liberate humanity from alienation, and Weber wanted to rescue "an ultimate human dignity".[60] In their analyses of the human predicament in modern society they were, if not in agreement, close to each other. They differ, however, in their attitude towards their respective analysis. Löwith interprets this difference in the following way:

> Marx promptly answers his own question by indicating the way in which men must 'regain control over the manner of their mutual relations'. Marx proposes a therapy while Weber has only a 'diagnosis' to offer.[61]

Löwith is surely right when he points to what Paul Honigsheim has called the "tragicism" of Weber.[62] Weber was not very optimistic about the possibilities of building a perfect human society on earth. He refuted any belief in the possibility of establishing the kingdom of God on earth, be it in a religious or a secularised manner. However, it is not therefore justified to assume that Weber was a pessimistic determinist who thought it was impossible to do anything at all to improve the situation of humankind in the modern world.

The rationalisation process is likely to continue, according to Weber, but it can be interrupted – temporarily at least – by charismatic phenomena. As will be shown in detail later, charisma is in Weber's eyes the real innovative force of history, a force which creates new values and new attitudes to life.[63] If Weber does not propose a therapy, it is because it is impossible to foretell what will happen in the distant future. But if charisma and ratio join forces in a constructive way, it is at least in principle possible to save some remnants of true humanity, according to Weber.[64] Weber should not be understood as if he had given up all hope, even if he thinks that the salvation from the "iron cage" of rationalism is distant and improbable.[65]

---

[60] Löwith, *op.cit.*, p. 22. In chapter 4, I argue that the notion 'alienation' can be applied also within a Weberian critique of modernity.

[61] Löwith, *op.cit.*, p. 25.

[62] Honigsheim, *op.cit.*, p. 237.

[63] Weber, Max: *Wirtschaft und Gesellschaft*, p. 142.

[64] It is Wolfgang Mommsens little book *The Age of Bureaucracy*, p. 20, which has made me see that Weber's solution to the problems of modernity lies in a combination of charisma and rationality. More on this in chapter 4.

[65] Weber, Max: "Wissenschaft als Beruf", *MWG I/17* pp. 110-111.

Theological Points of Contact

"Moreover, I am quite engaged in theology; I read Strauß, Schleiermacher and Pfleiderer ('Paulinismus') and besides that only Plato", the young Weber wrote to his mother in springtime 1882.[66] Weber kept this interest in theology for the rest of his life. His writings are full of allusions to or citations of biblical passages, theological classics or of the theologians of his own time.

Weber's relations to theology has been more and more noticed in the Weber research.[67] According to Graf, this relation can be understood along three main lines. Firstly, in his youth and during his early academic career, Weber met the liberal theology of his time, and especially its concern with the relation between religion and ethics and its ideas about religion as an autonomous sphere in the human consciousness. He also, secondly, co-operated closely with some theologians, notably Ernst Troeltsch, together with whom he developed a theory about religious sects. The third aspect of contact between Weber and the theologians of his time is, according to Graf, his and their interest in the fate of the individual personality in modernity.[68]

During his youth and in the beginning of his academic career Weber had close personal contacts with the liberal theologians, among others his cousin Otto Baumgarten, who later became professor of practical theology in Kiel. Through these contacts Weber learned to know the close relation between religion and ethics that many liberal theologians wanted to establish, and it gave him an understanding of the idea that religion is an autonomous part of human cognitive life. One of the most important contacts was with the History of religions school, and in many of his studies over the sociology of religion Weber refers to their works.

The theologians of the History of religions school were interested in studying *religion* as such. By understanding the religious history, they thought they would also get a better understanding of living religion.

---

[66] Weber, Max: *Jugendbriefe*, p. 48: "*Im übrigen bin ich ziemlich tief in die Theologie geraten; meine Lektüre besteht aus Strauß, Schleiermacher und Pfleiderer ('Paulinismus') und außerdem nur Platon.*"

[67] e.g. see: Graf, Friedrich Wilhelm: "Max Weber und die protestantische Theologie seiner Zeit", p. 122-147. Graf has also pointed to the fact that there are some implicit theological value judgements in Weber's writings, especially the analysis of the Protestant ethic. See his "Die 'kompetentesten' Gesprächspartner?" Graf makes the same point in "The German Theological Sources and Protestant Church Politics", pp. 27-49.

[68] Graf, Friedrich Wilhelm: "Max Weber und die protestantische Theologie seiner Zeit", pp. 122-147.

They were particularly interested in how religion and culture interacted and how religion helped to form the individual's life and society. Accordingly, these theologians strived to work strictly with common historical methods when they analysed religious material, a standpoint not uncontroversial among theologians in the beginning of the 20th century.[69] Common to many of the History of religions school theologians was furthermore the assumption of a religious *a priori* in human cognitive life; the concept "religion" became for many of these scholars a way to mediate between Christian faith and reason.[70]

A contact of special importance was Weber's relation to the Evangelical-Social Congress, an organisation of Protestant ministers and scholars, engaged in promoting an active social policy.[71] This social activism was motivated partly by the wish to avoid revolution, partly by the fact that there was a gulf between the church and the workers which the members of the Congress wanted to overbridge. Weber took part in the discussions and became friend with two Protestant ministers who were active in the Congress, Paul Göhre and Friedrich Naumann. Rita Aldenhoff has pointed out that Weber's reasons for engaging in the Congress's work were mainly political and scientific; he thought that it could be an effective political platform from which he could work for his own political ideal: a social-liberal imperialistic German Reich.[72] I think Aldenhoff is correct when she says that Weber's main reasons for participating were political and scientific, but from this one should not conclude that he had no interest what so ever in religious matters. There is no justification for labelling Weber a professing Christian, but he certainly was *personally* interested in religion and the church life of his time.

Sometimes Weber also co-operated in the liberal theological journal *Die christliche Welt*; among other articles he published his *"'Kirchen' und 'Sekten' in Nordamerika – Eine kirchen- und sozialpolitische Skizze"*, in the journal.[73] Another form of co-operation was that Weber assisted his cousin Otto Baumgarten, who was editor of the journal

---

[69] See e.g. Troeltsch, Ernst: "Ueber historische und dogmatische Methode in der Theologie".

[70] See e.g. Troeltsch, Ernst: "Zur Frage des religiösen Apriori", pp. 756-757.

[71] On The Evangelical-Social Congress, see Liebersohn, Harry: *Religion and Industrial Society*.

[72] Aldenhoff, Rita: "Max Weber and the Evangelical-Social Congress", pp. 198-199.

[73] in *Die Christliche Welt* 20 (1906). It is interesting to note that Weber at the end of this article criticised the religious life of the established churches in Germany. In Weber's eyes, they lacked 'religious motivation' compared to the charismatic sects. See pp. 581-583.

Evangelisch-soziale Zeitfragen, when Baumgarten should write the program for the journal.[74]

But perhaps the most important theological contact Weber had was that with Ernst Troeltsch. Sometimes it has been said that Weber strongly influenced Ernst Troeltsch, particularly Troeltsch's magnum opus *The Social Teachings of the Christian Churches*. This is an exaggeration grounded on the fact that Troeltsch adopts Weber's capitalism thesis. However, this is not the whole subject of his *Social Teachings*.[75] Troeltsch helped Weber to get to know much of the theological literature he needed to be able to write his *Die protestantische Ethik*.[76]

In the rest of this chapter I shall try to point to some affinities between Weber's thought and theological thought during the same period. I do this so as to gain resources for a more constructive theological interpretation of Weber's texts. I shall organise my investigation around three themes, namely 1) The origins of religion, 2) Religion, ethics and the interpretation of reality, and 3) Religion in modernity.

The Origins of Religion

Weber did not accept reductionistic explanations of religious phenomena. He repeatedly stated that it was an oversimplification to say that religious ideas were a product of economic or social phenomena, or that they could be totally explained by psychology.[77] According to Weber, religious experiences are, at least to a certain extent, autonomous (*endogen*).[78] Basically, this should be seen as a stress on multicausality. Such a complex phenomenon as religion cannot be reduced to just one set of causes. Religious teachings are of course causally related to social phenomena, but, Weber is eager to point out, religion cannot be reduced to social factors. Speculatively, one can say that it seems as if Weber thought that religion is a kind of basic human response to life.

Charismatic authority is the most innovative force in history,[79] according to Weber, and he appears to think that no religion can occur if it is

---

[74] Baumgarten, Otto: *Meine Lebensgeschichte,* p. 215. There is, however, no reference to this cooperation in Weber's own writings.

[75] Drescher, Hans-Georg: *Ernst Troeltsch. His Life and Work,* p. 125; see also Graf, Friedrich Wilhelm: "Max Weber und die protestantische Theologie seiner Zeit", pp. 133-134.

[76] Graf, Friedrich Wilhelm: "Max Weber und die protestantische Theologie seiner Zeit", p. 136.

[77] e.g. in Weber, Max: *Das antike Judentum,* p. 302.

[78] Weber, Max: *Das antike Judentum,* p. 308.

[79] See for example Weber, Max: *Wirtschaft und Gesellschaft,* pp. 142, 446.

not grounded in some sort of charismatic phenomenon.[80] The authority of a charismatic leader is however dependent on the followers' acceptance, and therefore charismatic leadership cannot be established if it does not proclaim a message that is relevant in the social context. Weber's idea of the origins of religion seems to be that certain individuals have extraordinary experiences of some sort which motivate them to preach a religious message. This message, however, is largely a product of the social context and cannot be otherwise, because if it did not relate to and answer the questions of the time in which it is preached, nobody would listen.

Furthermore, since one of the main psychosocial functions of religion is to help people cope with the ethical irrationality of the world, the message is constructed in such a way as to correspond to the need of the social stratum that is its main basis. The religion of farmers, for example, tend to focus on the forces of nature and lean towards magic, because of the farmer's dependence of the natural forces for his living. If farmers adopt a more developed form of religion, it is often because it gives them the possibility to oppose landlords that oppress them, according to Weber. The privileged groups of a society, on the other hand, seem to adopt a religiosity that legitimates and enforces their privileged status.[81]

Weber was very interested in the Old Testament prophets, because they were a sort of charismatic leaders. Since this area is the natural point of contact between Weber's theory of the origin of religion and the theology of his time, I shall analyse how he viewed the Old Testament prophets and compare his view with one of the central figures of the History of religions school, namely Hermann Gunkel. As will be evident, there are striking parallels between Gunkel's and Weber's view of Old Testament prophetism and also their theory of the origin of religion at large.

According to Weber, the beginning of Old Testament prophecy is to be found in the magicians and seers that played a central role in the tribe society of Israel, before the establishment of the Davidic kingdom. These older type of prophets were, according to Weber, charismatic figures who, in contrast to the scriptural prophets, deliberately brought about their ecstatic states with the help of dance and music.[82] These

---

[80] Weber, Max: "Wissenschaft als Beruf", *MWG I/17*, p. 110.
[81] Weber, Max: *Wirtschaft und Gesellschaft*, pp. 285-314.
[82] Weber, Max: *Das antike Judentum*, pp. 105-106.

older type of prophets were recruited on the ground of personal charisma, but they constituted a professional guild, pursuing common exercises at special places.[83] These prophets differed from the later, scriptural prophets in that they were mainly prophets of good fortune, not of doom. Except for prophesying good fortune, they helped people with various troubles, as indicated when Saul and his servant think of hiring Samuel to find Saul's father's lost donkeys (1 Sa 9). With the establishment of the kingdom, this prophecy of fortune gradually changed into a new form of prophecy, critical of the kingdom and especially of its rulers, who adopt foreign customs.[84] When the prophet Amos enters the scene, a new form of prophecy has occurred, according to Weber, namely the prophecy of doom, built on a theology characterised by ethical monotheism.

Weber characterises the pre-exilic prophets as political figures, concerned with the difficult situation of the state and of the people, due to the world-political situation.[85] The prophets explained, according to Weber, the power-political misfortunes that befell Israel as Yahweh's punishment for Israel's sins, and therefore they viewed foreign conquerors as God's instruments.[86] Weber points out that Jeremiah's preaching of submission to Nebuchadnezzar looks like high treason, if judged by modern standards.[87] Despite that the prophets were of different social origin, their attitudes to inner-political questions were quite similar: they were critical of the monarchy, stood on the side of the poor and underprivileged and preferably directed their curses towards the rich and powerful.[88]

Out of this characterisation it would seem as if the prophets were allied to certain political groups in the Israelite society, but according to Weber it would be totally wrong to draw such a conclusion from the fact that their message had political implications, even if the prophets' contemporaries sometimes understood them in that way. Weber justifies this view by pointing to the fact that the prophets were not consistent in their political loyalties, and he exemplifies with the fact that the same Isaiah that had seen the king of Assur, Sennacherib, as the instrument of Yahweh, and preached against the politically wise alliances with Egypt,

---

[83] Weber, Max: *Das antike Judentum*, p. 105.
[84] Weber, Max: *Das antike Judentum*, pp. 119-120.
[85] Weber, Max: *Das antike Judentum*, pp. 281-282.
[86] Weber, Max: *Das antike Judentum*, pp. 322-326.
[87] Weber, Max: *Das antike Judentum*, p. 288.
[88] Weber, Max: *Das antike Judentum*, p. 291.

turned against Assur and Sennacherib when it was religiously relevant to do so.[89]

The prophets understood their own charisma as consisting in the ability to understand Yahweh, and the possession of magical powers were not so important for them as it was for Jesus, according to Weber.[90] The prophets' interest lay, on Weber's interpretation, on ethics rather than cult. Their religion was characterised by a strict ethical monotheism, where Yahweh was regarded as the heavenly king who was the origin and custodian of the moral law, made known to humanity through the Torah.[91] This view of God as a heavenly king was, according to Weber, at least partly constructed on the model of kingship prevalent in the Orient at the time.[92]

Weber repeatedly stresses that the prophetic religion was related to and at least partly caused by the social context. The doom-prophetism was constructed because it was relevant in the social and political circumstances,[93] and the socially constructed theology of the time at least partly decided what kind of experiences that was recognised as religious experiences sent by God.[94] But even if Weber strongly emphasises the social construction of Old Testament prophetism, he also claims that prophetism to a certain extent is grounded in the autonomous, inner experiences of the prophets:

> The sacred states of the prophets were…truly personal and were thus experienced by them and their audiences, and not as the product of an emotional mass influence. No sort of external influence, but his personal God-sent condition placed the prophet in the ecstatic state.[95]

The prophets were, according to Weber, solitary ecstatics who had some sort of inner religious experiences which it is impossible to explain scientifically. In Weber's eyes, any effort to explain the prophets' experiences by reference to the social context will fail, since it seems that no social stratum or class really benefited from their teachings. It seems,

---

[89] Weber, Max: *Das antike Judentum*, p. 288.

[90] Weber, Max: *Das antike Judentum*, p. 312.

[91] Weber, Max: *Das antike Judentum*, pp. 319, 323.

[92] Weber, Max: *Wirtschaft und Gesellschaft*, pp. 273-274.

[93] Weber, Max: *Das antike Judentum*, pp. 322.

[94] Weber, Max: *Das antike Judentum*, pp. 326-328.

[95] AJ p. 293. Weber, Max: *Das antike Judentum*, p. 308: "*Die heiligen Zuständlichkeiten dieser Propheten sind…durchaus endogen, und wurden auch so, und nicht als Produkte einer emotionalen aktuellen Massenwirkung, von ihnen und den Hörern empfunden: nicht irgendeine Wirkung von außen her, sondern die eigene gottgesendete Zuständlichkeit versetzt die Propheten in den ekstatischen Habitus.*"

however, that the prophets interpreted their experiences with the help of the available religious symbol system as a mission from Yahweh to morally exhort the people.[96] They seldom spoke out of ecstasy in the way the Delphic oracle did, but they reflected over their experiences before preaching.

In Weber's view, this coming together of ecstatic and interpreter in the same person explained why the prophetic preaching had such a fundamental impact on Israelite society and religion: the prophets saw themselves as having been standing in "Yahwe's council" and this gave them a tremendous élan.[97] Their message, however unpopular, had relevance in the situation in which it was preached, because it offered an interpretation of the situation of the people.

Even if Israelite prophecy bore many common traits with other forms of prophecy, Weber thought that he could identify two characteristics of Israelite prophecy that made it different from other forms, namely the solitude of the prophets and the fact that they did not seek ecstasy, it came to them spontaneously.[98]

From this analysis of Weber's discussion of prophecy in the Old Testament some conclusions regarding his view of the origin of religion can be drawn.[99] It seems that he thinks that at least some forms of religiosity have their ground in autonomous experiences. These experiences are more or less void of cognitive content and have to be interpreted and understood with the help of the religious symbol system that is available. This language is a product of the historical and social circumstances, and the prophets' interpretation of their experiences with the help of the available religious language will be listened to insofar as it is experienced as relevant by the listeners. The prophets' preaching was relevant because it gave an explanation to the ethical irrationality of the world that manifested itself in the fact that misfortune befell the people of God. One could say that Weber thinks that the fact that the prophets were religious persons cannot be given a scholarly explanation, because it is

[96] Weber, Max: *Das antike Judentum*, p. 303.

[97] AJ p. 291. Weber, Max: *Das antike Judentum*, p. 305: "*Jahwes Ratsversammlung*".

[98] Weber, Max: *Das antike Judentum*, p. 306.

[99] From the fact that my discussion concerns Weber's treatment of Old Testament prophecy, it should not be concluded that Weber valued prophetic or charismatic elements in other religions as less interesting. For example, he characterises the Buddha as a charismatic prophet in *Wirtschaft und Gesellschaft* p. 273. It cannot be denied, however, that Weber's treatment of the Old Testament prophecy is the most developed discussion of the character of religious experiences that can be found in his writings.

grounded in an autonomous religious experience, but the content of the message they preached can be understood, if not wholly so at least to a great extent, as a product of the social context in which it was created.[100] Another way to interpret Weber's opinion would be to say that he holds that it is impossible to talk about unconceptualised religious experience, but that he still wants to stay clear of a reductive approach to religion.

Weber's understanding of Israelite prophecy would of course have been controversial to the conservative theology of his time, but it bear clear similarities to the work of theologians of the History of religions school. I shall now turn to Hermann Gunkel's view of prophecy in the Old Testament, to which Weber admits being highly indebted.

Hermann Gunkel was the father of form criticism, an exegetical tradition which sees the tales of the Pentateuch, for example, as folk tales that have been handed down between the generations long before they were written down. What interested Gunkel was not so much the text as it could be read in the Bible as the social milieu in which Old Testament religion had developed.

Gunkel developed his view of what religion is in a speech held on the *Fünfte Weltkongress für freies Christentum und religiösen Fortschritt* [The Fifth World Congress for a Free Christianity and Religious Progress]. He starts with the assertion that no religion can be without doctrine in some form. But this "objective" side of religion is secondary to a deeper, experiential side:

> We know, due to the teachings of pietism and the German theology since Schleiermacher, that every religious doctrine is an expression of something deeper, which stirs in the human heart; that the source, from which religion always has come and forever will come from, is the heart of the pious humans, who have been touched by God.[101]

In his book about the prophets of the Old Testament, Gunkel seems to adopt this view of what religion is to his analysis of what he calls the

---

[100] Weber's understanding of ancient Judaism and Old Testament prophecy has been severely criticised for laying to hard a stress on the solitude of the prophets and for having an evolutionist perspective of Judaism. See for example: Holstein, Jay: "Max Weber and Biblical Scholarship", pp. 159-179 and Berger, Peter: "Charisma and Religious Innovation. The Social Location of Israelite Prophecy", pp. 940-950.

[101] Gunkel, Hermann: *Die Religionsgeschichte und die alttestamentliche Wissenschaft*, p. 8: "*Wir wissen, durch den Pietismus und die deutsche Theologie seit Schleiermacher belehrt, daß alle religiöse Lehre der Ausdruck eines Tieferen ist, was sich im Herzen des Menschen regt; daß der eigentliche Born, aus dem die Religion stets geflossen ist und in Ewigkeit fließen wird, das Herz des frommen, von Gott berührten Menschen ist.*"

prophets' secret experiences.[102] Just as Weber, Gunkel holds that the
prophets were solitary ecstatics who thought of themselves as someone
"who has been standing in Yahweh's council".[103] Gunkel is, like Weber,
sceptical about efforts to explain the ecstatic character of the prophets as
psychopathological phenomena, even if he recognises that there are
resemblances between the behaviour of the prophets and what we would
call pathological behaviour. But Gunkel points to the fact that what
behaviour which is regarded as normal is different in different cultures,
and therefore one cannot in a simple way draw the conclusion that since
the prophets behaved in a way that seems pathological to us, they suf-
fered from mental diseases.[104]

For Gunkel, the ecstatic experiences of the prophets were impossible
to explain with scientific methods. Of course it was equally impossible
to explain them theologically as revelations from Yahweh.[105] What
could be said, according to him, was that the prophets had certain experiences of transcendence which they interpreted as revelations from Yahweh. Like Weber, Gunkel saw the content of the prophets' preaching as
mainly a product of the political and social circumstances.[106] This
preaching, however, was grounded in their experience of transcendence,
or, as Gunkel writes, the prophets' convictions came "from the depths of
their hearts".[107]

Just as Weber, Gunkel makes a distinction between the prophets of
good fortune, and the prophets of doom.[108] His interest concentrates on
the prophets of doom because he thinks that they are far more important
for the understanding of the essence of prophecy.[109] According to
Gunkel, the prophets preached that Israel's misfortune was due to divine
punishment for Israel's sins. The God of the prophets was an ethical God
who did not care for sacrifices, but wanted his people to live an ethical
life.[110] The new with the prophets' theology is not, according to Gunkel,
that they relate religion and morality, but that they see morality as the

[102] Gunkel, Hermann: *Die Propheten*, p. 2. Weber had a very high regard for
Gunkel's analysis of these "secret experiences". In *Das antike Judentum*, p. 281, he says
of Gunkel's study that it is *"glänzend wie immer"*.
[103] Gunkel, Hermann: *Die Propheten*, p. 7: *"wer im Rate Jahves gestanden hat"*. See
Jer 23:18.
[104] Gunkel, Hermann: *Die Propheten*, pp. 26-27.
[105] Gunkel, Hermann: *Die Propheten*, pp. 30-31.
[106] Gunkel, Hermann: *Die Propheten*, p. 77.
[107] Gunkel, Hermann: *Die Propheten*, p. 73: *"aus tiefstem Herzen"*.
[108] Gunkel, Hermann: *Die Propheten*, pp. 32-33.
[109] Gunkel, Hermann: *Die Propheten*, pp. 37-38.

essence of religion, and that they construct God as the personalisation of the moral ideal.[111]

The parallels with Weber's thought are obvious, and this is of course due to the fact that Weber to a large extent is dependent on Gunkel and other theologians of the History of religions school in his analysis of ancient Judaism. Weber and Gunkel agree that the prophets' religiosity is grounded in ecstatic experiences of transcendence, that the content of their preaching to a large extent is caused by the social and political circumstances and that the prophets' religion best can be characterised as ethical monotheism. It also seems that the evaluative developmental perspective, at least to a certain extent, is common: both Weber and Gunkel tend to regard the scriptural prophets as representatives of a 'higher' form of religion than the earlier prophets and sages of ancient Israel.

There is, however one important difference between Gunkel's and Weber's view of the Old Testament prophetism, and that difference is that Gunkel was a Christian theologian with theological ambitions, while Weber had no theological aims. For Gunkel the relation between religion and ethics which the prophets pointed to was an essential part of divine revelation and religiously relevant:

> We recognise God's revelation in the great personalities of religion, who in their inner depths experience the holy secret and speak of it in flames of fire. We see God's revelation in the great turns and wonderful connections of history.[112]

It should be noted, that the view of religion as a product of both autonomous experiences of transcendence and of the social context was quite common among theologians in the beginning of the 20th century. The common view seems to have been that which Troeltsch formulated as such: "For although religion is interwoven with life as a whole, in development and dialectic it has an independent existence."[113]

Similar ways of reasoning can be found in the writings of Weber's cousin, the theologian Otto Baumgarten. The underlying theme in Baumgarten's theological writings is, as Dietrich Rössler has said, his

---

[110] Gunkel, Hermann: *Die Propheten*, pp. 47-48.

[111] Gunkel, Hermann: *Die Propheten*, p. 80.

[112] Gunkel, Hermann: *Israel und Babylonien*, pp. 36-37: "*Gottes Offenbarung erkennen wir in den grossen Personen der Religion, die in ihrem tiefsten Innern das heilige Geheimnis erfahren und mit Flammenzungen davon Reden; Gottes Offenbarung sehen wir in den grossen Wendungen und wunderbaren Fügungen der Geschichte.*"

[113] *Social Teachings*, p. 43. Troeltsch, Ernst: *Die Soziallehren der christlichen Kirchen und Gruppen*, p. 25: "*Das religiöse Leben hat eben bei aller Verflechtung in das übrige Leben doch seine eigene Entwicklung und eigene Dialektik.*"

understanding of religion as a radically subjective phenomenon, grounded in the inner experiences of the religious person.[114] Religion is for Baumgarten grounded in the secret experiences of the individual, and the cognitive content of the religion has very little with the experiential core of religion to do.[115]

There are substantial contacts and parallels between Weber's view of the origin of religion and of views current among theologians in the beginning of the 20th century. There was common emphasis on the subjectivity of religion and its grounding in inner experience, especially the experience of religious geniuses like Jesus or the Old Testament prophets. There was also a widespread consensus about the fact that the concrete content of religious teaching was mainly a product of the social and historical context and that therefore religious experience and the social form in which it is embedded can hardly be separated from each other. What separates Weber from the theologians is thus not the understanding of religion as originating both in religious experience and social context, but the theological interpretation of the experiences.

Religion, Ethics and the Interpretation of Reality

For Weber, religions historically have had two main functions, namely to provide value orientation and an overall interpretation of reality. Weber repeatedly states that the motive for constructing religious belief systems is a deeply felt human need to come to grips with the problem of suffering.[116] One of the main functions of religion according to Weber is to provide a meaning that enables humanity to see the world as a rationally ordered cosmos, despite the fact that the empirical reality points in the opposite direction.[117] In the religious efforts to handle the problem of suffering, different types of solutions have been developed, according to Weber, for example the Hindu doctrine of karma, or the idea of predestination and of the *deus absconditus*.[118]

---

[114] Rössler, Dietrich: "Die Subjektivität der Religion", p. 21.

[115] Baumgarten, Otto: *Neue Bahnen*, p. 37.

[116] see for example Weber, Max: "Politik als Beruf", *MWG I/17*, p. 241. The term 'function' should not be taken in an explanatory way. Weber would never have accepted the idea that by interpreting the *function* of a phenomenon a sufficient causal explanation of the same phenomenon can be established.

[117] Weber, Max: *Wirtschaft und Gesellschaft*, p. 275.

[118] Weber, Max: *Wirtschaft und Gesellschaft*, pp. 317-318.

Another central function of religion is to guide human action in the world, that is, to provide value orientation.[119] This *function* of religion does not need to be seen as a central aspect of a religious faith by the believers. The most obvious example of this in Weber's thinking is his analysis of the relations between Protestantism and capitalism. Before my analysis of Weber's view of this relation, it should be noted what Weber does not say; he does not hold that Protestantism has caused capitalism, only that the Protestant ethos can be ideal-typically constructed as one factor that has contributed to the development of modern industrial capitalism.[120]

Weber observes that the economy has developed in a capitalistic direction earlier and easier in areas in which Calvinism has been the dominating religious tradition, than it has in other areas. The reason for this is that reformed Christianity has fostered an ascetic way of living, which promotes production and restricts consumption. The result of this was accumulation of capital and since this wealth could not be used for consumption, the only way was to reinvest it in production.

This way of economic behaviour was promoted by the Calvinist doctrine of predestination and the rationalistic character of Calvinism, which excluded any possibility to influence God or contribute to one's own salvation by magic or sacramentalism.[121] Weber assumed that this doctrine of predestination made the problem of *certitudo salutis* acute for the Calvinists.[122] In the Calvinist pastoral care this was solved by the theory that the behaviour of the individual was a sign of her or his election. Combined with the idea that leisure was sin, this created an industriousness that was tremendous, because if you could be said to live a sinful life, this was a sign that you did not belong to those elected for salvation.[123]

Weber's theory of the relation between Protestantism and capitalism is an example of his idea that human behaviour is guided by world views. In this case the Calvinist doctrine of predestination and the need for *certitudo salutis* that the doctrine created gave effectiveness to the values that Calvinism promoted. This interest in the practical side of

---

[119] Weber, Max: "Einleitung", *MWG I/19*, p. 101.

[120] Weber, Max: "Die protestantische Ethik", *GARS I*, p. 83. Weber's analysis of Protestant ethics is notoriously difficult to interpret. One recently published suggestion is that the 'Protestant ethic-thesis' rather should be conceived as an ideal-type out of which hypotheses can be formulated. See Agevall, *op.cit.*, p. 239.

[121] Weber, Max: "Die protestantische Ethik", *GARS I*, pp. 93-98.

[122] Weber, Max: "Die protestantische Ethik", *GARS I*, pp. 103-106.

[123] Weber, Max: "Die protestantische Ethik", *GARS I*, pp. 165-178.

religion is an obvious point of contact between Weber and theology.[124] In a wider sense, the question of the relation between religious faith and ethics was at the centre of liberal theological thinking, not least in the thought of Albrecht Ritschl (1822-1889), who can be described as the founding father of modern liberal theology.[125]

Ritschl's theological system is profoundly anti-metaphysical in character. Basically he subscribes to a Kantian form of epistemology, and claims that we cannot have any knowledge of the thing-in-itself, but only of the world as it appears to us in our conceptualisations of it.[126] Ritschl proposes that religious assertions should be seen as value-judgements, rather than as statements of facts. By this he means that we cannot know anything about the essence of God or of the nature(s) of Jesus Christ in themselves, but only about what God or Christ means for us. There is no point in speculating about what is hidden from human perception. Rather we should attend to the importance of God and Christ in our lives.[127] Ritschl confesses his belief in Christ as God, but this does not imply that he accepts the formula of Chalcedon as an adequate expression of this faith. Christ is God because Christians value him as God in their lives:

> If Christ, by what he has done and suffered for my salvation, is my Lord, and if, by having confidence in the power of what he has done for me, I honour him as my God, then that is a value-judgement of a direct kind. It is not a judgement which belongs to the sphere of disinterested scientific knowledge, like the formula of Chalcedon. When my opponents on this point demand a judgement of the latter sort, they show that they do not know how to distinguish between scientific and religious knowledge, that is, they do not really feel at home in the sphere of religion. All knowledge of a religious kind consists in value-judgements... We can only know anything about the essence of that which is God and divine if we determine its value for our salvation and bliss.[128]

[124] Graf, Friedrich Wilhelm: "Max Weber und die protestantische Theologie seiner Zeit", p. 126.

[125] I use the notion 'liberal theology' in a wide sense, as referring to various revisionist theological projects, aiming at making Christian faith acceptable to modern culture and reason. In my usage it includes both Ritschlianism and the theological outlook of Troeltsch, even if I acknowledge that they do differ on very important points. For an introduction to Ritschl's theological thinking, see Richmond, James: *Ritschl: A Reappraisal*.

[126] Ritschl, Albrecht: *Die christliche Lehre von der Rechtfertigung und Versöhnung III*, pp. 18-21.

[127] Ritschl, *op.cit.*, pp. 195-197.

[128] Ritschl, *op.cit.*, p. 376: "*Ist aber Christus durch das, was er zu meinem heil gethan und gelitten hat, mein Herr, und ehre ich ihn als meinen Gott, indem ich um meines Heiles willen der Kraft seiner Wohlthat vertraue, so ist das ein Werthurtheil directer Art.*

Ritschl thus abstains from interpreting Christian faith in theoretical terms. Christian faith, according to him, does not compete with scientific knowledge or try to explain the world ontologically. On such matters faith has nothing to say. Christianity rather offers a religious and ethical perspective on the world. Ritschl describes Christian faith as an ellipse with two focal points: on the one hand the reconciliation of humanity with God through Christ based on God's love, and on the other hand an ethical conception formulated in the idea of the kingdom of God as the moral goal of humanity.[129] Salvation, which Ritschl describes as justification (*Rechtfertigung*), should, according to him, be seen as something which renews the person who is tormented by feelings of guilt. When a person has experienced the justification, he or she is reconciled with God and can continue to strive towards the realisation of the kingdom of God.[130]

Ritschl presents a form of Christian theology whose main concern is the ethical dimension of human life. In accepting the boundaries of theoretical reason drawn up by Kant, Ritschl sees Christian faith as located within the sphere of practical reason. For him, Christian theology does not raise knowledge-claims in any ordinary sense. Rather it formulates a way of life based on the value of love. In the words of John Macquarrie, Ritschl seems to think that the word 'God' refers to an unknown x, of which we can have no theoretical knowledge. But Jesus Christ has revealed that God is love, and so gives a practical meaning to the word 'God'.[131]

The Ritschlian way of doing theology – antimetaphysically and ethically oriented – was characteristic for liberal Protestant thinking during Weber's life. Of course there was also conflict among radical theologians. At the end of the 19th century, this conflict took the form of a discussion between the Ritschlians and the advocates of the so called

---

Das Urtheil gehört nicht in das Gebiet des uninteressirten wissenschaftlichen Erkennens, wie die chalcedonensische Formel. Indem also die Gegner an dieser Stelle ein Urtheil der letztern Art erfordern, so geben sie kund, daß sie religiöses und wissenschaftliches Erkennen nicht zu unterscheiden wissen, also im Gebiet der Religion eigentlich nicht zu Hause sind. Alle Erkenntnisse religiöser Art sind directe Werthurtheile... Das was Gott und göttlich ist, können wir auch dem Wesen nach nur erkennen, indem wir seinen Werth zu unserer Seligkeit feststellen." My English translation closely follows the one provided in Macquarrie, John: *Jesus Christ in Modern Thought*, p. 254.

[129] Ritschl, *op.cit.*, p. 11. On the 'kingdom of God' as the moral goal of humanity, se also p. 267.

[130] Ritschl, *op.cit.,* pp. 503-504.

[131] Macquarrie, John: *Jesus Christ in Modern Thought*, p. 254. For the view that God is love, see Ritschl, *op.cit.*, p. 260.

History of religions school. For many historians of religion and biblical scholars, the Ritschlian way of doing theology tended to portray Jesus as a fine, educated and virtuous German university professor, rather than as the apocalyptical prophet which he in fact was. In the eyes of the History of Religions school, the Jesus of Ritschl had never existed in history. But many of the historians who criticised Ritschl did so because they thought his picture of the historical Jesus was incorrect, not because they had anything in principle against an ethically and antimetaphysically oriented interpretation of Christianity.[132]

Another line of conflict between liberal Protestant theologians was the divide between those who strictly adhered to Ritschl's antimetaphysical position, and those who wanted to preserve the idea that Christian dogma expresses truth-claims in an ordinary sense and therefore has to be integrated with the claims of science and continuously revised when science develops. Brent Sockness has provided a lucid analysis of this internal liberal conflict between what we in a modern philosophical idiom would label noncognitivists and cognitivists, in his analysis of the debate between Ritschl's follower Wilhelm Herrmann, and Ernst Troeltsch. Both Herrmann and Troeltsch were eager to respect the "eternal covenant" between liberal theology and science, implying that theology respects free scientific efforts and the results stemming therefrom. But they respected this covenant in two different ways. Wilhelm Herrmann located Christian faith in a more or less noncognitive realm of spiritual life, while Troeltsch took a more cognitive approach and accepted the fact that Christian theology continuously has to revise dogma in the light of new scientific findings.[133]

Troeltsch regarded the relation between religion and ethics as complicated and was suspicious against one-dimensional ways of presenting the relation between them.[134] But this does not mean that he did not think that the Christian ethos contained certain characteristic values, such as a strict individualism, pared with a sense for community, and a stress on the importance of charity.[135] The fact that Troeltsch took a different view

[132] See e.g. Weiß, Johannes: *Die Predigt Jesu vom Reiche Gottes,* pp. 7, 66-67. To this issue see Walter E. Wyman Jr.'s article "The Kingdom of God in Germany".

[133] Sockness, Brent: *Against False Apologetics,* pp. 214-215. Wilhelm Herrmann's view is stated in a clear way in his "Der Glaube an Gott und die Wissenschaft unserer Zeit", especially from page 197. Herrmann explicitly criticises Troeltsch on p. 207. Troeltsch's critique of Herrmann is clear from for example his "Zur Frage des Religiösen Apriori", pp. 764-766.

[134] Drescher, Hans-Georg: *Ernst Troeltsch. His Life and Work,* p. 184.

[135] Troeltsch, Ernst: *Die Soziallehren der christlichen Kirchen und Gruppen,* pp. 978-979.

on the relation between religion and science than did Ritschl and Wilhelm Herrmann, must thus not be taken as if he thought that religion and ethics have to be radically separated.

Harnack, as a follower of Ritschl, held, that the Christian Gospel can be seen as an ethical message, founded in Jesus' teaching about love.[136] According to Harnack, Jesus taught that love of God is the root of all good, and he states that "in this respect it is possible to view religion as the soul of morality and morality as the body of religion".[137] Even if Harnack admits that the Gospel does not proclaim another morality than the common ethics, he seems to think that Christianity in some sense provides another ground of morality, because it connects morality with love of God.

How are these ideas of Ritschl, Troeltsch and Harnack related to Weber's thinking about the relations between religion, morality and the human need to interpret reality? The most obvious contact is of course the simple fact that they all hold that there is an intimate relationship between religion and morality. Further, they all deny that religion can be reduced to morality. Of course, Weber would not have accepted Harnack's view that love of God is the root of all that is good. But he would have admitted that Christianity, as all religions, can create values and/or motivate us to implement certain values, as for example humility, a value especially appreciated by Harnack.[138]

Weber did not openly take sides in the conflict between Herrmann and Troeltsch, but his thought is highly suspicious of any form of metaphysics. In rationalised culture, there cannot be any plausibility structure for metaphysical beliefs in an ordinary sense. Theology, if it wishes to be a viable option in modernity, therefore has to be seen as something else than a system of metaphysical statements if it should be able to be integrated with Weber's thought. With a terminology borrowed from Loren R. Graham, one can say that both Weber, Ritschl and Wilhelm Herrmann advocates an epistemological *restrictionism,* that is the view that a sharp line between what can be seen as scientifically legitimate claims to knowledge, and what most appropriately can be termed religious wisdom must be drawn.[139] Initially, therefore, it seems that

---

[136] Harnack, Adolf, *Das Wesen des Christentums,* pp. 45-47.

[137] Harnack, *op.cit.,* pp. 47: *"in diesem Sinne kann man die Religion die Seele der Moral und die Moral den Körper der Religion nennen".*

[138] Harnack, *op.cit.,* p. 47.

[139] Graham, Loren R.: *Between Science and Values,* p. 8. The concept of epistemological restrictionism has also been used by the Swedish historian of ideas Kjell Jonsson in his *Vid vetandets gräns,* pp. 11-12.

Ritschl's and Herrmann's approach to the question of the relation between theology and science is in better agreement with Weber's thinking.

Religion in Modern Society

Karl Löwith claimed that one of the most important points of contact between Weber and Karl Marx was their mutual interest in the fate of the individual in modern society. There were, according to Löwith, similarities between their respective diagnoses of the situation, but differences when it came to the question about what to do about it. The same could be said of Weber's relations to the liberal theologians.

The most obvious point of comparison is the cultural analysis of Ernst Troeltsch. Troeltsch was not especially optimistic about the future of humanity in modern society. According to him, modern society could be characterised as contradictory. On the one hand, capitalism promotes individuality, but on the other hand it creates new dependencies that replace the bonds of the feudal society.[140]

As Graf concludes, this analysis of modern capitalism is not so very different from Weber's.[141] As was the case with Marx and Weber, what differs is not primarily the diagnosis but the proposed cure. For Weber, in modern society religion can only have relevance for the individual as a kind of personal, private cure against the meaninglessness of the world.[142]

Weber does not deny the possibility of religious experiences in the modern world, but he thinks that these experiences can only be private experiences that cannot be incorporated in a socially constructed religious world view that is able to dominate a whole society. Troeltsch, on the other hand, thinks that religion even in modern culture can be a formative factor in society at large. Troeltsch and Weber agree in assuming that religion in modern society can function as a way for the individual to preserve some sort of freedom and personal character. Troeltsch, however, also thinks that Christianity can have an integrative function and help to bridge conflicts in society.[143] This is a view that Weber cannot share; for him modern society is characterised by a never-ending conflict between mutually exclusive values.[144]

---

[140] Troeltsch, Ernst: "Das Wesen des modernen Geistes", p. 310.

[141] Graf, Friedrich Wilhelm: "Max Weber und die protestantische Theologie seiner Zeit", pp. 138-139.

[142] Weber, Max: "Wissenschaft als Beruf", *MWG I/17*, pp. 109-110.

[143] see for example: Troeltsch, Ernst: "Das Wesen des modernen Geistes", pp. 335-336.

[144] see for example: Weber, Max: "Wissenschaft als Beruf", *MWG I/17*, pp. 99-100.

As has already been stated, Weber was not very optimistic about the possibility of creating a truly humane world. The only way to radically change the trend towards a totally rationalised society would be a new outburst of prophetic charisma,[145] something that Weber judged to be unlikely, even if his political writings show that he did not regard it as impossible. The idea that prophetic charisma is one of the possible solutions to the problem of modernity can be found also in the writings of his contemporary theologians. A typical example is the following passage from Gunkel:

> The complaint that the personalities which the idealistic epoch brought forth in such a multitude are beginning to vanish and that it becomes more and more difficult to keep independent men in various enterprises are more and more heard today. Would not our spiritual life benefit from some old israelitic spirit? Yes indeed, may the prophets wake up![146]

When Weber discusses the importance of charisma and the character of religion in modern society he does not seem to assume that Christianity has any obvious role to play, more than as a refuge for those who cannot bear the fate of modernity; Weber recommends them to return into "the arms of the old churches" which "are opened widely and compassionately".[147] But in modern political life he sees a conflict between the Christian ethos and the ethos of politics, a conflict that he understands as a conflict between an ethics of conviction (*Gesinnungsethik*) and an ethics of responsibility (*Verantwortungsethik*).[148] As the social reality has developed, traditional Christianity cannot be more than an escape from modernity.

Weber points out that this does not mean that the person who adheres to an ethics of conviction is irresponsible or that a person who follows an ethics of responsibility has no convictions.[149] What differs is the

---

[145] This idea is expressed in Weber's writings foremost in relation to his discussions of the constitution of the Weimar republic, e.g. in "Politik als Beruf", *MWG I/17*, pp. 223-225.

[146] Gunkel, Hermann: *Was bleibt vom alten Testament?*, p. 31: "*Aber man hört gegenwärtig laut und lauter die Klage, daß die Persönlichkeiten, die das idealistische Zeitalter in so reicher Fülle erzeugt hat, auszusterben beginnen, und daß es selbstständigen Männern immer schwerer wird, sich in dem ungeheuren, alles vereinerleienden Getriebe zu behaupten. Sollte unserem geistigen Leben nicht ein Schuß altisraelitischen Geistes guttun? Ja, würden die Propheten wach!*".

[147] FMW p. 155. Weber, Max: "Wissenschaft als Beruf", *MWG I/17*, p. 110: "*die weit und erbarmend geöffneten Arme der alten Kirchen*".

[148] Weber, Max: "Politik als Beruf", *MWG I/17*, p. 237.

[149] Weber, Max: "Politik als Beruf", *MWG I/17*, p. 237.

character of the convictions and the responsibility.[150] The "Gesin-
nungsethiker" is primarily responsible to her or his principles, and
leaves the consequences of the actions to God, as Weber expresses it.
The "Verantwortungsethiker" is acutely aware of reality as it is, and
tries to accomplish her or his goals by using the adequate means, even
if these means from an ethical point of view can seem dubious. This
does not imply that followers of an ethic of responsibility always hold
that the ends justify the means, but that they are prepared to consider to
use means that they deem proper to achieve a given goal, even if this
implies that they has to use means that *per se* are in conflict with their
ideals. Simply stated, they accept means-end calculating.

Modern politics should, according to Weber, be an example of action
according to the principles of the ethics of responsibility.[151] A politician
has to strive for the realisation of her or his ideals as rationally as possible, which for Weber implies to use the most adequate means at hand.
Politics is the same as the striving for power and it is the art of the possible. Therefore the "spirit of politics" is in a permanent conflict with
the God of love:

> The genius – or demon – of politics lives in a state of inner tension with the
> god of love, and even with the Christian God as manifested in the institu-
> tion of the church, a tension that may erupt at any moment into irresolvable
> conflict.[152]

Politicians cannot avoid fighting what they think is evil with evil
means such as force; otherwise they will be responsible for the outcome.
Christians, ideal-typically, can avoid fighting the evil by evil means, and
if the consequences turn out to be bad, they can comfort themselves with
the fact that they did not violate their principles.

Despite Weber's claim that there is an irresolvable conflict between
politics and the Christian ethos, there were in fact theologians, contemporary with Weber, who expressed similar views. One example can be
found in a book that Weber's cousin Otto Baumgarten published in 1916
with the title *Politik und Moral*. Baumgarten holds that there is a sharp
difference between the morality of the private sphere and the morality of

---

[150] For a thoroughgoing analysis of Weber's distinction between the two types of
ethics, see Schluchter, Wolfgang: *Paradoxes of Modernity*, pp. 48-101.

[151] Weber, Max: "Politik als Beruf", *MWG I/17*, p. 235.

[152] PW p. 366. Weber, Max: "Politik als Beruf", *MWG I/17*, p. 247: *"Der Genius,
oder Dämon der Politik lebt mit dem Gott der Liebe, auch mit dem Christengott in seiner
kirchlichen Ausprägung, in einer inneren Spannung, die jederzeit in unaustragbarem
Konflikt ausbrechen kann."*

the state.[153] For Baumgarten, politics is the struggle for power with the most rational means available, and to have power is the same as to be correct – in the political sphere.[154] Politics should be rational and calculating, since the worst sin against the ethics of politics is to destroy the foundations of one's own power.[155]

In the end of his book, Baumgarten seems to retreat from this instrumentalist view of politics when he says that the personality stands above the state.[156] The state can and have the right to force the subjects to show outer loyalty, but it must not try to shape their inner convictions.[157]

The parallels between Weber's thinking about the different types of ethics and their relations to politics and Baumgarten's reasoning are obvious. Both Weber and Baumgarten claim that in modern society, politics has to be rational according to a means-end scheme, and that this technical rationality stands in conflict with the Christian ethos of love. As a liberal, Lutheran theologian, Baumgarten solves this conflict by saying that the ethics of love should only be applied to private life, while the political ethics is valid within the political, public sphere. Weber never explicitly discusses the relation between public and private morality, but it is quite clear that he prefers the ethics of responsibility and strongly recommends it when it comes to political action.

What then about Baumgarten's reservation that the state must not try to shape the personality of its subjects? Would this make him an advocate of the ethics of conviction in Weber's eyes? In one sense it seems to be so, since Baumgarten says that the state is not allowed to intrude in the personalities of the individuals, even if it is technically rational to do so.

But an ethic of responsibility cannot be equated with pure Machiavellian power politics. Nothing is so deplorable in politics as the striving for power for its on sake, according to Weber. Any politician has to have a goal, and strive for the realisation of a vision.[158] One such vision can be to develop a society where human personality and autonomy is respected and gets the opportunity to flourish. If that is the vision, which it seems to be in Baumgarten's case, it would be disastrous to use political means which destroy the vision. A *Verantwortungsethiker* should be

[153] Baumgarten, Otto: *Politik und Moral*, p. 141.
[154] Baumgarten, Otto: *Politik und Moral*, p. 114.
[155] Baumgarten, Otto: *Politik und Moral*, pp. 145-146.
[156] Baumgarten, Otto: *Politik und Moral*, p. 171.
[157] Baumgarten, Otto: *Politik und Moral*, pp. 171-172.
[158] Weber, Max: "Politik als Beruf", *MWG I/17*, p. 229.

loyal to her or his vision, but must not confuse vision with political reality. That seems to be Weber's point, with which Baumgarten agrees.

For Weber, religion has no given place in modern society, and this is due to two factors: rationalisation and the plurality of value-systems. Because of rationalisation, it will be more and more difficult for the knowledge claims of religious faith to gain plausibility, and because of this, a value pluralism and a religious pluralism characterise modern society. No religion can function as the integrative factor of a society, and no society can be grounded on a common value system. Rather, religions and value systems will be in a permanent state of conflict with each other.

Weber's provocative statements in *Politik als Beruf* about the irresolvable conflict between Christianity and modernity are partly due to the situation in which the lecture was held; he wanted to show that the utopias of Christian socialism, Marxism etc. were irrational and impossible ways forward for the new Weimar republic.[159] But nevertheless his statements of the conflicts between politics and the God of love seem to imply a negative view of the role of Christianity in modern society. The rest of this book is an effort to develop an alternative interpretation of Weber, showing that his perspective can be integrated with at least *some* forms of revisionist Christian theology. One aspect of Weber's thinking which provides a basis for such an alternative interpretation, is his view on the function of values in science, which will be the main object of study in the following chapter.

---

[159] Schluchter, Wolfgang: *Paradoxes of Modernity*, p. 49.

3. VALUES AND SCIENCE

Reality as an Infinite Multiplicity

Weber states in a footnote in *Roscher und Knies* that he considers Rickert's work as fundamental in the philosophy of science.[1] If one wants to make a coherent reconstruction of Weber's methodology, it is necessary to let Rickert provide the philosophical background, since Weber in his methodological writings purports to discuss the importance of Rickert's philosophy in his own field of research.[2] This does not mean that Weber has to be understood as being in total agreement with Rickert, as I will show in the section on the objectivity of the cultural sciences.[3]

As was stated in chapter two, Weber shared the Neo-Kantian idea of reality as an infinite manifold of phenomena. Reality shows itself as an unending flux of sensations to the human mind. How reality is *in se* is impossible to say, just because it shows itself as an infinity and it is impossible to grasp an infinity as it really is. In what follows, the term 'reality' thus does not designate reality *in se*, but reality as it shows itself in human perception. With "reality *in se*" I shall understand ontic reality, that is, as existent totally independent of how we humans conceive of it.[4]

Weber and Rickert reject the "picture theory of knowledge", which they understand as the idea that to have knowledge is to have a picture of reality *in se* in one's mind.[5] Humans can only have knowledge of their perceptions of reality, never of reality as it is *in se*, since in Rickert's view, reality *in se* is transcendent.[6] Neither Weber nor Rickert

[1] Weber, Max: "Roscher und Knies", *GAW*, p. 4, n. 2.

[2] Thomas Burger is perhaps the most ardent advocate of the view that Weber's methodology is in more or less total agreement with Rickert's views. See Burger, *op.cit.*, p. 7.

[3] Fritz Ringer has pointed to the relevant differences between Weber and Rickert in a lucid, albeit somewhat simplified, way. See his *Max Weber's Methodology*, pp. 49-52.

[4] On the concept "ontic" reality, see Herrmann, Eberhard: "Gud, verklighet och den religionsfilosofiska debatten om realism och antirealism", pp. 52-54.

[5] Weber, Max: "Roscher und Knies", *GAW*, p. 92, n. 1; Rickert, Heinrich: *Der Gegenstand der Erkentniss* (herafter: *Gegenstand*), pp. 44-45.

[6] Rickert, Heinrich: *Gegenstand*, p. 69. See also Nusser, Karl-Heinz: *Kausale Prozesse und sinnerfassende Vernunft*, p. 33.

defends epistemological realism, understood as the idea that the truth of
a statement can be judged by comparison with a reality independent of
human perception and conceptual construction.[7] However, there are
some passages in Weber's texts which can be said to support an interpretation implying that Weber conceived of the relation between reality
in se and our conceptual understanding of it in a slightly different way
than Rickert. These will be explored below.

The infinite manifold of reality is, according to Rickert, both *extensive*
and *intensive*.[8] Reality consists of an infinite number of phenomena.
Even if the quantity of matter in the universe is limited, reality must still
be seen as infinite, since both space and time are boundless, and therefore the material objects will occur in an infinite number of combina-
tions and relations.[9] Rickert labels this quantitative infinity reality's
extensive infinity.

But there is also an *intensive* infinity. Even if we focus our interest on
one single object, this object can be analysed from many perspectives.
Take the example of colours; a thing can be described as green, but if
you want you could try to define which nuances of green the object
reflects. Further, the object can be divided into smaller and smaller parts,
and perhaps not all parts can be described as green at all. Thus, every
single object can be said to consist of an infinite number of smaller
objects or aspects. This is in opposition to any 'picture theory of knowledge' which has to presuppose that reality consists of a limited number
of objects. In the contemporary debate, Hilary Putnam has taken a similar position as Weber and Rickert on such a 'picture theory': If we ask
how many objects there are in my study, we can answer that question in
different ways. Should we count every book as one object, or should we
count every page in a book as an object, just to mention one example.
We can construct reality in different ways, and therefore cannot claim
that our constructions are 'pictures' of reality *in se*.[10]

Weber accepts this distinction between intensive and extensive infinity, and tries to apply it in his methodology. An example of such an

---

[7] For a closer discussion of Rickert's critique of epistemological realism, see Oakes,
Guy: *Weber and Rickert,* pp. 56-61. See also Burger, *op.cit.,* p. 14. However, cf. Nial,
Tore: *Heinrich Rickerts kunskapsteori med hänsyn till närbesläktade fichteanska
tänkesätt,* pp. 193-211. Nials argues that Rickert *implicite* assumes a reality that exists
independent of human concept formation.

[8] Rickert, Heinrich: *Grenzen,* p. 36.

[9] Rickert, Heinrich: *Grenzen,* p. 33.

[10] The account of Putnam's example is based on Herrmann, Eberhard: "Gud, verklighet och den religionsfilosofiska debatten om realism och antirealism", p. 53.

application is his discussion of the phenomenon of economic exchange; he concludes that even a concrete act of exchange can be analysed from an infinite number of perspectives, and therefore a selection of what is worth knowing has to be done.[11]

Further, Weber and Rickert hold that the human mind is finite.[12] It is impossible for this finite mind to know something that is infinite, if knowledge is understood as having a picture of reality in the mind. The only way to gain knowledge of reality is to construct concepts which can grasp those parts of reality which human beings are interested in knowing. Of course this conceptualisation of reality is more than a scientific process. Every word in our language is a conceptualisation of phenomena, and so abstracts from and interprets reality as we immediately perceive it, according to Weber.[13] Our everyday language constitutes facts with which we can work scientifically.[14] Science is, accordingly, "the intellectual ordering of facts".[15]

To strive for total knowledge is of course a naive goal, since reality has no limits. Following Windelband's distinction between nomothetic and ideographic sciences, Weber holds that there are two ways of overcoming the gulf between concepts and reality. On the one hand are the natural sciences, which overcome this gap by the construction of universally valid laws and concepts.[16] These sciences are not primarily interested in the individual characteristics of phenomena, but only in what they have in common. They construct concepts with larger and larger extension, but with less and less content. This system of universally valid concepts and laws has very little to say about concrete reality. In that respect it has distanced itself from reality as we experience it. We do not experience empirical generalisations or natural laws, but concrete, individual phenomena.

---

[11] Weber, Max: "'Objektivität'", *GAW*, p. 171.

[12] Weber, Max: "'Objektivität'", *GAW*, p. 171; Rickert, Heinrich: *Grenzen*, p. 34.

[13] Weber, Max: "Roscher und Knies", *GAW*, p. 105, n. 1.

[14] see Burger, *op.cit.*, p. 62. According to Burger, Weber, in agreement with Rickert, understood the relations between direct experience, facts and science as a tripartition between formless experience, categorically formed facts and a scientifically formed presentation of facts.

[15] Weber, Max: "'Objektivität'", *GAW*, p. 157: *"die denkende Ordnung der Tatsachen"* ("analysis of facts", which is the translation in *MSS*, is totally misleading in this case); Rickert, Heinrich: *Gegenstand*, p. 68.

[16] Weber, Max: "Roscher und Knies", *GAW*, p. 4.

On the other hand are the sciences of concrete reality (*Wirk-
lichkeitswissenschaften*).[17] These sciences give up the goal of attaining
knowledge of reality in its totality, and concentrate on trying to understand a single object or a limited class of objects as fully as possible.
The sciences of concrete reality do not formulate laws, but try to approx-
imately represent the object under investigation by selecting its distinctive characteristics. Of course, this representation of the object is not a
"picture" of the object, which for Weber would be impossible due to the
intensive infinity of reality, but an approximation which highlights those
characteristics of the object that we are interested in knowing.[18] The
concepts of the sciences of concrete reality have a limited extension, but
are richer in content than the concepts of the natural sciences. One
example of such a concept in the sciences of concrete reality could be
'feudalism', which is used to describe certain forms of economy. It cannot be applied to all forms of production.

Given that human beings are interested in having complete knowledge
of reality, these different scientific methods have both gains and losses,
according to Weber and Rickert. The natural, nomothetic, sciences, in
their ideal form, give us knowledge of reality in its totality since the
laws and generalisations they provide are universally valid. Reality,
however, does not consist of generalities but of individual phenomena,
and therefore the nomothetic sciences fail to give us full knowledge. The
ideographic sciences of concrete reality, on the other hand, give us a
fuller picture of individual phenomena, but they fail to help us grasp
reality in its fullness, since they can only give us an understanding of
single phenomena and limited classes of phenomena.

It should be noted that Weber's and Rickert's view of the natural sciences is a bit old-fashioned in our eyes. In their view, the natural sciences proceed by an inductive method on the basis of which they gener-
alise and formulate laws.[19] In Weber's case, which is what interests me
here, the interest taken in the methodological problems of the natural
sciences is very limited. He just takes their nomothetic and inductive
character for granted. According to Weber, the nomological knowledge
thus established is important as a *means* to scientific knowledge within

[17] Weber, Max: "Roscher und Knies", *GAW*, p. 5. On the term *Wirklichkeitswis-
senschaft,* see for example Weber, Max: "Roscher und Knies", *GAW*, p. 113; "'Objektivität'", *GAW*, p. 170 and Rickert, Heinrich: *Grenzen*, p. 369.
[18] Weber, Max: "Kritische Studien", *GAW,* p. 272.
[19] See for example Rickert, Heinrich: *Grenzen*, pp. 636-637.

the humanities.[20] If historians, for example, want to explain the Battle of Marathon causally,[21] they have to have knowledge of causal regularities, which are established by the nomothetic sciences.[22] However, attaining nomothetic knowledge can never be the *goal* of the sciences of concrete reality. Rather, they strive to describe and causally explain single events.

Value Relevance

The cultural sciences, as Weber understands them, select phenomena from the unending flux of reality, study their individual characteristics and in the last instance should try to explain them causally.[23] But how should this selection be done? In the methodological tradition which was dominant in the humanities in Germany at the end of the 19th century the answer was that as little selection as possible should be done, and that the task of history was to describe as many individual phenomena as possible and thereby in a cumulative fashion create a better and better picture of reality. This view is often called *historicism* in the Weber literature, and is described as having been in deep conflict with what was then called *positivism* in the famous *Methodenstreit*.[24]

---

[20] See for example Weber, Max: "Roscher und Knies", *GAW*, pp. 90-91.

[21] Weber, Max: "Kritische Studien", *GAW*, pp. 274-275.

[22] Weber, Max: "'Objektivität'", *GAW*, p. 179.

[23] Causal explanation should not be understood too narrowly. Weber holds that motives should be counted as causes when explaining human action. Fritz Ringer's *Max Weber's Methodology* contains an analysis of Weber's view of causal explanations. See pp. 77-80. Weber's view diverges from views expressed in much philosophy of science since World War II, e.g. in von Wright, Georg Henrik: *Explanation and Understanding*, pp. 132-160. 'Cultural science' should primarily be understood as those sciences which work with an ideographic method, investigating individual phenomena in human culture. History would be an example of what Weber and Rickert understand with a cultural science. Social science, on the other hand, is a natural science if it employs a generalising method, and a cultural science if it employs an individualising one. See Rickert, Heinrich: *Grenzen*, p. 589.

[24] The concept 'historicism' is for example used by Käsler, *op.cit.* p. 187. On the *Methodenstreit*, see e.g. Homann, Harald: *Gesetz und Wirklichkeit in den Sozialwissenschaften*, pp. 94-245. An interesting analysis is also provided in Agevall, *op.cit.*, pp. 100-101. Ola Agevall rightly warns for the extremely ambiguous word 'historicism' (p. 70). In this context nothing more should be read into it than what is said in my definition. An alternative term could be 'historism' which is used by e.g. the Swedish historian of ideas Björn Skogar in his *Viva vox och den akademiska religionen* (pp. 19-21). However, in most of the literature referred to here, including Agevall's book, the term 'historicism' is used. In the English translation of Herbert Schnädelbach's book *Philosophy in Germany*, the translator has chosen to translate '*Historismus*' with 'historicism'. See translator's note on p. vii.

The positivists held that the law-seeking, generalising method of the natural sciences should be applied in all scientific work, even in the work of the cultural sciences. The 'positivists' should be clearly distinguished from the philosophical school emanating from the Vienna circle called logical positivism or empiricism. The positivists of Weber's days were interested in the unity of science and were negative to metaphysics, but was generally more positive to the use of theoretical models, like the model of rational economic man in classical economics, than their namesakes in the Vienna circle.[25]

Of course, Weber could not accept these solutions to the problem of the methodology of history. His and Rickert's idea of reality as infinite makes the historicist solution impossible, and his acceptance of the distinction between the purposes of the natural sciences and the cultural sciences makes him hostile to the idea of the unity of science. According to Weber it is necessary in every cultural science to select from reality, and it would be dishonest not to admit that. In Weber's eyes, it is of central importance for methodology to discuss how this selection should be done. He does not accept the idea that it is the causal 'effectiveness' of a historical phenomenon – understood as the idea that the fact that a given phenomenon can be shown to be causally significant in the historian's own time – which makes it worth studying.[26] Instead it is the phenomenon's relevance to values, its *Wertbeziehung*, that makes it an object of investigation.[27] The scholar within the field of cultural science approaches reality with a set of values which tells her or him which phenomena are worth studying. It is, according to Weber, our *values* which help us to select phenomena from the infinite manifold of reality and create objects of research.[28] Even if Weber does not explicitly say so, this is obviously also the case within the natural sciences. The research within nuclear physics during the thirties and forties, for example, was clearly motivated by values.

[25] Eliaeson, Sven: "Influences on Max Weber's Methodology", p. 16.
[26] Weber, Max: "Kritische Studien", *GAW*, pp. 259-260. For a comment on this, see: von Schelting, Alexander: *Max Webers Wissenschaftslehre*, pp. 241-244; and also Oakes, *op.cit.*, pp. 26-27.
[27] The English translation of the term *Wertbeziehung* is not uncomplicated. Bruun, in Bruun, *op.cit.*, translates it as 'value relation', while for example Burger, *op.cit.*, and Oakes, *op.cit.*, translate it with 'value relevance'. I shall adhere to Burger's way of translating.
[28] See for example: Weber, Max: "Roscher und Knies", *GAW*, p. 50; "'Objektivität'", *GAW*, pp. 170, 175-178; "Kritische Studien", *GAW*, pp. 262, 271-272; "'Wertfreiheit'", *GAW*, pp. 511-512. A good analysis of Weber's position is given in Germer, Andrea: *Wissenschaft und Leben*, pp. 104-114.

It is necessary to keep in mind that when Rickert writes about *values* he does not think of value judgements like "p is good" or "p is bad", but rather statements like "p is an aspect of human existence that all humans should be interested in". Politics is, according to Rickert, a cultural value, but my being of a socialist or liberal conviction is not. Values are not something that can be disputed, as subjective value judgements can: they are simply valid. Research should, according to Rickert, be value-neutral in the sense that it should not build on the researcher's personal appraisals of value, but it cannot be value-neutral in the sense that it should not establish its research object according to the principle of value relevance. Weber did not uphold such a strong distinction between acceptable value relevance and subjective value judgements, but that question will be further discussed in the section on scientific objectivity below.

According to Weber, scholars in the cultural sciences have their evaluative perspective on reality, grounded in their views of life. This evaluative perspective naturally makes them more interested in some phenomena than others. My positive evaluation of some forms of religious life, for example, makes me interested in Max Weber's theory of religion, but since I do not have the same evaluative interest in law, I do not take the same pains to try to understand Weber as a legal scholar, unless it helps me to understand Weber's theory of religion. With Weber's terminology: my own interest in religion helps me to form an object of research out of the infinite manifold of phenomena that is reality. This evaluative perspective does not have to be positive, however.[29]

I shall label this kind of interest, grounded in personal appraisals of value, *practical value relevance*.[30] Weber repeatedly stresses the importance of the scholar's own position in regard to value questions for scientific work.[31] Especially the social sciences, widely defined, cannot be understood at all if their relation to values and concrete political problems is not taken into account:

> ...in social sciences the stimulus to the posing of scientific problems is in actuality always given by *practical* "questions". Hence the very recognition of the existence of a scientific problem coincides, personally, with the possession of specifically oriented motives and values.[32]

[29] Weber, Max: "Kritische Studien", *GAW*, p. 246; see also "'Objektivität'", *GAW*, p. 181.
[30] Bruun, *op.cit.*, p. 105, employs a similar terminology.
[31] see for example Weber, Max: "'Objektivität'", *GAW*, p. 182; "Roscher und Knies", *GAW*, pp. 124-125.
[32] MSS p. 61. Weber, Max: "'Objektivität'", *GAW*, p. 158: "*...durch den Umstand, daß auf dem Gebiet der Sozialwissenschaften der Anstoß zur Aufrollung wissenschaftlicher*

But normally Weber sees the practical value relevance as a preliminary stage to another type of value relevance, which I, following Bruun, shall label *theoretical value relevance*.[33] When scholars have identified an object through their subjective value judgement, they should put themselves in a certain distance from the object to be able to analyse the object's *possible* relations to values, a process that Weber labels *Wertinterpretation* or *Wertanalyse*.[34] In the following, I shall translate these terms as *value-analysis*.[35]

When scholars conceive of their object, constituted on the ground of their value judgements, from a certain distance they can discover that the object can be related to other values than the value which they themselves proceeded from. My own interest in religion made me discover Max Weber as an object of research. But in removing myself from this interest I can see that Max Weber also can be related to an interest in law, in economics or history, for example. By such a value-analysis scholars will be able to create new objects of research and define new problems. This distance from the object is furthermore important since too much personal involvement in the object of research can threaten the value-freedom of scientific results.[36]

But there is also a kind of normative element in value-analysis. Weber, following Rickert, prescribes that the object should be related to cultural values, *Kulturwerte*.[37] A cultural value is empirically given, that is, it is commonly accepted as a value in a certain society or culture. As such, it should not be confused with an ethical imperative, according to Weber.[38] Rickert exemplifies with the value of politics. A deeply conservative *junker* in Prussia and a liberal have very different political

---

Probleme *erfahrungsgemäß regelmäßig durch* praktische 'Fragen' *gegeben wird, so daß die bloße Anerkennung des Bestehens eines wissenschaftlichen Problems in Personalunion steht mit einem bestimmt gerichteten Wollen lebendiger Menschen."*

[33] Bruun, *op.cit.*, p. 109.

[34] Weber, Max: "Kritische Studien", *GAW*, pp. 245-246. That the concepts *Wertinterpretation* and *Wertanalyse* are used interchangeably by Weber is obvious from e.g. "Kritische Studien", *GAW*, p. 248. On this kind of analysis, see also "Roscher und Knies", *GAW*, p. 89, n. 2.

[35] It is generally a problem that Weber's terminology can be and is translated in various ways. Weber himself is not very lucid either, as the example of the concepts *Wertinterpretation* and *Wertanalyse* shows. In my opinion it is convenient to use a single term for this process. In using the translation "value-analysis" I am following Burger, *op.cit.* Bruun, *op.cit.*, translates "value-interpretation".

[36] Weber's understanding of the concepts of value-freedom and scientific objectivity will be treated later.

[37] Weber, Max: "'Objektivität'", *GAW*, p. 181.

[38] Weber, Max: "'Wertfreiheit'", *GAW*, p. 504.

views. The junker is for example a protectionist and a monarchist, while the liberal is an advocate of free trade and parliamentary democracy. But both will accept the value of politics and constitute the *object* politics in the same way. Otherwise there would be no conflict between them, since they would not be discussing the same thing.[39]

Other examples could be taken from the field of historical research. A Roman Catholic and a Lutheran historian in Weber's time could be expected to have very different views on Martin Luther. But both could agree that Luther is worth studying as a historical object.[40] Or two persons could have very different evaluative standpoints on Goethe's letters to Charlotte von Stein, but agree on their importance as objects of research.[41] Or take the case of Caesar's death. A political historian constructs this event in a certain way that makes her or him able to disregard the medical aspects of the murder. Instead she or he is interested in the relation between the political struggles in Rome and the murder of Caesar, and in the political effects brought about by the murder.[42] This focusing on the political aspects of Caesar's death depends on the fact that the historian has constructed a theoretical value relevance which allows her or him to focus on the political aspects. Someone who is interested in the daggers of Roman antiquity could perhaps also be interested in the murder of Caesar, but would construct another value relevance and focus on other aspects.

The idea is that it would be problematical if every scholar constructed an own reality and did her or his research on objects which do not interest anyone else. Therefore the theoretical value-relevance should be established by relating phenomena to empirically given cultural values. But since there are many cultural values, the scholar's own appraisals of value will decide *which* cultural value she or he is interested in.

If, however, a scholar should constitute her or his object of research as relevant to a value that was held only by herself or himself, or only by a very small number of persons, this would not make the scientific results invalid. A family chronicle can be just as historically "correct" as a study of great cultural phenomena, to use Weber's own example.[43] What will differ is only the *interest* the readers of the scholarly publications will show.

---

[39] Rickert, Heinrich: *Grenzen,* pp. 364-365.
[40] Rickert, Heinrich: *Grenzen,* pp. 633-634, n. 1.
[41] Weber, Max: "Kritische Studien", *GAW,* pp. 245-246.
[42] Weber, Max: "Kritische Studien", *GAW,* p. 272.
[43] Weber, Max: "'Objektivität'", *GAW,* pp. 183-184.

Bruun has pointed out that there seems to be an inconsistency at this point in Weber's thought.[44] On the one hand, Weber says that a scientifically acceptable theoretical value-relevance should be established with reference to cultural values,[45] and on the other hand he says that if this is the case or not has no bearing on the validity of the scientific results. This sounds like a contradiction, if we read the former position as: without a relation to cultural values there cannot be any acceptable theoretical value relevance at all and accordingly no science. There is no obvious solution to this problem. A passage that seems to support the stress on cultural values is the following:

> When we require from the historian and social research worker as an elementary presupposition that they distinguish the important from the trivial and that he should have the necessary "point of view" for this distinction, we mean that they must understand how to relate the events of the real world...to *universal "cultural values"* [my italics, TE] and to select out those relationships which are significant for us.[46]

But it is also obvious that Weber stresses that the values that constitute the objects of the cultural sciences are purely subjective, and that scholars are free to choose among all possible values in creating a value-relevance.[47] If that aspect of Weber's thinking is stressed, it must be concluded that the validity of the scientific results is a separate question from the character of the value relevance.

A possible solution to the problem of how to regard the relation between value relevance and scientific validity could be to interpret Weber along the following lines. Weber can be understood as saying that scholars ought to relate to (*nota bene* not adhere to) values that are actually held in their society because such value relevancies will make their research most interesting, valuable and useful in their social context. Value relevancies based on cultural values is thus not a *conditio sine qua non* for granting scientific status to the research effort. Weber's

---

[44] Bruun, *op.cit.*, p. 124.

[45] Weber, Max: "'Objektivität'", *GAW*, p. 178.

[46] MSS pp. 81-82. Weber, Max: "'Objektivität'", *GAW*, p. 181: "*Wenn wir von dem Historiker und Sozialforscher als elementare Voraussetzung verlangen, daß er Wichtiges von Unwichtigem unterscheiden könne, und daß er für diese Unterscheidung die erforderlichen 'Gesichtspunkte' habe, so heißt das lediglich, daß er verstehen müsse, die Vorgänge der Wirklichkeit...auf universelle 'Kulturwerte' zu beziehen und danach die Zusammenhänge herauszuheben, welche für uns bedeutsam sind.*" It should be noted that the expression *universal cultural values* in this context could mean either empirically universal *or* normatively universal. The implication of this vagueness will be discussed in the section on the objectivity of the cultural sciences.

[47] E.g. in Weber, Max: "'Objektivität'", *GAW*, p. 182.

view of the importance of values as guides in scientific work could then
be described as a kind of hermeneutical circle, in the following way.

First, scholars approach reality with their own value judgements, and
choose areas of research that they think are interesting on the basis of
these. Then, by performing a value-analysis, they can notice that the area
of research can be interesting from a number of different perspectives,
and that very different questions can be asked to the same material. In
actual research, scholars may choose to constitute the object of research
in relation to a cultural value, because such a theoretical value-relevance
will make the results maximally interesting and relevant. But at the same
time the choice among possible cultural values is subjective. Both religion and law are for example cultural values in the Western world of
today, in the sense that most people have to confront them, but the fact
that I study Weber from a theological point of view and not a legal,
depends on my own personal valuations and interests.

Weber is not blind for the fact that the choice of theoretical value-relevancies can influence those values that dominate a society or an
epoch.[48] There is a reciprocal relationship between cultural values and
scientific efforts, since the cultural sciences create theoretical value-relevancies in relation to cultural values but at the same time influence
which values that becomes prevalent. This gives special weight to the
practical value-relevance, the scholar's own evaluative starting-point. In
a passage in *Objektivität*, Weber expresses this by saying that "the
refraction of values in the prism of his mind" will, in the last instance,
decide the direction of the scholar's work.[49]

Values and Understanding

The cognitive functions of values are not exhausted with their importance for the constitution of the research object. According to Weber,
they are also indispensable for understanding and analysing certain phenomena. In a passage in *Wertfreiheit* Weber states that the capacity to
take an evaluative standpoint is a prerequisite for the understanding (*Verstehen*) of certain phenomena, such as art.[50] Further, in certain scientific

[48] Weber, Max: "'Objektivität'", *GAW*, p. 182.
[49] MSS p. 82. Weber, Max: "'Objektivität'", *GAW*, p. 182: "*die Farbenbrechung der
Werte im Spiegel seiner Seele*".
[50] Weber, Max: "'Wertfreiheit'", *GAW*, p. 524.

analyses of social policy the scientific critique can be inspired by the critic's own personal ideals.[51]

Weber's comments on this topic are not very clear, and his idea has to be reconstructed from scattered remarks in several of his writings. The most lucid passages can be found in *Wirtschaft und Gesellschaft,* even if Weber speaks of *Verstehen, Deutung* or *Interpretation* in many passages in his works.[52] On some points, these other passages can shed light on the comprehensive exposition of the concept of *Verstehen* which Weber offers in *Wirtschaft und Gesellschaft,* but often they are written as responses to what others have written, and therefore not very systematic.

Underlying this concept is Weber's conception of the social and cultural sciences as concerned with *meaningful* material. A sociological analysis of human action, for example, is primarily interested in actions which have a purpose according to the acting and willing person. The action must be oriented towards a value in some way in order to become an object of a cultural/social scientific investigation. Actions that are mere biological reactions to certain stimuli, for example, are interesting as phenomena for the natural sciences, since they can be conceived as material for establishing nomological regularities. But the cultural sciences are interested in phenomena seen as individual events, and therefore only in meaningful material.

Accordingly, it is important to try to understand the motives which have guided an actor. These motives are at least co-determinants of the action in question, even if other causes in no way can be excluded. It is a gross misunderstanding to see Weber as an advocate of a sharp distinction between an explanatory method (*Erklären*) and a method of interpretative understanding (*Verstehen*).[53] Rather, Weber conceives of understanding as an essential part of causal explanation.[54]

Weber distinguishes between two types of understanding: *direct* understanding (*aktuelles Verstehen*) and *explanatory* understanding (*erklärendes Verstehen*).[55] Instances of direct understanding are for example

[51] Weber, Max: "'Objektivität'", *GAW,* pp. 156-157.

[52] Käsler, for example, chooses to proceed from the passages in *Wirtschaft und Gesellschaft* when discussing Weber's concept of *Verstehen.* See Käsler, *op.cit.,* p. 176. The same holds for e.g. Johansson, Sten: "Max Weber", pp. 49-51.

[53] Käsler, *op.cit.,* pp. 175-176.

[54] Weber, Max: "Roscher und Knies", *GAW,* p. 89, *Wirtschaft und Gesellschaft,* p. 4. On Weber's view of motives as causes, see Huff, Toby: *Max Weber and the Methodology of the Social Sciences,* pp. 35, 67-69; Burger, *op.cit.,* p. 112 and Ringer, Fritz: *Max Weber's Methodology,* p. 94.

[55] Weber, Max: *Wirtschaft und Gesellschaft,* pp. 3-4.

when we understand the meaning of situations like when a hunter aims at an animal with a rifle, or when a person reaches for the door handle in order to shut the door. Of course, this does not exclude that we have acquired this capacity for understanding. It is, as Ringer points out, based on previous experiences.[56]

Explanatory understanding is of a different kind, though. It is about understanding the motives that guide an action. We can directly understand what an outburst of rage is, but we understand it in an explanatory way if we know that it is caused by jealousy. We can directly understand that a person who aims at an other person with a rifle probably intends to shoot her or him, but we understand the situation in an explanatory way if we know that the situation is an execution where the person with the rifle acts on given orders.[57]

Sometimes, according to Weber, we have difficulties in understanding the motives and values of others, even if we can grasp them intellectually. This is due to the fact that certain values and feelings are unknown to or very alien to us. For someone who has never experienced love it can be hard to understand actions made by a person deeply in love, for example.[58] The aim of all explanatory understanding is to interpret a person's actions with reference to her or his motives.

If we want to understand an irrational action, the best way to do this is to construct an ideal-type of how the action would have been if it had been totally rational; "rational" should here be understood as choosing the most effective means to reach a given end. An ideal-type can for example be a model of the progression of behaviour on the stock exchange, describing how a completely rational person would behave. When confronted with the often irrational behaviour of stockbrokers, the ideal-type can help us understand their irrational actions by providing the base for a counterfactual reasoning in regard to what caused the deviation from the expected 'ideal-typical' behaviour.[59] An ideal-type should, accordingly, be understood as an analytical tool for ordering the infinite flux of phenomena that we find in reality. It is a one-sided accentuation of certain phenomena found in empirical reality for heuristic and expository

[56] Ringer, Fritz: *Max Weber's Methodology*, p. 104.
[57] Weber, Max: *Wirtschaft und Gesellschaft*, p. 4.
[58] Weber, Max: *Wirtschaft und Gesellschaft*, p. 2.
[59] The example of the stock exchange comes from Weber, Max: *Wirtschaft und Gesellschaft*, p. 2. To this, see Agevall, *op.cit.*, pp. 172-177 and Ringer, Fritz: *Max Weber's Methodology*, pp. 114-115.

purposes.[60] The ideal-type can almost never be said to exist in its pure form. However, as a theoretical construct it can help us first to order reality and then to generate hypotheses for explaining phenomena. In scientific work of that kind, empathic ability can sometimes be necessary if the scholar is to be able to understand deviations from the ideal-typical model. Thus, empathic ability (*Einfühlung*) is only a prerequisite for explanatory understanding in certain cases, not a distinctive method for the cultural sciences.[61]

Weber seems to hold that there are certain aspects of reality that we cannot fully understand or have knowledge about without being emotionally involved in phenomena that resemble our object of understanding, and therefore he can be interpreted as accepting a very modest form of an involvement theory of knowledge.[62] An involvement theory of knowledge assumes that we can have knowledge of reality through certain forms of experience of involvement. Through being in love we can understand what love really is, or through a religious experience we can come to the conclusion that there is a spiritual dimension in reality. According to Jeffner, an involvement theory of knowledge can be combined with an acceptance of the primacy of empirical knowledge, which functions as a check on what can be asserted on the ground of an involvement theory of knowledge.[63]

There is no ground for assuming that Weber thought of experiences of involvement as a central path to knowledge. He can not reasonably be held to assume that religious experiences are necessary to understand religious phenomena in a scientific way, since he described himself as religiously unmusical and still devoted a large part of his research efforts to investigate religious phenomena. But, as I have shown, he considered it important to have some evaluative and/or emotional acquaintance with certain phenomena in order to be able to understand them as meaningful. If such an acquaintance is lacking, some phenomena cannot be seen as more than brute facts (*Gegebenheiten*), lacking meaning to the researcher.[64]

---

[60] Weber, Max: "'Objektivität'", *GAW*, pp. 190-191.

[61] Käsler, *op.cit.*, p. 178; Ringer, Fritz: *Max Weber's Methodology* p. 95.

[62] On this concept, see Jeffner, Anders: *Att studera människosyn*, p. 15. The term in Swedish which I have translated as 'involvement theory of knowledge' is '*engagemangs-teori för kunskap*'.

[63] Jeffner, Anders: *Att studera människosyn*, p. 16.

[64] Weber, Max: *Wirtschaft und Gesellschaft*, p. 2.

Objectivity and Value Freedom

It is a disputed question to what extent Weber is dependent on Rickert's view when it comes to the question of the objectivity and value-freedom of the cultural sciences. One line of interpretation holds that Weber follows Rickert,[65] another that this is the decisive point where Weber diverges from Rickert.[66] Before discussing Weber's view, it will therefore be necessary to briefly sketch Rickert's opinion on the objectivity of the cultural sciences.

For Rickert it is impossible to construe scientific objectivity as correspondence with facts due to reality's extensive and intensive infinity. Reality can, according to this view, never be perceived apart from our conceptual construction of it, and therefore it is impossible to use a correspondence criterion of truth as a check on the objectivity of scientific propositions.[67] Instead, it is the objective character of the values which are the ground of the value relevance that guarantee the objectivity of the cultural sciences.[68] In Rickert's view "the true judgement is the judgement that *should* [my italics, TE] be made".[69]

Rickert recognises that this view of scientific objectivity presupposes that there are objective values, and he sets out to demonstrate this claim by a transcendental deduction. Rickert argues that the knowledge-seeking subject stands before a categorical imperative, which demands the acceptance of the value of truth. Anyone who seeks knowledge has, on logical grounds, a duty to accept the value of truth, since this value is logically contained in any act of knowledge-seeking. It would be absurd, Rickert argues, to want knowledge at the same time as you do not accept the value of truth as unconditionally valid. On this ground he claims that there is at least one unconditionally valid value, namely the value of truth.[70]

Another way to express Rickert's transcendental reasoning could be the following. Whenever we make an assertion we acknowledge the value of truth, since without this value it would be pointless to make any

[65] e.g. Burger, *op.cit.,* p. 93.

[66] e.g. von Schelting, Alexander: *op.cit.,* p. 232-241; Bruun, *op.cit.,* pp. 131-142; Ringer, Fritz: *Max Weber's Methodology,* pp. 49, 124-125; Owen, *op.cit.,* p. 92; Germer, *op.cit.,* pp. 130-131.

[67] Rickert, Heinrich: *Grenzen,* p. 660.

[68] Rickert, Heinrich: *Grenzen,* pp. 640-641, 682.

[69] Rickert, Heinrich: *Gegenstand,* p. 64: " [D]*as wahre Urtheil ist das Urtheil, welches gefällt werden soll.*"

[70] Rickert, Heinrich: *Grenzen,* pp. 697-698.

assertions at all. And when we doubt an assertion, we also acknowledge the value of truth, since without such a value, it would be pointless to doubt anything. And if we question these propositions, we do so on the ground that we think that they are false, and then we have to presuppose the value of truth. So the value of truth is unconditionally valid, *quod erat demonstrandum*.[71]

But the value of truth is not the only value that constitutes value relevancies, so it seems that Rickert still has not solved the problem of the objectivity of the cultural sciences. He holds that value relevancies are constructed on the ground of values which are held as normative in the culture to which the scholar belongs. But this seems to mean that what is claimed as scientific truth in one culture can be seen as unscientific in another culture with different cultural values, and that therefore science cannot be objective, if objectivity is understood as demanding universal validity.

Therefore, Rickert demands that the cultural values have to stand in a more or less approximate relation to unconditionally valid values:

> Anyone who studies the singular development of the human culture and holds this to be a necessary scientific task elevated above all human arbitrariness has to assume that all empirically observable normative universal values are more or less close to what unconditionally *should* be. Accordingly it must be assumed that human culture has some, perhaps forever disclosed for us, objective meaning in regard to unconditionally valid values. Only if that is the case, is it at all possible to relate the historical process to values.[72]

The meaning of this argument seems to be that it may be impossible to actually determine all absolutely valid values, but that we have to or are allowed to postulate that empirically valid cultural values stand in some relation to objectively valid values, and that therefore it is reasonable to assume that we can approximate the ideal of scientific objectivity if we construe value relevancies with reference to values that are as universally accepted as possible. The ground for this assumption is that

---

[71] Rickert, Heinrich: *Gegenstand,* pp. 74-75.

[72] Rickert, Heinrich: *Grenzen,* p. 640-641: "*Wer die einmalige Entwicklung der menschlichen Kultur erforscht und dies für eine über alle menschliche Willkür erhabene nothwendige Aufgabe der Wissenschaft hält, muss voraussetzen, dass alle empirisch konstatirbaren normativ allgemeinen Werthe dem, was unbedingt sein* soll, *näher oder ferner stehen, und dass daher die menschliche Kultur irgend einen, uns eventuell gänzlich unbekannten objektiven Sinn mit Rücksicht auf unbedingt gültige Werthe hat, denn nur dann ist es unvermeidlich, den geschichtlichen Verlauf auf Werthe überhaupt zu beziehen.*"

at least some values can be transcendentally deduced, such as the unconditionally valid value of truth.

This view is of course problematic in several respects. Rickert's theory comes into conflict with what is commonly called Hume's law,
namely the principle that "...no pure value judgement can logically follow from a consistent set of purely empirical premises".[73] There is simply no way to conclude that there are universally valid values from the
existence of empirically observable values. Even if every human being
could be shown to construct the value of politics in exactly the same
way, this does not show that there is a corresponding ultimate value.[74]
And even if the absolute validity of the value of truth can be demonstrated, it is impossible to infer from that fact that there are any other
absolute values.

It can also be questioned if not those kind of values with the help of
which value relevancies are constructed are linked with value judgements in such a way that it practically becomes impossible to differenti-
ate them. There is for example not *one* construction of the concept *political*, and it seems impossible to find out which construction of such
concepts which is the valid one. There is obviously a risk that Rickert's
view of universally held cultural values leads to what Iris Marion Young
has called *cultural imperialism*, which means that one dominant group's
view of cultural meanings is established as a norm.[75]

Rickert's formulation of the principle of objectivity in science thus
cannot be accepted for moral and logical reasons. Perhaps there is also
an empirical reason for not accepting his formulation. It is doubtful if
people really construct values in the same way. Can it really be said that
an orthodox Marxist and a neo-liberal, when arguing with each other,
construct the political domain in the same way? Is it not rather so, that
their constructions of the political differ from each other in certain
respects, but are similar in others, so that one can say that there is some
sort of family resemblance between their respective conceptions of the
political domain in human life?

Weber never explicitly takes a stand on Rickert's view of scientific
objectivity. In his writings one can find references to Rickert, and comments saying that Rickert's work is good and interesting, but never a

---

[73] Bergström, Lars: *Grundbok i värdeteori*, pp. 21-22. "*...inget rent värdeomdöme
kan följa logiskt från en konsistent uppsättning rent empiriska premisser*".
[74] Critical commentaries similar to this has been put forward by e.g. Bruun, *op.cit.*, p.
94 and Eliaeson, Sven: *Bilden av Max Weber*, pp. 92-93.
[75] Young, Iris Marion: *Justice and the Politics of Difference*, pp. 58-59.

thorough discussion of Rickert's view on objectivity. Not even in the essay *Die 'Objektivität' sozialwissenschaftlicher und sozialpolitischer Erkenntnis* does Weber discuss the problem of objectivity more than in a few passages, and there are never any explicit comments on Rickert's ideas about unconditionally valid values as ground for objectivity, or any remarks about his transcendental deductions.

This has lead many of Weber's interpreters to conclude that he either did not accept Rickert's ideas or that he did not think them to be relevant for his methodological considerations. There have also been some suggestions that he did not really understand what Rickert wanted to say or the full consequences of Rickert's thought.[76] Others have concluded that since it can be established that Weber was deeply influenced by Rickert when writing his methodological essays, it is reasonable to conclude that he accepted Rickert's overall view of the philosophy of science, including his view on objectivity. Thomas Burger, perhaps the most ardent advocate of this line of interpretation, argues for this in roughly the following way.

Weber's methodological views are never coherently formulated anywhere in his writings, and it cannot be shown that Weber was very much interested in methodological or epistemological questions; rather he only wrote on methodological problems when he thought he had to oppose someone else. It can, however, be shown that Weber was deeply influenced by Rickert and appreciated his works, and if one assumes that Weber accepted Rickert's philosophy of science, it is possible to explain every problematic and unclear statement that Weber makes in regard to methodology. Therefore it seems, according to Burger, reasonable to hold that Weber *in toto* accepted Rickert's philosophy of science and only elaborated it in a few aspects with relevance for his own field of research.[77]

A totally different view was put forward by Alexander von Schelting in 1934, and it has been followed by a number of Weber's interpreters.[78] von Schelting holds that Weber does not claim that the values by which the research object is constituted have to be objectively valid. A scientific proposition is objectively true if it fulfils certain formal conditions

---

[76] e.g. Oakes, *op.cit.*, p. 145.

[77] Burger, *op.cit.*, pp. 5-7, 87-93. A similar view has been put forward by Segady, Thomas: *Values, Neo-Kantianism and the Development of Weberian Methodology*, p. 81.

[78] e.g. Bruun, *op.cit.*, p. 131; Ringer, Fritz: *Max Weber's Methodology*, p. 49. See also Owen, *op.cit.*, p. 92 and to a certain extent Oakes, *op.cit.*, pp. 147-148.

that are immanent in the theoretical sphere of thinking.[79] von Schelting understands these formal conditions in Max Weber's methodology as the requirement that causal explanations have to be constructed in a certain, logically necessary way, and that they must not contain any value judgements as premises.[80] The procedure for causal explanation that Weber, according to von Schelting, requires for the cultural sciences to be objective is the analysis of objective possibility (*objektive Möglichkeit*).[81]

According to Weber, the main aim of historical investigations is to produce causal explanations. When historians want to explain a phenomenon X, established by its value relevance, they should try to imagine as many *possible* causes of X as possible.[82] Then they, according to Weber, shall try to conceive some cause or causes changed, and on the grounds of their nomological knowledge ask themselves if X still would be the case.[83] By this contrafactual process, which first isolates the *possible* chain of causes from factors that are presumed to be causally irrelevant, then on the basis of nomological knowledge judges what causes are necessary for X to happen, the *adequate* causation of X can be established.[84] This kind of causal knowledge, is, according to von Schelting's interpretation, the locus of objectivity in Weber's methodology.[85]

The tradition of interpretation of which von Schelting is the grand old man sees the main difference between Weber's and Rickert's methodologies in the status of the cultural values that through value relevance constitute the research objects. For Rickert, there are absolute, eternally valid values which can be established by transcendental deductions, while for Weber values ultimately are dependent on what acting and willing human beings construct as ultimately valid. Therefore the objectivity of the cultural sciences cannot be dependent on the values which constitute the value relevance, but has to be located in the formal process of causal imputation.

[79] von Schelting, *op.cit.,* p. 234.
[80] von Schelting, *op.cit.,* p. 259.
[81] von Schelting, *op.cit.,* p. 262; Weber, Max: "Kritische Studien", *GAW*, pp. 266-277. On the theoretical background for Weber's discussion of objective possibility and adequate causation, see Turner, Bryan: *Max Weber*, pp. 163-179 and Agevall, *op.cit.,* pp. 148-166. Fritz Ringer has suggested a model of Weber's view on historical explanations. See his *Max Weber's Methodology*, pp. 78, 115.
[82] Weber, Max: "Kritische Studien", *GAW*, p. 275.
[83] Weber, Max: "Kritische Studien", *GAW*, p. 273.
[84] Weber, Max: "Kritische Studien", *GAW*, p. 286.
[85] von Schelting, *op.cit.,* p. 266 and Bruun, *op.cit.,* pp. 135-136.

Is it possible to decide which of the interpretations offered by Burger and von Schelting that is the correct one? In my opinion, the character of Weber's texts, fragmentary and often obscure as they are, makes a final decision on the matter impossible. It is even impossible to find an explicit definition of the concept "objectivity" in his article on *Die 'Objektivität' sozialwissenschaftlicher und sozialpolitischer Erkenntnis*. Perhaps it is significant that Weber himself has put the word *Objektivität* between quotation marks. However, I shall try to build up a cumulative argument for von Schelting's line of interpretation. In what follows, I shall label von Schelting's interpretation A, and Burger's interpretation B.

Interpretation A has to solve a serious difficulty if it should be plausible, and that is the obvious fact that Weber's methodology shares the phenomenological starting-point of Rickert's philosophy of science, namely that reality is an extensive and intensive manifold of phenomena. If reality is understood as absolutely impossible to grasp otherwise than through concepts constructed by the knowledge-seeking subject, how could a causal analysis of the type referred above be said to be objective? Will it not necessarily follow that the causes too have to be seen as constructed with the help of value relevancies?[86] The only way of solving this problem seems to be to claim that the scientific results somehow can be checked against reality, but, as I have shown, both Rickert and Weber repudiate epistemological realism. There are, however, a few passages in Weber's texts which could be interpreted as an indication of that he conceives of this repudiation of realism in a different way than Rickert does.

In a footnote in *Roscher und Knies*, Weber discusses to what extent poetry can be said to be a direct picture of reality.[87] He remarks that the novels of for example Émile Zola do not really depict reality as it is *in se*, but that the degree of conceptualisation is relatively low. How can one say that the degree of conceptualisation is low, if it is not somehow possible to test the claim with reference to reality *in se*? On the basis of this passage it is of course not possible to claim to have proven that Weber accepts epistemological realism, but perhaps he can be understood as assuming that reality *in se* can function as somewhat of a check on our conceptualisations. Reality *in se* will resist certain forms of conceptual formation, even if we cannot really perceive it without our concepts.

---

[86] Weber touches upon this in "Roscher und Knies", *GAW,* p. 51.

[87] Weber, Max: "Roscher und Knies", *GAW,* p. 105, n. 1. For an other passage in line with this interpretation, see "Roscher und Knies", *GAW,* p. 92, n. 1.

This position could be described as a kind of *weak metaphysical realism*. The assumption of an independent reality is not so much a statement of what exists, as a logical presupposition for such statements.[88] In my opinion, such a view must be ascribed to Weber if it is accepted that he does not follow Rickert's view on objective values, but holds on to Rickert's idea of a reality as infinite. If not, no reasonable interpretation of Weber's view on objectivity can be given, since it would mean that there is nothing against which claims to objectivity could be measured.

Wagner and Zipprian have claimed that Weber's use of the method of objective possibility forces him to depart from Rickert's epistemology, since Rickert's view of concept formation does not allow concepts to have a denotation, but only connotations, and that therefore any argument from objective possibility would be fallacious, since the phenomenon in question always could be constituted in another way and thereby acquire other adequate causes.[89] From this Wagner and Zipprian conclude that Weber must have accepted some sort of realist conception of reality.[90] According to them, Weber tried to create a synthesis between Rickert's transcendental philosophy and J. S. Mill's idea that proper names have denotations but not (when the reference is first established) connotations. By thinking of concepts as referring to real objects, Weber saved his idea of objective possibility, since such a view allows him to regard the adequate causes as related to an objectively *given* object, and not just an object constructed on the basis of value relevance.[91]

From these deliberations, it seems clear that the method of objective possibility is inconsistent with Rickert's philosophy, and therefore one is forced to give priority either to the theory of objective possibility or to the transcendental philosophy of Rickert when trying to reconstruct a consistent view out of Weber's writings. I think it is reasonable to claim that Weber is a metaphysical realist in the sense that he heuristically assumes that there is a reality independent from our knowledge of it. This reality can only be known through our conceptual construction, but reality can resist certain forms of conceptual constructions, that is, it can resist certain ways of acting implied by the conceptual constructions. In that way it functions as somewhat of a check on our concept formation. This kind of reasoning would be in line with interpretation A.

---

[88] On weak metaphysical realism, see Herrmann, Eberhard: "A Pragmatic Approach to Religion and Science", p. 131.

[89] Wagner, Gerhard & Zipprian, Heinz: "Methodologie und Ontologie", p. 127.

[90] Wagner, Gerhard & Zipprian, Heinz: *op.cit.*, p. 129.

[91] Wagner, Gerhard & Zipprian, Heinz, *op.cit.*, p. 127.

Weber repeatedly stresses that scientific inquiries should be value neutral (*wertfrei*). The reason for this is that he regards 'is' *(Sein)* and 'ought' *(Sollen)* as logically absolutely heterogeneous.[92] Therefore, a *conditio sine qua non* for every science is that it is kept free from value judgements.[93] For Weber there is

> simply no bridge which can span the gap from the *exclusively* "empirical" analysis of given reality with the tools of causal explanation to the confirmation or refutation of the "validity" of *any* value judgment.[94]

Rickert's theory of the relation between empirically valid cultural values and universally valid values comes into conflict with this fact-value distinction. If Weber had fully understood the implications of Rickert's reasoning (which he perhaps not did) could he really have emphasised this logical heterogeneity as strongly as he does? Anyway, a reconstruction of Weber's thinking has to come to terms with this problem, either by devaluing Weber's stress on value neutrality, or by accepting interpretation A. If one considers the *pathos* with which Weber defended his principle of value neutrality in scholarly conflicts with his colleagues,[95] it does not seem reasonable to devalue this principle in Weber's thought, and therefore interpretation A seems to be a better alternative. According to interpretation A, Weber's principle of value-freedom mainly consists in the demand that value judgements may not be premises in a causal explanation,[96] and that the scientific concepts employed may not be formulated in such a way that they covertly support a value judgement.[97] Another argument that speaks in favour of interpretation A is that Weber holds that there is no inherent meaning in the world, and that therefore all meaning that the world may be seen to have, is a human construct:

---

[92] e.g. Weber, Max: "'Wertfreiheit'", *GAW,* p. 501.

[93] e.g. Weber, Max: "Roscher und Knies", *GAW,* p. 57.

[94] R&K p. 117. Weber, Max: "Roscher und Knies", *GAW,* p. 61: *"...schlechterdings keine Brücke, welche von der wirklich* nur *'empirischen' Analyse der gegebenen Wirklichkeit mit den Mitteln kausaler Erklärung zur Feststellung oder Bestreitung der 'Gültigkeit' irgendeines Werturteils führt..."*

[95] On the *Werturteilsstreit* see e.g. Käsler, *op.cit.,* pp. 184-193. cf. Gouldner, Alvin: "Anti-Minotaur: The Myth of a Value-Free Sociology", pp. 199. Gouldner claims that Weber's demand for value-neutrality in science to quite a large extent can be explained as an effort to handle a problematic aspect of the German university system in the beginning of the 20th century. The *Privatdozenten* were dependent on the attendance rates on their lectures for their income, and this fact made them more inclined to hold spectacular and value-laden lectures, according to Gouldner.

[96] Bruun, *op.cit.,* p. 41; see also Weber, Max: "'Wertfreiheit'", *GAW,* p. 524.

[97] Bruun, *op.cit.,* p. 38.

> The fate of an epoch which has eaten of the tree of knowledge is that it must know that we cannot learn the *meaning* of the world from the results of its analysis, be it ever so perfect; it must rather be in a position to create this meaning itself.[98]

As is obvious, this contradicts Rickert's theory of universally valid values, since Rickert holds that these values give human culture an objective meaning.[99]

Bruun has pointed out, that Weber seems to be much more interested in the practical value relevance than in the theoretical.[100] This observation is yet another argument for interpretation A, since the practical value relevance is constituted by the value judgements of the individual scholar. Weber just does not seem to pay much attention to Rickert's discussion of universally and eternally valid values. But on the other hand, this can also – as a kind of *argumentum ex silentio* – be interpreted in favour of B, since it could be understood as if Weber sees no need of discussing at length what he has already found in Rickert's texts.[101]

There are many passages in Weber's texts that seem to support interpretation A, while interpretation B to a much wider extent has to build on what can *not* be read in Weber's texts, even if there are some passages that support B too, such as a part of the following.

> The *objective* validity of all empirical knowledge rests exclusively upon the ordering of the given reality according to categories which are *subjective* in a specific sense, namely, in that they present the *presuppositions* of our knowledge and are based on the presupposition of the *value* of those *truths* which empirical knowledge alone is able to give us. The means available to our science offer nothing to those persons to whom this truth is of no value. It should be remembered that the belief in the value of scientific truth is the product of certain cultures and is not a product of man's original nature. (...) The objectivity of the social sciences depends rather on the fact that the empirical data are always related to those evaluative ideas which alone make them worth knowing and the significance of the empirical data is derived from these evaluative ideas. But these data can never become the foundation for the empirically impossible proof of the validity of evaluative ideas. The belief which we all have in some form or other, in the meta-empirical validity of ultimate and

---

[98] MSS p. 57. Weber, Max: "'Objektivität'", *GAW*, p. 154: "*Das Schicksal einer Kulturepoche, die vom Baum der Erkenntnis gegessen hat, ist es, wissen zu müssen, daß wir den* Sinn *des Weltgeschehens nicht aus dem noch so sehr vervollkommneten Ergebnis seiner Durchforschung ablesen können, sondern ihn selbst zu schaffen imstande sein müssen...*"

[99] Rickert, Heinrich: *Grenzen*, pp. 640-641. See also Barker, Martin: "Kant as a Problem for Weber", p. 242.

[100] Bruun, *op.cit.*, p. 108.

[101] Burger, *op.cit.*, pp. 6-7.

final values, in which the meaning of our existence is rooted, is not incompat-
ible with the incessant changefulness of the concrete viewpoints, from which
empirical reality gets its significance. Both these views are, on the contrary, in
harmony with each other.[102]

In this passage, there seems to be one comment that supports interpretation B, since Weber in the beginning of the citation relates the
objectivity of empirical knowledge to values. On such an interpretation
the latter part of the passage has to be understood as referring to the
scholar's choice among different acceptable value relevancies, that is
when Weber points out that we all *believe* in certain values.

But on the same time he seems to hesitate to follow Rickert. There is
for example no reference to Rickert's transcendental deduction, nor does
Weber try to perform such an argument himself. Instead he says that we
believe in ultimate values, and that it is impossible to *prove* the validity
of values with the help of empirical science. Perhaps the only way to
interpret this passage is to conclude that Weber himself is in doubt
whether he shall follow Rickert to the bitter end or not. In any case, this
passage is no definitive argument for interpretation B.

Perhaps the most central passage in Weber's texts in favour of interpretation A is a statement in *'Objektivität'*, where Weber says that if a
scientific argument is to be considered as objectively valid, it has to be
valid also for a Chinese, who perhaps does not at all agree with or understand the values which are the ground for the value relevance which constitutes the object of research.[103] The idea is that the Chinese can follow
and judge the causal imputation, even if he or she can not or will not
accept the value which makes the investigation worth undertaking.

---

[102] MSS pp. 110-111. Weber, Max: "'Objektivität'", *GAW*, pp. 212-213: "*Die* objektive *Gültigkeit alles Erfahrungswissens beruht darauf und nur darauf, daß die gegebene
Wirklichkeit nach Kategorien geordnet wird, welche in einem spezifischen Sinn* subjektiv,
nämlich die Voraussetzung *unserer Erkenntnis darstellend, und an die Voraussetzung des*
Wertes *derjenigen Wahrheit gebunden sind, die das Erfahrungswissen allein uns zu
geben vermag. Wem diese Wahrheit nicht wertvoll ist – und der Glaube an den Wert wissenschaftlicher Wahrheit ist Produkt bestimmter Kulturen und nichts Naturgegebenes -,
dem haben wir mit den Mitteln unserer Wissenschaft nichts zu bieten. (...) Die 'Objektivität' sozialwissenschaftlicher Erkenntnis hängt vielmehr davon ab, daß das empirisch
Gegebene zwar stets auf jene Wertideen, die ihr allein Erkenntnis*wert *verleihen, aus-
gerichtet, in ihrer Bedeutung aus ihnen verstanden, dennoch aber niemals zum Piedestal
für den empirisch unmöglichen Nachweis ihrer Geltung gemacht wird. Und der uns allen
in irgendeiner Form innewohnende* Glaube *an die überempirische Geltung letzter und
höchster Wertideen, an denen wir den Sinn unseres Daseins verankern, schließt die
unausgesetzte Wandelbarkeit der konkreten Gesichtspunkte, unter denen die empirische
Wirklichkeit Bedeutung erhält, nicht etwa aus, sondern ein...*"
[103] Weber, Max: "'Objektivität'", *GAW*, pp. 155-166.

There are numerous other passages throughout Weber's texts that make the same point. In a footnote in *Roscher und Knies*, Weber points out that the historian is always free in the choice of guiding values, but strictly bound by the principles of causal explanation,[104] and in the discussion of the scientific status of a family chronicle Weber declares that

> In the *method* of investigation, the guiding "point of view" is of great importance for the *construction* of the conceptual scheme which will be used in the investigation. In the mode of their *use*, however, the investigator is obviously bound by the norms of our thought just as much here as elsewhere.[105]

The idea that Weber tries to express in these and other passages seems to be that there are certain norms of a purely formal character that a historical or cultural scientific investigation has to follow, if it should be able to be regarded as objective and scientific, and that it is the adherence to these norms that guarantee the objectivity of the scientific results. Interpretation A can thus be supported by a larger number of textual evidence than interpretation B. Moreover, if one wants to interpret Weber in a way that makes him maximally interesting for an integrative theological effort today, it seems that interpretation A is the best line to follow, since that interpretation loosens the ties between Weber's thinking and the somewhat outdated philosophy of Rickert. In what follows, I will proceed from interpretation A, for the reasons discussed above.

Interpretation A, as presented so far, seems to confine objectivity to causal explanations. This, however, is not a reasonable interpretation, since it denies the possibility to regard many aspects of scientific praxis as objective and intersubjectively valid, aspects to which Weber obviously grants such a status. As will be shown later on, he holds that it is possible to formulate a scientific and philosophical critique of views of life in a way that can lay claim to intersubjective validity, and he seems to hold that the construction of heuristic instruments like the ideal type can be objective or intersubjectively valid in the sense that they can be used and understood by scholars of very different evaluational standpoints. He also seems to hold that descriptions or reconstructive interpretations of

---

[104] Weber, Max: "Roscher und Knies", *GAW*, p. 124, n. 1.

[105] MSS p. 84. Weber, Max: "'Objektivität'", *GAW*, p. 184: "*...in der Methode der Forschung, ist der leitende 'Gesichtspunkt' zwar...für die Bildung der begrifflichen Hilfsmittel, die er [the scholar] verwendet, bestimmend, in der Art ihrer Verwendung aber ist der Forscher selbstverständlich hier wie überall an die Normen unseres Denkens gebunden.*"

phenomena, such as anarchism, can be intersubjectively valid, or at least get fairly close to such an ideal.[106]

But when Weber really approaches the problem of objectivity he retreats to the method of objective possibility, which for him is the ideal form of how to attain objectively valid causal explanations in the cultural sciences, and he does not give his readers much help in trying to understand how this type of objectivity is related to the type discussed in the above paragraph. Hence, in my opinion, it is necessary to construct a more explicit understanding of objectivity out of Weber's writings.

On the one hand, objectivity cannot be defined as the correspondence between our statements about the world and the world as it is *in se*. But on the other hand, it cannot be understood in Rickert's way as a value relevance which stands in some relation to an unconditionally valid value. Rather, a scientific statement will be objective if it is claimed on rational grounds. This means that there can be different degrees of objectivity. Statements which can be tested by empirical experiments such as the statement that water boils at 100° Celsius is objectively true in a 'hard' sense, while the statement that King Louis XVI was beheaded during the French revolution is objective in a weaker sense. Philosophical analyses and critiques can also be called objective, but in a still weaker, soft sense.

A claim to soft objectivity would then imply a claim that the analysis follows logical rules, which is at least one example of the norms to which our thinking is bound, according to Weber.[107] Among those rules are for example Hume's law. A soft objective assertion has to follow commonly accepted norms of logic and criteria for a rational discourse, and it has to be transparent in such a way that every scientifically or philosophically trained person can follow the argument.

Values and Views of Life

In a letter to Adolf Harnack, Weber says that Lutheranism in its historical manifestations is the most terrible of all horrors, because it does not give enough resources for coping with life, at least not for Germans. Weber argues that Lutheranism has not fostered asceticism and discipline, necessary for a successful life in the modern world. Lutheranism

---

[106] Weber, Max: "'Wertfreiheit'", *GAW*, p. 515.
[107] Weber, Max: "'Objektivität'", *GAW*, p. 184.

has not, on the whole, according to Weber, provided humans with an orientation in the world that has made it easier for them to cope with the harsh realities of human existence. Calvinism and what Weber calls sects, such as Baptists and Quakers, have provided their adherents with a value-structure that has fostered industriousness and thereby helped them to create a (materially and politically) better life than what has been possible for Lutherans, because Lutheranism does not foster activity, but passivity.[108]

Of course, this does not mean that Lutheranism has had no social and political effects, but rather that the character of human action that Lutheranism fosters in Weber's eyes is negative. Regardless of how Weber evaluates different ideological or religious convictions – a matter that to some extent will be treated later – is it obvious that he thinks that belief-systems like Calvinism and Lutheranism provide human beings with meaning in life and with values that guide their action in the world.

Weber's theory of action is based on the assumption that what makes an action human is that it is consciously oriented towards a value or several values, while action based on instincts and affects cannot be said to be specifically human.[109] Weber distinguishes between four types of action, namely ends-rational action, value-rational action, traditional action and affectual action. Ends-rational action (*zweckrationales Handeln*) is oriented towards an end, and uses the most effective means the agent can conceive of to produce the desired end. Value-rational action (*wertrationales Handeln*) is oriented towards the action as such, because the performance of the action is thought to be intrinsically valuable, irrespective of the consequences. Traditional action is based on what is common or traditional in a given society, and the actor, according to Weber, does not normally reflect over her or his action, but performs it more or less automatically. This means that traditional actions are borderline cases between meaningful actions and meaningless actions (n.b. not pointless). Affectual actions, lastly, are close to instinctual behaviour, and are performed without prior reflection, as for example when I cry out loudly if I happen to smash my thumb with a hammer.[110]

---

[108] Weber, Max: Letter to Adolf Harnack 5/2 1906, *MWG II/5*, p. 32. Ernst Troeltsch seems to analyse the social effects of Lutheranism and Calvinism in a similar way. See Troeltsch, Ernst: *Die Soziallehren der christlichen Kirchen und Gruppen*, pp. 605-608. For a comment, see e.g. Hecht, Martin: *Modernität und Bürgerlichkeit*, p. 221.

[109] Brubaker, *op.cit.*, p. 92.

[110] Weber, Max: *Wirtschaft und Gesellschaft*, pp. 12-13.

Weber holds that an ideal human life is a life which consists in free and conscious actions, motivated by an orientation towards values.[111] It is this orientation towards values that makes human life possible to understand in an interpretative way as meaningful, and not just a natural event that can be subsumed under natural laws.

As I have pointed out above, Weber does not think that it is possible to demonstrate the values which ought to direct the actions of human beings. Every choice between different values is for Weber to quite a large extent a choice between different beliefs or convictions, for which no ultimate reason can be given.[112] However, according to Weber an effective way of action demands that different values and preferences that we have can be organised towards a focal point or some ultimate values.[113] Otherwise it is impossible to handle conflicts between different values that we may adhere to and to act in a consistent and effective manner.

A properly human personality, according to Weber, is organised through one or several internally consistent values, which, in the last instance, can motivate other values and guide an individual's life.[114] In an interesting comparison between Max Weber's and Thomas Mann's understanding of the concept of 'calling', Harvey Goldman has identified four 'hallmarks' in Weber's view on personality. A true human personality is determined by *ultimate values*, has an intrinsic *relation to these values*, is characterised by a *constant will* and *acts rationally*.[115]

This system of values that Weber seems to think about, is often called *value-orientation* in the literature on Weber.[116] Weber himself does not use a single term, but several, which makes it a bit difficult to decide whether he is writing about the same thing or not; for example he often uses the word *Weltanschauung* without any definition, but obviously thereby implying some sort of value-orientation.[117]

---

[111] Weber, Max: "'Objektivität'", *GAW*, p. 152. Brubaker, *op.cit.*, pp. 95-96.

[112] Weber, Max: "'Objektivität'", *GAW*, pp. 152, 213. Brubaker has pointed out that this line of reasoning in Weber's thought has some similarities with for example R.M. Hare's moral philosophy. See Brubaker, *op.cit.*, p. 113. One example of a passage in Hare's writings which has clear affinities with Weber's thought can be found in *Freedom and Reason*, pp. 150-154. I contend that what Hare calls "ideals" is close to Weber's "values".

[113] Weber does not discuss organisation of values more than in a few sketchy passages, e.g. in "'Wertfreiheit'", *GAW*, pp. 510-511.

[114] Weber, Max: "'Objektivität'", *GAW*, p. 152.

[115] Goldman, Harvey: *Max Weber and Thomas Mann*, p. 142.

[116] e.g. in Brubaker, *op.cit.*, p. 62.

[117] e.g. Weber, Max: "'Objektivität'", *GAW*, p. 154.

To make this idea of value-orientation a bit more fruitful for my integrative theological purpose, I shall propose that we by value-orientation understand a view of life, according to Anders Jeffner's definition of what a view of life is. In the following, I shall try to show that it is reasonable to equate *value-orientations* with *views of life*. If that equation holds, it will be easier to establish contact between Weber's reasoning and theological discourse.

According to Jeffner it is possible to distinguish three components in such views that normally are called views of life. A view of life consists of certain *theoretical beliefs,* for example about what differs humans from animals or how the universe came into being, a *central system of values*, which provides some ultimate norms which we should follow, and, finally, a view of life expresses a *basic mood*, as for example optimism or pessimism. It should be noted that Jeffner does not hold that every theoretical belief is part of an individual's view of life, but only those beliefs that give us an overall picture of our situation.[118] Jeffner arrives at the following definition of a view of life:

> A view of life is the theoretical and evaluative assumptions which constitute or have central impact on an encompassing view of humanity and the world and that constitute a central system of values and expresses a basic mood.[119]

The most difficult component in a view of life is of course the theoretical, since it seems to contain knowledge-claims which cannot be justified by scientific reasoning. Jeffner's own position is that it can be rational to reckon with an extended concept of knowledge, so that for example religious experience can be regarded as sufficient justification for raising religious truth-claims.[120] Personally, I am not as optimistic as Jeffner about the possibility of justifying religious truth-claims by recourse to religious experience for reasons which I provide in chapter five. Further, I do not believe that such a position could be integrated with Weber's thought. However, I still find Jeffner's definition fruitful, for two reasons. First, it is a good analytical tool for analysing people's belief-systems. Justified or not, most religious people actually raise truth-claims in regard to their faith. Secondly, I do think that we in our

---

[118] Jeffner, Anders: "Att studera livsåskådningar", p. 12.

[119] Jeffner, Anders: "Att studera livsåskådningar", p. 13: "*En livsåskådning är de teoretiska och värderingsmässiga antaganden som utgör eller har avgörande betydelse för en övergripande bild av människan och världen och som bildar ett centralt värderingssystem och som ger uttryck åt en grundhållning.*"

[120] See e.g. Jeffner, Anders: *Theology and Integration*, p. 41.

cognitive life have to make certain assumptions about reality which cannot really be made probable by scientific methods. Weber's own weak metaphysical realism is one example of such an assumption. He does not try to prove the existence of a noumenal reality. Rather, he presupposes reality *in se* as a kind of basis for his concept of science and objectivity. Such heuristic assumptions may be counted as parts of the theoretical component of a view of life.

If Jeffner's definition of views of life is applied to Weber's discussion of Calvinism and Lutheranism in his letter to Harnack, the following picture can be said to emerge. The basic theoretical belief in Calvinism, according to Weber, is the conviction that God predestines human beings to either salvation or damnation. Connected to this view is the idea in some forms of Calvinist pastoral care that the fate of human beings in the world to come can be disclosed by the way they live or act here and now. In Calvinism there are also, according to Weber, some important central norms, such as the fundamental goodness of industriousness, and the prohibition against unnecessary consumption. The basic mood of Calvinism as Weber conceives it would be optimism. This might seem strange in face of the rather austere doctrine of predestination. But in Reformed praxis, as understood by Weber, there is also a basic faith in the possibility of ends-rational action. Society can be changed *ad majorem Dei gloriam.*

In Weber's eyes, Lutheranism seems to operate in the opposite way. The most important theoretical conviction in Lutheranism is the idea of salvation *sola fide*, and thereby the idea that one's actions have no impact on salvation. The central system of values in Lutheranism contains an idea that everything should better be left as it is, and since the salvation is given by God's grace and the idea of predestination has not had the same central position as in Calvinism, the basic mood of Lutheranism seems to be pessimism. In Weber's view, the Lutherans, ideal-typically, have no incentives for rational action, since the stress on a personal relation to Christ tends to orient them towards inward contemplation. Taken together, the construction of the Lutheran view of life does not give any strong motives for action, but rather impels the individual to passivity and quietism.

It is reasonable to assume that what mainly interests Weber is the aspect of views of life that motivates us to action. The central system of values in different views of life is the aspect of Weber's analyses of religious ideas that he always focus on, and he seems to regard the theoretical beliefs in a view of life as interesting only to the extent that it has any impact on the central system of values and thereby on human action.[121] Of course, this is not to say that Weber holds that the only important thing with a view of life is the central system of values. There are much evidence to the contrary in his writings. For example, he argues that one of the main reasons for humanity to construct religious beliefs is the deeply felt need to come to grips with the problem of suffering.[122] But these theoretical beliefs will influence the central value system and indirectly create values that can guide action. On the basis of these observations, it is possible to interpret Weber's texts as saying that views of life have two main functions: they help us to create cosmos out of chaos, because they give meaning and purpose to human existence, and they provide us with values which can guide our action in the world.

The letter to Harnack and other similar passages in Weber's texts give evidence, however, to the assertion that Weber regards the value-providing function as the main function of views of life. It is this function which makes views of life absolutely necessary in human life and thereby also in scholarly work. Science cannot exist without the acknowledgement of values, since, according to Weber, the values of scholars and their society are what constitute the research objects and give scientific work its direction. With the words of the Swedish philosopher of religion Eberhard Herrmann, science has to accept something that lies outside itself to be able to perform its work.[123]

Views of Life and Value Spheres

An aspect of Weber's thinking that is very often commented on and criticised is his idea about irresolvable value conflicts.[124] Since the values that we adhere to are grounded in our views of life, between which, according to Weber, it is necessary to choose on the basis of faith, conflicts between opposing values will be impossible to solve completely by recourse to rational argument.[125] In a very lucid discussion of Weber's

[121] see for example Weber, Max: "Einleitung", *MWG I/19*, pp. 85, 109-110.

[122] Weber, Max: "Politik als Beruf", *MWG I/17*, p. 241 and "Einleitung", *MWG I/19*, pp. 94-95.

[123] Herrmann, Eberhard: *Erkenntnisansprüche*, p. 120.

[124] For a classic critique of Weber's idea of the irresolvability of value conflicts, see Strauss, Leo: *Natural Right and History*, pp. 36-78, especially from p. 64. See also MacIntyre, Alisdair: *After Virtue*, p. 26.

[125] There is, however, some evidence in Weber's texts which shows that he thought that there is a limited possibility of a rational discussion of views of life. This will be explored below.

view of conflicts between value-orientations, Brubaker identifies three factors which, according to Weber, assure conflict between views of life.

First, views of life are "*inner properties* of individuals". A view of life is what constitutes the personality of an individual, and this makes her or him eager to defend it against competing views of life. Secondly, views of life are "subjectively *generated*". According to Weber, no view of life can be intellectually demonstrated in such a way that an individual, however rational, feels compelled to adhere to it. Rather, individuals have to choose for themselves which view of life they will follow. Third, "only a *subjective validity* can be claimed for value-orientations". The beliefs and values of a view of life cannot be demonstrated with objective validity, given Weber's understanding of objectivity, and therefore the 'knowledge' contained in a view of life is valid only for the person who believes in it.[126] Science, which is the only human activity capable of creating *objective* knowledge, according to Weber, can teach us nothing about the meaning of our life or the world.[127]

This conflict between different views of life is a very serious matter for Weber, since it can threaten the stability of any human community. This potentiality for conflict increases rapidly in modern society, since people more and more tend to create their own views of life, instead of taking over a common view, like Christian faith in the age of Christendom. There are of course various institutions in modern society which can handle value conflicts, such as the parliamentary system or the courts of law, but they can only fulfil this function as long as they are not themselves the object of value conflict.[128]

But in Weber's texts it is also possible to find discussions of an other type of conflict, namely the conflict between *value spheres (Wertsphäre)*.[129] Weber never properly defines this concept, and sometimes uses the concept value order (*Wertordnung*) instead of value sphere in such a way that it is not always easy to determine whether he is discussing the same thing or not.[130] However, the clearest and most comprehensive treatment of conflicts between value spheres can be found in *Zwischenbetrachtung*, and therefore I will confine my analysis here to Weber's discussion in that text.

---

[126] Brubaker, *op.cit.*, pp. 66-67. Note that Brubaker does not speak about 'views of life' but of 'value-orientations'.
[127] Weber, Max: "'Objektivität'", *GAW*, p. 154.
[128] Brubaker, *op.cit.*, p. 68.
[129] e.g. in Weber, Max: "Zwischenbetrachtung", *MWG I/19*, p. 485.
[130] e.g. in Weber, Max: "Wissenschaft als Beruf", *MWG I/17*, p. 99.

In *Zwischenbetrachtung* Weber discusses which tensions and conflicts that can occur between religion, considered as an autonomous value sphere, and other value spheres, such as economics, erotics and politics. A value sphere in Weber's sense can, with the words of Brubaker, be defined as a "distinct realm of activity which has its own inherent dignity, and in which certain values, norms and obligations are immanent".[131] A discussion of the value sphere of economics and how it can come into conflict with what Weber calls religions of brotherhood (*religiöse Brüderlichkeit*) can serve as an example.

The economic sphere in its typical form is an ends-rational organisation of the interest-struggle – oriented to money – of human beings on the market, according to Weber.[132] In a completely technically rational market personal relations do not exist, and moral reflections are not relevant. The only thing that counts on a rational market is how successfully you uphold your interests in the market. The ethics of brotherliness advocated by some religions, such as Christianity or Islam, will inevitably clash with the norms of the economic sphere, and with different warnings and prohibitions try to keep the economic sphere in check. Any religion who can say to the poor "Blessed are you who are poor, for yours is the kingdom of God" (Lk. 6:20b) will inevitably come into conflict with the economic sphere. The same will, according to Weber, *mutatis mutandis*, hold for other value spheres, such as the intellectual, political or erotic sphere.

The idea underlying this thinking is that the different spheres are autonomous (*eigengesetzlich*).[133] Weber does not explicate exactly what he means by saying that value spheres are autonomous. One possible line of interpretation could perhaps be to assume that he conceives of this autonomy as if the different spheres could be transcendentally deduced as *a priori* forms of human life, somewhat in the way the Swedish theologian Anders Nygren argued for his idea about religion as an autonomous and valid sphere in human consciousness by way of a transcendental deduction.[134]

But such an interpretation is contrary to the textual evidence. Weber himself hints at another interpretation in the beginning of *Zwischenbetrachtung*, commenting on the discussion of value spheres:

---

[131] Brubaker, *op.cit.*, p. 69.
[132] Weber, Max: "Zwischenbetrachtung", *MWG I/19*, p. 488.
[133] Weber, Max: "Zwischenbetrachtung", *MWG I/19*, p. 485.
[134] Nygren, Anders: *Religiöst apriori*, pp. 238-241.

The constructed scheme, of course, only serves the purpose of offering an ideal typical means of orientation. It does not teach a philosophy of its own. The theoretically constructed types of conflicting 'life orders' are merely intended to show that at certain points such and such internal conflicts are possible and 'adequate'. They are not intended to show that there is no standpoint from which the conflicts could not be held to be resolved in a higher synthesis.[135]

As Brubaker has pointed out, it would be wrong to take Weber totally at face value here. He does not in fact regard his description of value spheres in *Zwischenbetrachtung* as *only* a heuristic tool. In practice, Weber claims that he has described real tendencies in the development of the modern world, in which human life becomes more and more fragmented.[136] Weber's point with labelling the value spheres *autonomous* is that in modern society, different spheres tend to follow norms which are in some sense inherent in the kind of activity that constitutes the sphere in question. The spheres of religion and ethics will have less and less influence over spheres like politics and economics, for example. This differentiation makes society fragmented, and erodes the possibility for humans to see their lives as meaningful totalities. Systems of thought which are structured around certain values and beliefs, like religion, will in their turn come into more and more conflict with what Weber calls the irrational spheres of life, such as art and erotics, which develop as protests against the instrumental rationality of modern society.[137]

Perhaps one could conclude that Weber's discussion in *Zwischenbetrachtung* is a mix of construction of ideal-types and empirical generalisations. The conflict between the religious sphere and the other spheres which Weber discusses, should then not be understood as a conflict *a priori*. Rather Weber *constructs* the conflict in a typical way, on the basis of empirical generalisations that he has done. The *summa* of

---

[135] FMW p. 323. Weber, Max: "Zwischenbetrachtung", *MWG I/19*, p. 480: "*Das konstruierte Schema hat natürlich nur den Zweck, ein idealtypisches* Orientierungsmittel *zu sein, nicht aber eine eigene Philosophie zu lehren. Seine gedanklich konstruierten Typen von Konflikten der 'Lebensordnungen' besagen lediglich: an diesen Stellen sind diese innerlichen Konflikte möglich und 'adäquat'* – nicht *aber etwa: es gibt keinerlei Standpunkt, von dem aus sie als 'aufgehoben' gelten können.*" N.b. that "Lebensordnung" is another equivalent to "Wertsphäre", at least in this passage. I also think that this more nuanced passage should be given priority over Weber's rather dogmatic opposition between the value spheres of science and religion in "Wissenschaft als Beruf", p. 108. The main reason for this is that *Wissenschaft als Beruf* was put forth as a lecture in a context where Weber wanted to argue against any romantic flight from modernity into religion.

[136] Brubaker, *op.cit.*, p. 83.

[137] Weber, Max: "Zwischenbetrachtung", *MWG I/19*, p. 499.

Weber's discussion of the conflict between religion and economics is that a consistent and radical ethic of brotherliness inevitably will come into conflict with a totally ends-rational economic system. He does not, however, say that all religion will be in conflict with every economic system, or that there are no ways to resolve conflicts of this type.[138] But by constructing this typical conflict we have an instrument to interpret real conflicts that we find in history or in the contemporary world. I thus do not agree with those of Weber's interpreters who hold him to say that it is more or less impossible to find a position where religion and science could coexist in peace and co-operation in modern society.[139] If Weber's philosophy of science is taken into account when trying to interpret his discussion of the future of religion in modern society, such a view has to be modified.

What then is the relation between views of life and value spheres in Weber's thinking? A view of life is a personal system of values and beliefs, which can be totally individual or shared by many people. These views of life can come into conflict with each other in a way that is impossible to totally resolve, since it is impossible to establish which (if any) view of life that is the correct one. Value spheres, on the other hand, are conceptual instruments for describing and analysing human conduct and conflicts between different values and views of life. As a true follower of Luther, X may hold that the taking of interest is immoral. X's type of Lutheranism will then inevitably clash with a modern capitalistic economy. Weber's discussion of the conflict between the economic and the religious value spheres can then be helpful if one wants to understand X's behaviour. Perhaps X is vehemently fighting Y, who holds that it is a duty to earn money in the most technically rational manner possible, and considers the lending of money at an interest the best way to do so.

When discussing Weber's idea of the irresolvability of value conflicts, it is therefore crucial to be clear about what kind of conflict that is discussed. Is it a conflict between different views of life, or is it a conflict between different value spheres? Of course, conflicts between value

---

[138] Wolfgang Schluchter has pointed out that Weber himself deals with two ways of overcoming this conflict. Either one absolutifies the religious sphere and forces the economic sphere to adapt. This will inevitably in the long run create more intensive conflict. Or one can relativise religion, like in Luther's doctrine of the two realms, or in the Hindu caste system. See Schluchter, Wolfgang: *Rationalism, Religion and Domination*, pp. 146-148.

[139] e.g. Schluchter, *Rationalism, Religion and Domination*, pp. 254-255.

spheres cannot be resolved, since they are constructed as being absolute, for the sake of clarity and analysis. But what about conflicts between different views of life? Can they be resolved? Or can science and philosophy help us to choose between different views of life? To these questions and the implicit answers in Weber's thinking I shall now turn.

Views of Life and Science

In one of the concluding paragraphs of *'Objektivität'*, Weber asserts that "life with its irrational reality and its store of possible meanings is inexhaustible".[140] In Weber's eyes, there is no objective meaning of life: in other words, it is impossible to establish intersubjectively, by way of rational analysis, what the true meaning of life is. Human life can, according to Weber, be constructed as meaningful in many ways, and it is inevitable that ultimately we have to choose between various possible views of life. Weber strongly emphasises that every individual has to choose for herself or himself,[141] but this does not imply that he thinks that *every* individual actually makes a conscious choice. Most people take over their view of life from their social context. But, Weber insists, theoretically and ideally every individual can and should make a conscious choice.

Can science, as Weber conceives it, be of any help for an individual who wants to make a choice between different views of life? Even if Weber never explicitly gives an answer to that question, I think it is reasonable to hold that his thinking implies a *limited* affirmative answer. A prerequisite for this affirmation is of course that the individual who wants to make a choice accepts the value of scientific knowledge, an acceptance which in no way can be taken for granted.[142] But scientific knowledge is valid for anyone who seeks the truth, since, according to Weber, there is no path to objective knowledge beside science.[143] One can easily imagine a person who is not interested in knowing what science has to say about reality. It is, according to Weber, impossible to

---

[140] MSS p. 111. Weber, Max: "'Objektivität'", *GAW*, p. 213: "*...das Leben in seiner irrationalen Wirklichkeit und sein Gehalt an* möglichen *Bedeutungen sind unausschöpfbar...*"

[141] This stress on personal choice in Weber's thinking has led some scholars to describe him as an existentialist. e.g. Cuneo, Michael: "Values and Meaning", p. 92.

[142] Weber, Max: "Roscher und Knies", *GAW*, pp. 60-61.

[143] Weber, Max: "'Objektivität'", *GAW*, p. 184.

compel her or him to accept the value of scientific knowledge, and for that person science can be of no help in the choice among different views of life. It should be noted, however, that Weber does not think that all efforts to accomplish a metaphysical interpretation of the world a priori are meaningless. He explicitly states that metaphysical speculation and reflection can fulfil cognitive functions.[144] But this does not imply that he is prepared to recognise that such metaphysical claims have the same cognitive and logical status as scientific propositions. Rather, they must be seen as heuristic devices, as I have pointed out above.

In *Wertfreiheit* Weber discusses which functions a scientific discussion of value judgements and – implicitly – views of life can fulfil. First, scientific and philosophical analysis can investigate which basic values lurk behind concrete value judgements made by a certain person or group. Scientific and philosophical analysis can provide a consistent structure to a view of life and thereby make it easier for a person who wants to take a stand towards the view of life in question to see what the view of life really implies. This is also a valuable service to the adherents of a specific view of life.

Secondly, science and philosophical analysis can deduce implications of the ultimate values of a view of life, both theoretically and practically. It is, according to Weber, possible to say – with legitimate claims to objectivity – that *if* you hold the value X, you logically will have to accept value Y, and you ought to perform the action Z. For example, if a person holds that all humans, irrespective of the colour of their skin, have the same value, he or she is logically bound to deem it immoral to discriminate against black people on the labour market. To point out such connections is a perfectly legitimate scientific task, according to Weber.

Thirdly, it can be scientifically possible to determine the factual consequences that the performance of a specific action will have. This analysis of consequences has, according to Weber, two aspects. First, it can show that the realisation of a certain value necessarily is bound to some indispensable means, and secondly, it can show that the actualisation of a certain value will have some unavoidable repercussions, which were not intended from the outset. This analysis can be a critical instrument, if it shows A) that there are absolutely no possible means to realise a certain value, or B) that the realisation of the value in question

---

[144] Weber, Max: "'Objektivität'", *GAW*, p. 156.

is highly improbable, either because of insufficient means for its realisation, or because it will have such repercussions that it will come into
conflict with other values that are deemed to be ultimate by the person
or group in question, or C) that there are means or repercussions that the
advocate of the value did not at all consider and that these means and/or
repercussions, given the view of life of the person in question, will create new problems for her or him.

Fourth, a scientific and philosophical analysis can show that the view
of life of the person in question implies values that she or he did not
consider, and which are relevant to her or his actions.[145] This fourth
function seems to me to be a specification and elaboration of the first
function, and it does not seem to be necessary to distinguish between
them. One could summarise the first and fourth functions by saying that
scientific and philosophical analyses can help to formulate consistent
views of life. The point with constructing consistent views of life is of
course, as has been mentioned, that they enable people to act effectively
in the world.

In *Wissenschaft als Beruf* Weber in a similar way discusses if science
has anything valuable to contribute to practical and personal life, and he
formulates four functions, but with a little different character from the
functions discussed in *Wertfreiheit*, that science can fulfil in regard to
views of life.

First, science can provide us with technical knowledge, that is it can
show us how to realise our values. Secondly, science provides us with
methods and instruments for our thinking. Thirdly, science can provide
us with clarity, especially with respect to our views of life, the values
that they imply and the means necessary to realise those values. And
fourth, science can help us to deduce theoretical and practical consequences out of our views of life.[146]

In *Wissenschaft als Beruf* Weber tries to summarise his view of what
kind of help science and philosophy can offer us with respect to our
views of life in the following way:

> Thus, if we are competent in our pursuit...we can force the individual, or
> at least we can help him, to give himself an *account of the ultimate mean-
> ing of his own conduct*. This appears to me as not so trifling a thing to do,
> even for one's own personal life.[147]

---

[145] Weber, Max: "'Wertfreiheit'", *GAW*, pp. 510-511.

[146] Weber, Max: "Wissenschaft als Beruf", *MWG I/17*, pp. 103-104.

[147] FMW p. 152. Weber, Max: "Wissenschaft als Beruf", *MWG I/17*, p. 104: "*Wir
können so, wenn wir unsere Sache verstehen...den einzelnen nötigen, oder wenigstens*

Science and philosophy help to clarify our views of life and their consequences, and provide us with the knowledge necessary to realise the values that our views of life provide us with. One could say that Weber's thinking bears some resemblance to the philosophy of religion of Eberhard Herrmann, who proposes a division of labour between science and our views of life, saying that science provides us with knowledge, and our views of life provide us with values that guide our action.[148]

The argument put forward in the above paragraphs may lead one to think that Weber conceives of the relation between views of life and science as at least in principle harmonious and co-operative. But there are textual evidence in his writings that disturb such an interpretation. Several times Weber repeats that religious faith in modern society requires a *sacrificium intellectus*.[149] Weber recommends those who cannot bear the meaninglessness of modernity to return to the open and merciful arms of the old churches, which will inevitably require a sacrifice of the intellect, since membership in a Christian church presupposes the acceptance of a "positive" theology, that is a theology that claims to know things about a transcendent realm with a cognitive security that properly can only be ascribed to science.[150]

The problem with a theology of this type is that it regards revelation as an axiom, according to Weber. Theological axioms are of a totally different kind than presuppositions used by science, and they "do not represent 'knowledge', in the usual sense, but rather a 'possession'" (*Haben*).[151] This 'possession'-character of theological claims – that is claims to have access to a revelation that provides special knowledge not available for everyone – makes it impossible for any theological statement of metaphysical character to lay claim to intersubjective validity. Science can for example never accept claims to special knowledge through revelation or certain miracles.[152] To accept such claims *as if*

<hr/>

ihm dabei helfen, sich selbst Rechenschaft zu geben über den letzten Sinn seines eigenen Tuns. *Es scheint mir das nicht so sehr wenig zu sein, auch für das rein persönliche Leben.*"

[148] Herrmann, Eberhard: *Scientific Theory and Religious Belief*, p. 61; see also Herrmann, Eberhard: "The Trouble with Religious Realism", p. 42 and "A Pragmatic Approach to Religion and Science", p. 146.

[149] e.g. in Weber, Max: "Wissenschaft als Beruf", *MWG I/17*, p. 108.

[150] Weber, Max: "Wissenschaft als Beruf", *MWG I/17*, p. 110.

[151] FMW p. 154. Weber, Max: "Wissenschaft als Beruf", *MWG I/17*, p. 107-108: "...*sind kein 'Wissen' im gewöhnlich verstandenen Sinn, sondern ein 'Haben'*".

[152] Weber, Max: "Wissenschaft als Beruf", *MWG I/17*, p. 98.

they were valid in the same sense as a scientific proposition would then be a *sacrificium intellectus*.

As I have hinted at in chapter two, Weber had deep contact with and knowledge of the theological world of his time, and he cannot reasonably be said to have been unaware of the radical character of much of the liberal theology of his own time. Of course, much liberal theology would have been criticised by Weber for requiring a *sacrificium intellectus*, for example if it presupposed that the world had an inherent meaning,[153] but at least I think it is reasonable to assume that he found liberal theology to be an interesting effort to create an intellectual picture of a religiosity relevant in the modern world.[154] Views of life are necessary for both human life in general and for scientific work according to Weber. A reasonable interpretation of his view on the relation between views of life and science has to recognise this fact. Therefore an effort to reconstruct his view in a consistent and coherent manner has to provide an interpretation that makes it possible both to have a view of life and to respect the scientific domain fully.

A possible interpretation of Weber's texts seems to be that religious life as it typically functions in the "old churches" requires a sacrifice of the intellect. The churches and their members normally hold that it is an intersubjectively valid fact that Jesus was born of a virgin, that he walked on water or that he rose from the dead in some sort of bodily form on Easter day. Given the acceptance of the modern world-view it is not possible to accept such knowledge-claims with honesty, and therefore the believers have to make a sacrifice of the intellect, that is they have to choose to live outside modernity. Weber was of course aware of that not all church members (e.g. many of his friends and relatives among the liberal theologians) believed metaphysical propositions of this kind, but a typical church member would. His reasoning about religion requiring a *sacrificium intellectus* can then be seen as the construction of an ideal-type.

As Weber hinted at in *Zwischenbetrachtung*, conflicts between different value-spheres must not be seen as being absolute other than in an ideal-typical way. It cannot be concluded *a priori* that there is an irresolvable conflict between science and religion or other types of views of life, and that there is no way of overcoming such a conflict. If there is to be a conflict or not will depend on exactly how the view of life in

[153] Weber, Max: "Wissenschaft als Beruf", *MWG I/17*, pp. 105-106.
[154] Weber, Max: Letter to Ferdinand Tönnies 19/2 1909, *MWG II/6*, pp. 65-66.

question is structured, which theoretical beliefs it contains and which claims to validity it has for these beliefs, which values that belongs to the central value-system etc. Given the reasonableness of the interpretation of Weber's texts that says that views of life are necessary for science, it cannot at the same time be claimed that Weber's texts necessarily have to be understood as pointing to an irresolvable conflict between science and views of life, at least not if the ambition is to construct a consistent theory out of his thinking.[155]

In an influential article, Alvin Gouldner proposed that Weber tried to find a solution to the problem with the competing claims of faith and reason in a way that respected the distinctive character of both.[156] Such a solution, as I see it, would then imply that the claims of science to be the only provider of intersubjectively valid knowledge must be respected by faith (understood in a wide sense, as referring to views of life in general), and that science respects the legitimate claims of faith to create values that guide human action and bestow meaning upon human existence.

Several scholars have suggested that Weber's main ambition is to secure the integrity and dignity of the views of life against the imperialism of science.[157] As I have mentioned, there is an existential trait in Weber's thinking, and he regards the free choice of views of life as a moral ideal. As I have said above, Weber holds it to be impossible to solve conflicts about values in a completely rational manner. This has cost him accusations of being a relativist. Others have defended him from this charge with much fervour. Ringer, for example, has said that someone who holds that actors should have consistent and coherent ultimate objectives (views of life) hardly can be called a relativist. Rather, Weber should be seen as a champion of the necessity of applying rational criteria in our deliberations on how to act.[158] Stephen Turner has criticised Ringer's anti-relativistic interpretation of Weber for providing "a Weber for the right-thinking". In Turner's view, Weber's position does not allow for any wide-ranging claims in regard to the possibility of applying universal criteria when judging between different value-positions.[159]

---

[155] I thus diverge from the interpretation put forward by Wagner and Krech, *op.cit.*, p. 764.

[156] Gouldner, *op.cit.*, p. 214.

[157] e.g. Bruun, *op.cit.*, pp. 21-22, Gouldner, *op.cit.*, pp. 214-215.

[158] Ringer, Fritz: *Max Weber's Methodology*, p. 141.

[159] Turner, Stephen: "A Weber for the Right-Thinking", pp. 267-274.

In my opinion, Turner's critique of Ringer is to a large extent justified. When Ringer claims that Weber was "in no sense" a relativist, he
clearly overstates his case. Weber clearly held that it is impossible to
give compelling arguments for any basic value. If equality is good or
not, is for Weber a matter of faith, for example. But this does not mean
that he despairs of science's possibility of giving *any* help when it comes
to value-choices. Science can test the consistency of a view of life, it can
point out practical consequences of certain ways of acting, and it can
criticise obviously erroneous positions in regard to facts. Weber's position is thus far too complicated for being described as either 'relativist'
or 'non-relativist'.

Any scientific claim to be able to *prove* what the meaning of life is,
or that certain values are true, would threaten human liberty and dignity, since, for Weber, it is the capacity to provide existence with meaning that makes humans human. Therefore Weber's own view of life
contains a value that demands that science and views of life should be
kept separate, since that is the best way of preserving the dignity and in
some sense superiority of views of life. In this respect, Weber would
follow Wilhelm Herrmann rather than Ernst Troeltsch in the conflict
over how Christian faith should be integrated with science.[160] Weber
has an ambition to secure "faith" against the imperialistic claims of
"reason" because he regards this dignity as essential for humanity.
However, one should not therefore underestimate his logical and epistemological reasons for drawing such a sharp line between science and
views of life.

Theological Relevance

In this chapter I have tried to construct an interpretation of Weber's
thinking about the relation between science and views of life, and I
believe that I have shown that it is possible and reasonable to interpret
his texts as saying that views of life and science have two separate but
interrelated functions in modern society: science provides us with facts
and views of life provide us with values that can guide our action and
help us to bestow meaning upon our existence. What implications such
an idea would have for Christian theology I have not yet discussed. The
full treatment of that question will be performed in chapters five, six and

---

[160] See chapter two.

seven. Here I shall only try to hint at an answer by relating Weber to two contemporary thinkers whose ideas about the relation between views of life and science have a great affinity with Weber's thought, namely the Swedish philosopher of religion Eberhard Herrmann and the North American theologian Gordon Kaufman.

Herrmann proceeds from what he calls the dilemma of the Western religious intellectual. This intellectual person is a person who cannot help being religious, but at the same time cannot accept such religious beliefs which conflict with the contemporary scientific world-view. In Herrmann's view, it is impossible for the modern Western religious intellectual to regard central themes in Christianity as involving "knowledge-claims at the same logical level as ordinary statements".[161]

For Herrmann, views of life provide us with formulations and symbols that help us understand what he calls the contingencies of life. Contingencies of life are such phenomena in life that we experience as real, but which cannot be given an ultimate explanation. Such phenomena are for example death and love.[162] By providing these formulations, views of life give us insights in what it means to be a human being. These insights are not to be regarded as knowledge at the same level as knowledge produced by scientific activity, but rather as a kind of intuition, for which universal validity cannot be claimed, even if they to a certain extent can be generalised.[163] By giving us insights in what it means to be a human being, our views of life give us a vision of what life could be at its best, that is a kind of utopian picture of human existence. It is when we experience the contrast between this kind of visions and reality that we create values.[164] Views of life thus, in Herrmann's understanding, belong to the domain of values, and not of knowledge. But there are intimate connections between values, views of life and science. The aspect that Herrmann discusses mostly is the fact that we need values to be able to apply our scientific knowledge to the problems which confront us in our life. Knowledge of facts is about how reality is. Science can never tell us what we ought to do, other than in an instrumental way of the form: if you want to achieve the end X, you ought to apply the means Y. To establish ends, towards which human action can be directed, we need

---

[161] Herrmann, Eberhard: *Scientific Theory and Religious Belief*, pp. 17-18.
[162] Herrmann, Eberhard: *Scientific Theory and Religious Belief*, p. 19.
[163] Herrmann, Eberhard: *Scientific Theory and Religious Belief*, pp. 99-100.
[164] Herrmann, Eberhard: *Scientific Theory and Religious Belief*, pp. 61, 109. A similar, albeit not identical, position is taken by Drees in "The Significance of Scientific Images", p. 110.

values, which are provided by our views of life.[165] But Herrmann also points to what Weber called value relevance:

> There is an important kind of relationship between views of life and the sciences in the sense that the scientists' views of life help to influence their interest for certain fields of research and investigation. The interests which scientists have, involve of course not only their personal views of life. There is also a relation of agreement or disagreement with the dominant view of life in society.[166]

In a Weberian terminology, one could say that Herrmann in the above quotation distinguishes between practical and theoretical value relevance. It is both inevitable and necessary that scholars choose their object of research on the basis of values, both their personal values and by relating themselves to cultural values. However, Herrmann does not explore this kind of relation between science and views of life very much.

Herrmann concludes his essay *Scientific Theory and Religious Belief* with a short remark saying that if the function of views of life is to provide us with values, created on the basis of the expressions of what it means to be a human being and our experience of the discrepancies between life as it is and how it would be at its best, it is an important task to develop, criticise and invent such expressions.[167] Given Herrmann's understanding of views of life, the task of theology (both Christian and academic, according to their respective character) could be seen to do just this: develop, invent and criticise expressions of our understanding of human life.[168]

According to Gordon Kaufman, Christian theology should be praxis-oriented. It is not primarily a question of what is true, but a question about how we should live our lives.[169] In Kaufman's view, theology's main task is to provide us humans with an orientation for our lives. According to Kaufman, theology is a human imaginative construct which aims at fulfilling this task. Human reflection on the ultimate mysteries of life has created imaginative pictures and stories which we call religions. These collections of pictures and stories have for a long time provided humans with values towards which they have oriented their

---

[165] Herrmann, Eberhard: *Scientific Theory and Religious Belief,* pp. 60-61.
[166] Herrmann, Eberhard: *Scientific Theory and Religious Belief,* p. 96.
[167] Herrmann, Eberhard: *Scientific Theory and Religious Belief,* pp. 125-126.
[168] Herrmann has indicated this in his "A Pragmatic Approach to Religion and Science", pp. 154-155. However, I do not think that he accepts my division between academic and Christian theology.
[169] Kaufman, Gordon: *In Face of Mystery,* pp. 15-16.

actions and from which they have got a sense of meaning for their existence.[170] Given this view of theology and religious life, Kaufman understands the task of modern theology to construct a "focus for orientation, devotion, and service" that facilitates human flourishing and fulfilment. In Kaufman's opinion, the Western tradition has labelled this focus with the concept *God*.[171]

Of course, Kaufman is not unaware of the fact that this conception of what theology is and should be differs quite radically from how many Christians conceive of their faith. Kaufman rejects most of traditional Christian metaphysics on roughly the same grounds as Herrmann, and for that matter, Weber. Much of the content of traditional Christian dogma is, according to him, simply not tenable given the acceptance of the modern world-view.[172] However, he is eager not to throw out the baby with the bath-water. The fact that much of traditional religious belief is no longer tenable or reasonable should not be made to a hindrance for humanity to make use of valuable aspects in the religious and theological traditions. We need orientation in our lives, and our religious traditions have provided that for thousands of years. As Kaufman sees it, religious traditions are much more effective as providers of values and meanings and as motivators for actions than other kinds of views of life and the world. Non-religious world-pictures often seem to be lifeless in comparison with religions, which create and sustain a "wholehearted allegiance".[173]

If theology shall be able to fulfil this task, however, it has to become a truly *critical theology*. Sectarian theology, as pursued in anti-intellectualistic religious groups, can never in the long run provide resources for orientation in life. According to Kaufman, theology has to radically accept the world in which humans really live if it should be able to give direction and meaning to life. A theology which does not face the cultural and social reality in which it tries to speak, will be irrelevant, since it cannot address the problems that people really have. Proper theology therefore has to be critical. It must open itself to every sort of criticism, and it must be ready to criticise current religious symbols and practices.[174] A main task for such a theology would also be to propose new and better symbols for religious life.[175]

---

[170] Kaufman, Gordon: *In Face of Mystery*, pp. 28-29.
[171] Kaufman, Gordon: *In Face of Mystery*, pp. 42-43, 311.
[172] see e.g. Kaufman, Gordon: *In Face of Mystery*, pp. 3-4, 12.
[173] Kaufman, Gordon: *In Face of Mystery*, pp. 227-228.
[174] Kaufman, Gordon: *God – Mystery – Diversity*, p. 207.
[175] Kaufman, Gordon: *God – Mystery – Diversity*, p. 209.

If Kaufman's position is interpreted in the terminology of my distinction between Christian and academic theology, one can say that he advocates a kind of combination between them. In a sense, this is my position
too. There is a need for a detached academic theology, which tries to
judge Christian theology critically and suggest ameliorations in the
belief-systems of religious faith. But we also need a theology that con-
structively tries to orient us in life. In practice, it is not always possible
to separate Christian and academic theology, however. This is especially
so since reasonable Christian theology always has to reckon with the
critical perspective offered by the academy.

One important point which both Weber, Herrmann and Kaufman have
in common, is the repudiation of what Rickert called the 'picture theory
of knowledge'. All three authors agree that we cannot have any unconceptualised access to reality. Experience is thus not to be seen as the primary factor in our knowledge-seeking, but as the last instance, by which
our conceptual constructions of reality can be tested.[176] We can experience if reality *in se* resist certain conceptualisations, but we cannot say
that our concepts are some sort of depictions of phenomena. From a
Christian theological perspective, such a position has radical consequences, if accepted. The concept 'God' cannot, on such a view, be seen
as a *name* which points out a cosmic being. Rather, it must be seen as a
conceptual construction, useful for the ordering of certain aspects of our
experiences.

As my reconstruction of Max Weber's view on the relation between
science and views of life has shown, he holds consistent and coherent
views of life to be both desirable and necessary for scientific work, since
values produced by views of life constitute the objects of research and
give scientific work its direction. There is therefore in his thinking no *a
priori* conflict between science and views of life, not even religious
ones. But, according to this interpretation of Weber, not every view of
life can exist peacefully together with science, but only such views that
fully respect the claims of modern science.

This of course means that traditional Christian theology has to be
thoroughly revised and reconstructed if it should be compatible with
Weber's thinking. In my opinion, Eberhard Herrmann's and Gordon
Kaufman's views provide resources that are valuable when trying to
construct a model of theological thinking that can be integrated with

---

[176] Kaufman, Gordon: *An Essay on Theological Method*, p. 8; Herrmann, Eberhard:
"A Pragmatic Approach to Religion and Science", pp. 136-139.

Weber's thought. Herrmann's idea of a division of labour between views of life and science offers a perspective on religion that is acceptable to science as Weber understands it, and shows a great affinity with Weber's own thinking. In the light of Herrmann's philosophy of religion, Weber's view of the relation between science and religion can be seen as relevant in modern discussions of this relation.

Kaufman's vision of a critical academic theology could be seen as an elaboration of Weber's ideas about what science and philosophy can offer views of life, namely a constructive criticism that helps to create viable symbols and a consistent and coherent view of life. Since, in Weber's view, such views of life are of utmost importance to science and to human life in general, theology, understood as critical philosophical analysis of Christian teachings, can be regarded as a respectable academic activity.

But Weber's thinking can also offer critical reflections which have bearing on Herrmann's and especially Kaufman's view. Can a theology – and in the long run a religion – which is a [intellectual] construction fulfil its task to give orientation to human life? How should the relation between constructed theology and experienced religious reality be seen, and what kind of importance can be ascribed to innovative religious leaders such as Jesus or Mohammed? Weber's answers to such questions will be discussed in chapters five and six. Before that, however, it will be necessary to analyse Weber's picture of modern society and the place and function of views of life in the modern world. I have shown that Weber regards values as necessary for scientific work. But what kind of relation does he see between our views of life, science and political or economic action? Is consistent and coherent views of life necessary or desirable in all human activities in the modern world? And even if they are theoretically possible, can they be realised and lived in a world that Weber characterises as enclosed in the iron cage of rationalism? To such questions I shall turn in the next chapter.

4. RELIGION AND MODERNITY

The Processes of Rationalisation

The idea that human culture for a long time has undergone a process of rationalisation is a central theme in Weber's writings.[1] Weber adopts a universal historical perspective in his study of the process of rationalisation. However, this must not be understood as if Weber advocates a simple evolutionist scheme. In this chapter I shall explore Weber's view on the function and fate of religion in modernity. By modernity I understand, following Giddens, such "modes of social life or organisation which emerged in Europe from about the seventeenth century onwards and which subsequently became more or less world-wide in their influence".[2]

The concept rationalisation (*Rationalisierung*) is ambiguous. As Weber himself notes, 'rationalism' (*Rationalismus*) can mean several things. Weber roughly distinguishes between 1) intellectual systematisations of views of life and world-views (*Weltbilder*) and 2) rationalisation of action by a development towards a more technical and instrumental way of acting for the attainment of given goals.[3] In discussing the theory on rationalisation in Weber's texts, I shall make extensive use of Brubaker's lucid interpretation in his book *The Limits of Rationality*.

Brubaker distinguishes between two pairs of concepts regarding *rationality* in Weber's thought. The first pair is the distinction between formal

---

[1] See e.g. Brubaker, *op.cit.*, p. 1; Mommsen, Wolfgang: *The Social and Political Theory of Max Weber*, p. 133 and Turner, Bryan: *Max Weber*, p. 115. This idea about the rationalisation process as a central theme in Weber's writings is however not uncontested. See e.g. Tenbruck, *op.cit.*, pp. 238-240.

[2] Giddens, Anthony: *The Consequences of Modernity*, p. 1. The concept 'modernity' is of course very wide and not very precise. This is, in this context, more of an advantage than a deficiency, since it allows the concept to sum up very various trends in contemporary culture. More hazardous is of course my total omission of any usage of the concept 'post-modernity'. I omit this concept for two reasons. First, I do not believe that modernity has gone away. As Göran Therborn says in his *European Modernity and Beyond* (p. 268), it may have come under siege in the Western world, but it has not surrendered. Second, post-modernity seems to continue the demagification of the world, since it questions even the metaphysics of progress inherent in much of modern culture and may thus be described more as ultra-modernity than post-modernity. Se Turner, Bryan: *Max Weber*, pp. 15-16.

[3] Weber, Max: "Einleitung", *MWG I/19*, p. 117.

and substantial rationality. Formal rationality is a rationality of calculation. It is about applying the most adequate means to attain a given end
and can therefore be judged by scientific means: if a certain pattern of
action can be said (on empirical grounds) to be the most effective way to
attain a goal and is calculable, it is maximally formally rational. By substantive rationality is meant rationality from the point of view of a certain
value or a certain belief. According to this type of rationality, a pattern of
action is rational if it is consistent with the value or belief in question,
and irrational if it is not.[4]

In Weber's own terminology, the distinction between formal and substantive rationality can be seen in the difference between ends-rationality (*Zweckrationalität*) and value-rationality (*Wertrationalität*), ends-
rationality being related to formal rationality, and value-rationality to
substantive rationality. Value-rational action is determined by a belief in
the intrinsical value of a certain way of action. Calculations of a means-
end character is totally alien to such action. Ends-rational action, on the
other hand, means that the agent, with the best knowledge to her or his
disposal, tries to conceive of the most effective means to achieve a certain end.[5] According to Weber, from the point of view of ends-rationality, value-rationality is always irrational.[6]

Formal rationality is characterised by the stress on *calculability*. In,
for example, a formally rational economy, everything can be calculated, both the production process and the society's legal system.[7] In a
formally rational legal system, for example, the outcome of a legal
process can *in principle* be judged by calculation. In an amusing
metaphor, Weber describes the judge in a formally rational legal system as a "paragraph-machine into which one throws the documents on
a case together with the costs and fees so that it will then spit out a
judgement along with some more or less valid reasons for it".[8] In a

---

[4] Brubaker, *op.cit.*, pp. 35-36. Brubaker uses the concept formal rationality in a
broader sense than Weber himself does.

[5] The misunderstanding that Weber by *Zweckrationalität* meant the rationality of *ends*
must be avoided. What Weber has in mind when writing about *Zweckrationalität* is what
Mikael Stenmark has called means-end rationality, which he understands as consisting
"in the efficient pursuit of means for achieving certain implicit or explicit ends or goals".
See Stenmark, Mikael: *Rationality in Science, Religion and Everyday Life*, p. 27.

[6] Weber, Max: *Wirtschaft und Gesellschaft*, pp. 12-13.

[7] Brubaker, *op.cit.*, p. 12.

[8] PW pp. 148-149. Weber, Max: "Parlament und Regierung", *MWG I/15*, p. 454:
"...*Paragraphen-Automat...in welchen man oben die Akten nebst den Kosten und
Gebühren hineinwirft, auf daß er unten das Urteil nebst den mehr oder minder stich-
haltigen Gründen ausspeie...*", see also *Wirtschaft und Gesellschaft*, p. 565.

formally rational legal system, there is no room for *moral* considerations in the legal process.

In a substantive rational legal process, on the other hand, moral considerations are central. A case will not be judged by formal rules, but by moral criteria, applied to individual cases. Weber exemplifies this with the 18th century case of the Prussian miller Arnold who had not paid his rent to the landlord and therefore had been evicted. Arnold complained in a court of law, but was not listened to. The king then imprisoned the judges and made them liable to pay damages to Arnold, since their judgement had been unfair, even if it was in formal accordance with the law.[9] Such a legal system can never be calculated in advance, and is therefore irrational from the formal point of view.

In a society where formal rationality is developing, there is, according to Weber, a risk that *calculability* and formal rationality becomes the main end in itself. Effectiveness will then not only be a way to attain ends, but will in itself be the ultimate end.[10] According to Weber, there will always be a potential conflict between formal and substantive rationality in modern society, since what is formally rational may be highly dubious from a substantive point of view.[11] A totally ends-rational economic system, for example, can potentially be very irrational from an ethical point of view.[12] The good business manager does not have to be a moral manager, or perhaps cannot be, given a totally ends-rational economic system.[13]

The second pair of concepts which Brubaker develops is the distinction between objective and subjective rationality. Subjective rationality is rationality from the point of view of the agent. Both ends-rational action and value-rational action can thus be seen as subjectively rational. Agents act ends-rationally if they try to use the most effective means known to them in order to achieve a given end, and they act value-rationally if they act on the belief in the intrinsic value of the action. In both these cases the action is rational given certain qualities of the purpose of the agents. If, for example, an agent uses magic as a means to achieve a

---

[9] Weber, Max: *Wirtschaft und Gesellschaft*, p. 471. The full information on the story has been gathered from the editorial note in the Swedish edition of *Wirtschaft und Gesellschaft*. See *Ekonomi och samhälle II*, p. 339.

[10] This seems to be the ultimate content of Weber's dooms-prophecy in the end of "Die protestantische Ethik", *GARS I*, pp. 203-205.

[11] Brubaker, *op.cit.*, p. 38.

[12] See chapter 3 on the conflict between different value spheres.

[13] This example came to my mind when reading Sundman, Per: "The Good Manager – A Moral Manager?"

certain end, and personally believes that magic is effective, her or his action is ends-rational from a subjective point of view.[14]

Objective rationality, on the other hand, can only be applied to ends-rational action, since, according to Weber's view, there is no way to decide scientifically which values are correct. If an action is objectively rational, it applies the most objectively adequate means to achieve a given end, in accordance with scientific knowledge.[15] Magical acts, which Weber understands as ends-rational, can serve as an example.[16] From the subjective point of view, a magical act, say rain-dance, is a perfectly rational means given that the actor believes that it is the most effective way to create rain. From a scientific point of view, on the other hand, rain-dance cannot be said to be a very effective way to bring rain about, and so, from the objective standpoint, is irrational.[17] Objective rationality is exclusively a question of applying the correct technique, that is a technique which is able to achieve the desired end.[18]

What characterises the universal process of rationalisation in human culture is, according to Weber, that human action tends to become more and more ends-rational and objectively rational, and that human belief systems become more and more systematised.[19] The process is not simple, however. Magic, which Weber conceives as being prior to religion in time, is characterised by ends-rational actions, while religion is characterised by value-rational thinking, for example. It should be held in mind that there are striking similarities between the stage of magic and modern culture in Weber's thinking. Ends-rationality and fragmentation of value spheres are salient features of both stages. What separates them is primarily the degree of objective rationality inherent in respective stage. This makes a simple evolutionist interpretation of Weber's thinking inadequate.

[14] Brubaker, *op.cit.*, p. 53. Fritz Ringer uses the concept 'right rationality'. See his *Max Weber's Methodology*, pp. 97, 106. Weber's usage is not consequent, as is evident from e.g. Weber, Max: "'Wertfreiheit'", p. 525, where Weber writes about "...*rational 'richtigem', d.h. die objektiv, nach der wissenschaftlichen Erkenntnis, richtigen Mittel...*"

[15] Weber, Max: "'Wertfreiheit'", *GAW*, p. 525; *Wirtschaft und Gesellschaft*, p. 32; Brubaker, *op.cit.*, pp. 53-55.

[16] Weber understands *magic* as the attempt to influence the forces of nature. It should be distinguished from what he calls *symbolism*, a more "advanced" and symbolical use of magic. See *Wirtschaft und Gesellschaft*, p. 248.

[17] Weber, Max: *Wirtschaft und Gesellschaft*, p. 245.

[18] Brubaker, *op.cit.*, p. 57.

[19] Wolfgang Schluchter has called this systematisation *value rationalisation*. See e.g. his *Paradoxes of Modernity*, p. 67.

Further, the process of rationalisation is not only a universal historical process: it is also a process that takes place in a micro-perspective. A new, charismatically founded, religious movement tends to become more and more rationalised, for example. The small group of followers around the charismatically inspired person often develops into an institution with a rational administration.[20]

A contemporary example of a rationalisation process in micro-perspective could be the development of the New Age movement, as understood by Wouter J. Hanegraaff. According to Hanegraaff, the New Age has one of its roots in the cultural criticism of the 1960s, and started out as an idealistic movement, opposed to Western commercialism. But during the 1990s, the New Age has been more and more commercialised, according to Hanegraaff.[21] If his analysis is correct, the fate of the New Age Movement would be an illustrative example of a rationalisation process, where idealistic values undergo a process of formal rationalisation and ends up as little more than means to the end of effective profit-making.

In his book *Max Weber and the Sociology of Culture,* Ralph Schroeder suggests that Weber's view of universal history can be seen as containing three stages: magic, religion and science.[22] This typology can be useful for analytical reasons, and I shall use it in trying to explore Weber's idea of how the modern Western society has come into being through the world-wide process of rationalisation. But the typology also has some disadvantages: there is a risk that Weber is interpreted as advocating a very simple developmental scheme in which human history has to be pressed. That is absolutely not the case: Weber's view of human history is complicated, and the following sketch must not be considered as anything more than a simplified analysis, undertaken for the sake of the arguments following later in this chapter. What especially has to be borne in mind is that Weber's view of human history is not future-inclusive.[23] Weber's discussion of rationalisation is not a prophecy about the distant future of human society, but a generalising description of how history hitherto has developed, and a *hypothesis* about future developments.

---

[20] Weber, Max: *Wirtschaft und Gesellschaft,* p. 143. For a contemporary discussion of this phenomenon, see e.g. McGuire, Meredith: *Religion: The Social Context,* pp. 133-134.

[21] Hanegraaff, Wouter J.: *New Age Religion and Western Culture,* p. 523.

[22] Schroeder, *op.cit.,* p. 11.

[23] On the concept future-inclusive, see Jeffner, Anders: *Theology and Integration,* pp. 49-50.

Early human culture was, according to Weber, characterised by *magic*, understood as the belief that nature could be mastered through the use of certain rituals, performed by the magician or wizard.[24] Nature was conceived as being manipulable through the charisma of the magician, and the forces which were manipulated were conceived as immanent in the world. This magical acting, was, according to Weber, oriented to inner-worldly goals, like protection from enemies, creation of good weather, wealth, etc.[25]

The next step in this development was the belief in different spirits, who were conceived as standing behind the mystical forces that were manipulated by magic.[26] Step by step this belief in different spirits developed to the belief in a pantheon of different functional gods.[27] Through several complicated processes this pantheon came to be hierarchically ordered, so that one god (e.g. Zeus) became the ruler over the other gods. Different political circumstances, as the creation of a confederation between different groups, could create monolatry as a way of holding the confederation together.[28]

In ancient Judaism the emergence of the *prophet* became a decisive step toward the rationalisation of religion, according to Weber. The prophet can be separated from the magician as a preacher of a certain revelation, rather than as the performer of a certain ritual.[29] In Weber's view, the Jewish prophets preached an *ethical* religion – and in more advanced form: ethical *monotheism* – in contrast to earlier forms of religion and magic. For the prophets of ethical monotheism, magic is meaningless or evil, since the universe is governed by a wholly transcendent, omnipotent God. In their eyes, salvation can only be gained through a meaningful and ethical relation to this God, who says: "For I desired steadfast love and not sacrifice, the knowledge of God rather than burnt-offerings" (Hos 6:6).[30]

---

[24] Weber, Max: "Einleitung", *MWG I/19*, p. 105.

[25] Weber, Max: *Wirtschaft und Gesellschaft*, pp. 245-246. Weber's view on magic has, at least partially, been abandoned in modern anthropology, especially in regard to his strict separation of religion and magic. However, it must be noted that Weber does not regard magical practices as irrational. Rather they are perfectly subjectively rational. For an overview of the modern discussion about magic, see e.g. Schäfer, Peter & Kippenberg, Hans (eds.): *Envisioning Magic*.

[26] Weber, Max: *Wirtschaft und Gesellschaft*, p. 246.

[27] Weber, Max: *Wirtschaft und Gesellschaft*, p. 250.

[28] Weber, Max: *Das antike Judentum*, pp. 86-87.

[29] Weber, Max: *Wirtschaft und Gesellschaft*, p. 269.

[30] Weber, Max: *Wirtschaft und Gesellschaft*, p. 278.

The acceptance of ethical religion is, according to Weber, furthered by the fact that it promotes an ordered and rational way of living. The ethical demands on the gods, and in the long run the belief in an omnipotent ethical god, increase as the importance of ethical and pre-dictable behaviour of individuals increases. In a more developed econ-omy it is crucial that agreements can be trusted, and the ethical deity stands as the ultimate source and guardian of the ethical order.[31]

Thus the primal magical ends-rationality undergoes a value-rationali-sation, which in turn (unintendedly) increases formal rationality and in the long run objective rationality, since it successively eliminates magi-cal behaviour. Value-rationalisation creates the demagification of the world (*Entzauberung der Welt*).[32] As has been said before, rationalisa-tion, which primarily takes place in the Occident, is not unilinear. In Weber's eyes, Old Testament prophetism is the main origin of this process, which is developed and furthered by Protestantism, especially in the Reformed tradition. Medieval Catholicism, on the other hand, rep-resents a magical "backlash".[33]

Calvinist Protestantism takes this process a decisive step forward, according to Weber. For the Calvinist, God is utterly transcendent, and religion is devoid of all magical elements.[34] Reformed Christianity also created a rationalised theology, most obvious in its solution to the prob-lem of theodicy: the doctrine of *predestination*. For the Calvinists there existed no magical or mystical forces – everything that happened was a product of the will of God; even the eternal fate of individuals. Posi-tively expressed, the ultimate rationalisation of religious belief can be said to be the conviction that the world is completely governed by divine providence.[35] The Calvinist doctrine also contained a very high evalua-tion of professional work; the Calvinist God demanded that belief in him should be expressed in an ethically ordered, systematic way of life. This laid the ground for a methodical and ascetic way of life, necessary for a production-oriented capitalism.[36]

---

[31] Weber, Max: *Wirtschaft und Gesellschaft,* p. 263.

[32] Weber, Max: "Einleitung", *MWG I/19,* p. 114.

[33] Weber, Max: "Die protestantische Ethik", *GARS I,* p. 114. Se also *Wirtschaft und Gesellschaft,* p. 338.

[34] Weber, Max: "Die protestantische Ethik", *GARS I,* pp. 94-95.

[35] Weber, Max: *Wirtschaft und Gesellschaft,* p. 317.

[36] Weber, Max: "Die protestantische Ethik", *GARS I,* pp. 116-120. On modern Protestant work ethics, see Grenholm, Carl-Henric: *Protestant Work Ethics.* Grenholm's book also contains a discussion of Weber's analysis of Protestant work ethics, especially pp. 47-50.

But, as has been discussed in chapter three, the belief in such a God creates the need to know what this God has decided about one's own fate. In some forms of Calvinist pastoral care the idea that this could be determined by the degree of success in earthly business developed, and this, combined with a moral prohibition against luxury consumption and a high evaluation of professional work created a tremendous industriousness and accumulation of wealth which in turn could be invested in production. Thus a modern capitalist economy was furthered by Protestant religiosity.[37]

Protestantism thus was one of the driving forces behind the rationalisation of the way of life of individuals. If it was tremendously important to create wealth, people tried to find out the most effective way to do so, and, gradually, human behaviour came to be more and more formally and objectively rational. Eventually, this rationalisation eroded the substantive rationality of this kind of behaviour. Profit-making and success became ends in themselves, free from the connection to belief in God, or, as Weber expresses it, Bunyan's pilgrim was replaced by Robinson Crusoe.[38]

It deserves to be mentioned, that Weber's analysis of the Protestant ethic and its relation to the spirit of capitalism has been widely debated ever since it was first put forth. I cannot comment on the vast literature on the topic here, but the matter is in no ways settled. Kurt Samuelsson has criticised Weber's thesis, while, for example, Gordon Marshall finds some empirical evidence for Weber's thesis in his analysis of business records in Scotland during the seventeenth century.[39]

Hand in hand with the development of western capitalism followed the dominance of modern science. In Weber's view, science provides the knowledge and the techniques necessary for instrumental mastery over the world, and was therefore a natural consequence of the intensification of the rationalisation process. From the point of view of Protestantism, science was a dangerous ally, however.[40]

---

[37] It would be totally wrong, however, to assume that Weber thought of ideal factors such as Protestantism as sufficient causes for the growth of modern capitalism. See e.g. *Wirtschaft und Gesellschaft*, p. 349.

[38] Weber, Max: "Die protestantische Ethik", *GARS I*, pp. 197-206. The comment on Robinson Crusoe can be found on pp. 197-198.

[39] Samuelsson, Kurt: *Religion and Economic Action,* e.g. p. 153; Marshall, Gordon: *Presbyteries and Profits*, pp. 221-262, esp. 260-261. Richard Swedberg has commented upon this in his *Max Weber and the Idea of Economic Sociology*, pp. 130-132. See also the comments of Bryan Turner in Turner, Bryan: *Max Weber*, p. 116.

[40] Weber points out that Protestantism during the 16th and 17th centuries conceived of the natural sciences as *ancillae fidei* rather than threats. See Weber, Max: "Wissenschaft als Beruf", *MWG I/17*, p. 91; "Zwischenbetrachtung", *MWG I/19*, p. 512.

In the modern world, science has come to dominate society, by monopolising what can be called intellectual honesty. Only that which can lay claim to be 'scientific' in some sense or another will be accepted as universally valid in the modern world.[41] One example of this trend could be the so called New Age-movements and their strive for social recognition. Since science is the sole source of intellectual legitimity, even systems of thought that cannot reasonably lay claim to scientific status often try to present themselves as '*alternative* sciences', but still as *sciences*.[42] Another example of a somewhat awkward respect for modern science, is the scientism of Christian fundamentalism, which is both very critical towards modern biblical scholarship and deeply desires scholarly legitimation of its own ideas.[43]

The rationalisation process turns modern culture into a culture of experts. Expert knowledge becomes increasingly dominant because efficiency in terms of ends-rationality and calculability develops into salient features of society. The dominance of expert knowledge is a consequence of the expanded role of technical efficiency, according to Weber. This culture of experts often tends to become tyrannical, since it invades all spheres of life. People are moved towards pursuing short-term goals instead of long-term ones by this dominant kind of rationality, and this is what, according to Weber, has negative effects on freedom and humanity.[44] In Weber's eyes, there is a risk that the 'skeleton hands' of rationalism, as he puts it, destroy human autonomy and turn us into to nothing more than replaceable cogs in a big and lifeless machine.[45]

Weber's Nightmare

For Weber, the autonomy of the individual is the highest of all values. Human beings should organise their life around values that they consciously and freely have chosen, and struggle to realise them in everyday reality. In fact, Weber understands 'personality' as signifying a human being that has organised her or his life around certain consciously chosen

---

[41] Weber, Max: "Zwischenbetrachtung", *MWG I/19,* p. 517.

[42] For a discussion of the view of science in the New Age movement, see e.g. Hanegraaff, Wouter J.: *op.cit.,* pp. 62-76 and Hammer, Olav: *På spaning efter helheten,* pp. 222-229.

[43] Barr, James: *Fundamentalism,* p. 120.

[44] Schroeder, Ralph: *op.cit.,* p. 13.

[45] Weber, Max: "Zwischenbetrachtung", *MWG I/19,* p. 507.

values.[46] A true human personality creates her or his own meaning in life since

> ...we regard as *objectively* valuable those innermost elements of the "personality", those highest and most ultimate value-judgments which determine our conduct and give meaning and significance to our life. We can indeed espouse these values only when they appear to us as valid, as derived from our highest values and when they are developed in the struggle against the difficulties which life presents. Certainly, the dignity of the "personality" lies in the fact that for it there exist values about which it organizes its life...[47]

Weber's reasoning proceeds from a certain anthropological standpoint, according to which humans have freedom of choice, and he assumes that our intentions guide and influence our actions. It is this freedom of choice which is threatened in modern culture, which is characterised by an increasing depersonalisation. Accordingly, there is a risk that we are turned into something less than human.[48]

Especially two trends in the development of modern culture are, on Weber's account, dangerous from the point of view of the value of human freedom, namely the differentiation of life spheres and the bureaucratisation of societal life. Both these trends are consequences of the overarching process of rationalisation. When a certain sphere of life (value sphere) becomes more and more formally and objectively rational, it will be separated from other spheres, since relations with other spheres tend to make rationalisation incomplete. A formally rational political order cannot function effectively if it has too strong relations to ethics, for example. A modern rational legal system operates *sine ira et studio*, and the outcome of a legal process cannot, as was mentioned above, be calculated if it is subject to moral considerations. The same

---

[46] Weber, Max: "Roscher und Knies", *GAW*, p. 132. To be a personality is to have exercised the human capacity for conscious choices of desires and values. But Weber expressively rejects a romantic concept of personality. (see *ibid.*). An example of the linking together of a romantic concept of personality and the view that a personality is constituted by the values she or he consciously hold, can be found in Möller, Göran: *Etikens landskap*, pp. 85-95, especially pp. 90-91.

[47] MSS p. 55. Weber, Max: "'Objektivität'", *GAW*, p. 152: "...*gerade jene innersten Elemente der 'Persönlichkeit', die höchsten und letzten Werturteile, die unser Handeln bestimmen und unserem Leben Sinn und Bedeutung geben, werden von uns als etwas 'objektiv' Wertvolles empfunden. Wir können sie ja nur vertreten, wenn sie uns als geltend, als aus unseren höchsten Lebenswerten fließend, sich darstellen und so, im Kampfe gegen die Widerstände des Lebens, entwickelt werden. Und sicherlich liegt die Würde der 'Persönlichkeit' darin beschlossen, daß es für sie Werte gibt, auf die sie ihr eigenes Leben bezieht...*"

[48] Hennis, Wilhelm: "Personality and Life Orders", pp. 67-69.

holds for the economic sphere of life. In a society where economic efficiency in terms of profit maximisation is the ultimate goal, it is extremely difficult to be a businessman who also adheres to a Christian ethos, at least if this ethos has some affinities with the ethics of the Sermon of the Mount.[49] The rationalisation process thus ends in a fragmented culture, in which it is difficult to find any meaning.

Related to this fragmentation of life is the successive growth of a culture of experts (*Fachmenschentum*).[50] This is a necessity since culture becomes more and more complex, and different activities demand extensive knowledge. Modern banking, for example, cannot be runned in the bohemian way I handle my housekeeping money – it demands both extensive knowledge about the economic system, technical know-how, and a rational and effective organisation. This unavoidable need for experts, is the root and cause of the *bureaucratisation* of modern society, according to Weber. Bureaucracy is the hitherto most effective and rational way to organise any human activity, and therefore it is indispensable in a rationalised culture.[51]

The word bureaucracy may have certain negative connotations in our contemporary ears, such as inefficiency, capriciousness and arbitrariness. This is not what Weber had in mind, however. In Weber's usage, the concept 'bureaucracy' is an ideal type for describing certain ways of organising administration of human activity and implement the authority of a leader or a group of leaders. Weber identifies ten salient features of a bureaucratic organisation, features that can be present in different degrees in actual bureaucratic organisations, but nevertheless can be said to constitute a *typical* bureaucratic system. It should be noted, that 'bureaucracy' in Weber's usage does not exclusively refer to the civil service, but also to private enterprises, like rationally and bureaucratically organised companies or welfare organisations as for example the Red Cross. Accordingly, there are both official and private bureaucracies in modern society.[52]

Modern bureaucracy is, ideal-typically, organised as consisting of individual (civil) servants or white-collar workers, who, according to Weber, operate along the following lines. 1) They are personally free, and are only obliged to obey their employers in matters regarding their position in the organisation. 2) They are organised hierarchically, and

[49] Weber, Max: "Zwischenbetrachtung", *MWG I/19*, pp. 491-492.
[50] Weber, Max: *Wirtschaft und Gesellschaft*, p. 576.
[51] Weber, Max: *Wirtschaft und Gesellschaft*, pp. 560-562.
[52] Weber, Max: *Wirtschaft und Gesellschaft*, pp. 127, 562.

3) every position has a clearly defined area of competence. 4) The holder of a position has her or his position due to a contract with the employer. The employment is therefore principally grounded on a free choice among candidates on the basis of 5) qualifications, which normally are rationally controlled by examinations, degrees etc. 6) The work performed is compensated through a fixed salary in money. 7) The holder of a position regards the position as her or his only or main profession, and she or he 8) looks forward to a career in the organisation. 9) The employees in a bureaucratic organisation perform their tasks without owning the means which are necessary, that is they are separated from the means of production. 10) The employees in a bureaucratic organisation are obliged to work according to a strict discipline and their performance is constantly controlled.[53]

This kind of organisation creates, combined with the expertise that the bureaucrats possess, an effectiveness not hitherto seen in human society. Other forms of administration, as for example feudal forms or administration through notables who perform their administrative tasks as a spare-time occupation, can never achieve the same degree of efficiency and calculability that a bureaucratic form of administration can.[54]

However, the effectiveness of the bureaucratic apparatus is a two-edged sword, according to Weber. On the one hand, effectiveness and technical mastery over the world makes it easier to realise visions and values. An irrational societal organisation, based on, for example, magic, cannot normally achieve the same level of goal implementation as a modern, rationally organised society can. Therefore rationalisation and bureaucratisation are potentially good things according to Weber.[55] In politics, for example, the politician is always dependent on the professional expert for carrying out the political decision in everyday reality. When it comes to practical implementation, the bureaucrat is always the expert, and the politician is almost always a dilettante.[56]

But, on the other hand, it is unavoidable that "influence is exercised by the person who does the work".[57] In modern society, concrete rule will always be in the hands of the civil service.[58] Due to their special

---

[53] Weber, Max: *Wirtschaft und Gesellschaft,* pp. 126-127.

[54] Weber, Max: *Wirtschaft und Gesellschaft,* p. 562.

[55] see e.g. Weber, Max: "Parlament und Regierung", *MWG I/15,* pp. 460, 490.

[56] Weber, Max: *Wirtschaft und Gesellschaft,* p. 572.

[57] PW p. 171. Weber, Max: "Parlament und Regierung", *MWG I/15,* p. 479: "*wer die Arbeit tut, hat den Einfluß*".

[58] Weber, Max: "Parlament und Regierung", *MWG I/15,* p. 450.

knowledge, the experts will often have the possibility to block political decision-making, or change the political agenda irrespective of what the politicians want or intend.[59] The bureaucratic apparatus is not simply a neutral machine, but has interests of its own, and it often has no reservations about guarding those interests, even at the expense of the political bodies. These interests can include simple preservation of the status and power of the bureaucracy, but the bureaucratic apparatus can also serve political interests, as for example when a certain class or political interest group dominates the bureaucracy.[60] This was for example the case in Prussia during the 19th century and at the beginning of the 20th century, where the landed nobility had almost a monopoly on positions in the civil service and used them to guard the economic interests of the aristocracy, even against the will of the formal head of the civil service, the Kaiser.

One effect of the bureaucracy's wish to preserve its own existence and its own power is that it wants business to go on as usual, without disturbances. This may be a threat to the main aim of politics, namely to try to implement visions in the actual reality of society. There is a risk, as was said above, that the main aim in society becomes efficiency in itself, and bureaucracy is a main factor in such a development. The crucial question for Weber when it comes to the organisation of modern society is then how to combine the good sides of bureaucracy with a sufficient political room of manoeuvre.[61]

This task is not easily solved. The rationalisation process is a product of human activity, but to a very large degree it has gone out of hands of humanity and goes on automatically. For the Calvinist of the 16th century, the care for material well-being and, implicitly, technical efficiency should only be as a thin coat, hanging over the shoulders of the elect, a coat which they could take off at will. This is not possible any longer, according to Weber. The coat has been transformed into an iron cage, of which he writes:

> No one knows who will live in this cage in the future, or whether at the end
> of this tremendous development entirely new prophets will arise, or there

---

[59] This is the main occupation of Sir Humphrey Appleby in the amusing novels by Jonathan Lynn and Anthony Jay, *Yes Minister* and *Yes Prime Minister,* which can be recommended to everyone who wants to get a grip on what Weber really meant with the dangers of modern bureaucracy.

[60] A modern analysis of the relation between bureaucracy and political policy-making which mainly follows the tradition from Weber has been provided by for example Page, *op.cit.* His solution to the problem has some affinities with Weber's, see e.g. p. 169.

[61] Weber, Max: "Parlament und Regierung", *MWG I/15,* pp. 465-466.

will be a great rebirth of old ideas and ideals, or, if neither, mechanized petrification, embellished with a sort of convulsive self-importance. For of the last stage of this cultural development, it might well be truly said: "Specialists without spirit, sensualists without heart; this nullity imagines that it has attained a level of civilization never before achieved."[62]

I propose that what Weber views as the threat facing humanity in modern culture can be understood as *alienation*.[63] In a dissertation about the problem of alienation in Karl Marx, Lars Andersson has developed what he calls an *abstract model of alienation*.[64] In what follows, I shall try to show that it is reasonable to interpret Weber's view of the iron cage of modern capitalism along the lines laid down in Andersson's model. This is not to say, however, that Weber and Marx had identical views on alienation as phenomenon; they had not.[65] I only want to claim that Andersson's model can be useful for understanding Weber's view of modern culture. Let H = humanity and o = modern, rationalised culture.

In Andersson's model, for H to be alienated from o, means that

1) o is created by H
2) o satisfies a need in H
3) o takes control over H
4) o is harmful to H
5) H does not recognise o as a human creation, and
6) o is independent of H.[66]

---

[62] PE, p. 182. Weber, Max: "Die protestantische Ethik", *GARS I*, p. 204: "*Niemand weiß noch, wer künftig in jenem Gehäuse wohnen wird und ob am Ende dieser ungeheuren Entwicklung ganz neue Propheten oder eine mächtige Wiedergeburt alter Gedanken und Ideale stehen werden, oder aber – wenn keins von beiden – mechanisierte Versteinerung, mit einer Art von krampfhaftem Sich-wichtig-nehmen verbrämt. Dann allerdings könnte für die 'letzten Menschen' dieser Kulturentwicklung das Wort zur Wahrheit werden: 'Fachmenschen ohne Geist; Genußmenschen ohne Herz: dies Nichts bildet sich ein, eine nie vorher erreichte Stufe des Menschentums erstiegen zu haben.'*"

[63] Löwith, in Löwith, *op.cit.*, avoids using the concept alienation in connection with Weber. See e.g. p. 51. It should be stressed that Weber himself never seems to have spoken about his thinking as a theory of alienation.

[64] Andersson, Lars: *Alienation*, pp. 33-36.

[65] see e.g. Löwith, *op.cit.*, p. 58.

[66] Andersson, *op.cit.* p. 35. There is a discrepancy between how Andersson formulates component (3) in his model in the summary on page 35 in his book, and how he formulates it on page 34, where he discusses the component. According to what Andersson has suggested to me, it is the formulation on page 34 which is correct, and therefore I have used that variant in my account of the paradigmatic model of alienation. Andersson's summarises his model of alienation in English on p. 187.

For Weber, human beings risk becoming alienated from the rational (Western) culture in which they live.[67] Human culture, including the rationalisation process, is a human artefact according to Weber (1), and the rationalisation of culture satisfies the human need for mastery over the world (2). But somewhere in the development of the ends-rationality of modern culture, the rationalisation process becomes self-generating and takes control over human life (3). Since what characterises true *human* beings is that they determine their own lives, the modern rationalised culture is harmful to humanity (4).[68] In a totally rationalised culture most humans do not recognise the demand for ends-rationality as a human artefact, but just regard it as the way things are (5), and the process of rationalisation of cultural phenomena becomes so inevitable, that even protests against rationalisation tend to become rationalised. The process of rationalisation then becomes more or less independent from what human beings want (6). This independence can of course not be understood as a causal independence, since culture is a human artefact (cf. component 1). The sixth component should rather be understood as pointing to the self-reproducing character of rationalised culture: modern society has become so complicated that it seems more or less impossible to change its fundamental operations, even if people would like to.

From the standpoint of certain values, the rationalised modern society can be seen as irrational. If one, like Weber, values the freedom, autonomy and dignity of the individual, modern society as Weber depicts it is utterly irrational. And the values of 16th century Calvinism, which played an important role in bringing modern Western culture about, have become unnecessary and even impossible to hold in our time. So from the standpoint of Calvinism, the process that should be a celebration of God's glory, has become demonic. And the values which normally are associated with the Western capitalistic democracies, like freedom and individuality, become overruled by rationalisation's need of standardisation and homogeneity.[69] It is thus no exaggeration to say, that Weber's view of the risks of modernity is like a true nightmare.

---

[67] Bryan Turner in his *Max Weber*, points out that there is a connection between rationalisation and alienation in Weber's texts. See p. 177.

[68] Component (4) is of a different logical order than the other components, since it expresses a value judgement and cannot in the same way as the other components be tested. In Weber's eyes, it is *because* components (1), (2), (3), (5) and (6) that component (4) is the case. This was suggested to me in a discussion with Lars Andersson, Stefan Eriksson and Mattias Martinson.

[69] Löwith, *op.cit.*, pp. 40-41.

Escape from Modernity

Faced by the alienated situation created by the rationalisation of culture, human beings have two fundamental options; either they can try to
flee from rationality, or they can accept it. If they accept it, they can
either just follow the trend and loose what Weber would see as their true
humanity, or they could try to save human freedom and dignity in a
rationalised world. In this section I shall explore Weber's view of some
flight options, and in the next section his view of the possibility of an
acceptance of modernity that does not erode humanity. Basically, Weber
can be understood as saying that in fleeing from modernity, humanity
gets alienated, since it is virtually impossible to consistently opt out
from modern culture. The out-option is thus self-deceptive.[70] The third
way, to uncritically accept the rationalised culture, will not be explored
further.

One way of fleeing from modernity, as Weber sees it, is by *eroticism*.
In modern society, sexuality offers humans a possibility to escape from
the rational order of the world, since it offers a kind of 'sacramental'
union with another human being.[71] Sexuality offers experiences that are
außeralltägliche, it offers a possibility of transcending everyday rou-
tine.[72] This character of erotic experiences makes them more and more
desired the more rationalised culture becomes. This does not mean that
Weber had an over-romantic view of human sexuality, thinking that sex
is just a quasi-religious experience. He also pointed out that sexual relations often have dimensions of power and brutality, not always consciously recognised by the lovers themselves.[73]

Of course, human sexuality can also be exploited as a means for
profit-making, and thus be a means to other ends, and in a certain way
be appropriated by rationalised culture. It seems to me that Weber did
not explore this possibility very much, perhaps because it was impossible for him to foresee the extreme eroticism of today's Western society,

---

[70] For a contemporary account of the impossibility of opting out from modernity, see
Giddens, Anthony: *The Consequences of Modernity*, p. 84.

[71] Weber, Max: "Zwischenbetrachtung", *MWG I/19*, p. 507. See also Scaff,
Lawrence: *Fleeing the Iron Cage*, pp. 108-112.

[72] Weber, Max: "Zwischenbetrachtung", *MWG I/19*, p. 503. A similar interpretation
of Weber has been provided by e.g. Collins, Randall: *Max Weber. A Skeleton Key*, pp.
78-79.

[73] Weber, Max: "Zwischenbetrachtung", *MWG I/19*, p. 517. Weber's view of erotics,
sexuality and rationalisation has been discussed in e.g. Bologh, Roslyn W.: *Love or
Greatness*, especially pp. 195-209.

where almost every TV-commercial is full of erotic associations. Paradoxically, even the flight from rationalisation can be rationalised.

Somewhat parallel to the eroticism of modern western culture is the trend of *privatisation*. People more and more tend to find meaning in life in their intimate circles (*kleine Gemeinschaftskreise*), and withdraw from public life.[74]

Another way to escape the iron cage of rationalism is through *art* and *aesthetics*, according to Weber. Manifestations of art, such as literature, film, and music are, like sexuality, ways of transcending everyday reality.[75] As Randall Collins has pointed out, what Weber had in mind "...was the concert-going, museum-visiting, and book-reading audiences of his own day...".[76] But I think Collins is pointing to something important when he says that Weber's account of the aesthetic flight from modernity can equally be applied to "...the cults of popular music, sports entertainment, and television drama that have become so dominant today".[77] In the pressing reality of modernity, people tend to long for *panem et circenses*, rather than actively try to shape culture.

Another possibility for flight from modernity is religion. In the concluding words of his lecture *Wissenschaft als Beruf*, Weber states that

> To the person who cannot bear the fate of the times like a man, one must say: may he rather return silently, without the usual publicity build-up of renegades, but simply and plainly. The arms of the old churches are opened widely and compassionately for him.[78]

The fate of the modern time is rationalisation and bureaucratisation. Perhaps the most disturbing consequence of rationalisation is that there can be no *objective* meaning of life. Rather every individual has to make a choice for herself or himself and accept the rationalised culture of today – look it in the face, as Weber expresses it.[79] In Weber's eyes, traditional Christianity, as believed and lived in the traditional churches, can serve as a kind of therapy for those persons who cannot bear the fate of the times. The churches will provide an understanding of the life and

---

[74] Weber, Max: "Wissenschaft als Beruf", *MWG I/17*, p. 110.
[75] Weber, Max: "Zwischenbetrachtung", *MWG I/19*, p. 500.
[76] Collins, *op.cit.*, p. 78.
[77] Collins, *op.cit.*, p. 78.
[78] FMW p. 155. Weber, Max: "Wissenschaft als Beruf", *MWG I/17*, p. 110: "*Wer dies Schicksal der Zeit nicht männlich ertragen kann, dem muß man sagen: Er kehre lieber, schweigend, ohne die übliche öffentliche Renegatenreklame, sondern schlicht und einfach, in die weit und erbarmend geöffneten Arme der alten Kirchen zurück.*"
[79] Weber, Max: "Wissenschaft als Beruf", *MWG I/17*, p. 101.

of cosmos that allows the believer to perceive them as meaningful and coherent.

At the end of the 20th century, it seems that not only traditional religion offers such an escape option from modernity. In his study *The New Age Movement* Paul Heelas has pointed out that one possible explanation of the attractiveness of various New Age practices could be their character of offering a counter-culture to the "iron cage characteristics" of mainstream Western culture.[80] Perhaps it might be said that on a Weberian account, it is always possible to resist modernity and create a new meaning in life by taking recourse to such religious outlooks which programatically oppose the ends-rational character of modern culture.

This idea of religion as a flight from modernity might account for the fact that increasing modernisation in the West has not led to a corresponding decrease in religious practice, at least not in the United States.[81] If modern culture gets too pressing, it can be imagined that people will follow Weber's recommendation and return to the old churches, or, *mutatis mutandis*, to new religious movements which offer similar escape options. The incompatibility of religion and modernity in Weber's thinking must, accordingly, not be understood as saying that religious practice *is bound to* decline quantitatively. Rather Weber claims that it is impossible to *consistently* live in modernity and still adhere to traditional forms of religion.[82] This lack of consistency aggravates the possibility for effective action in the world.

There is however a price for the experience of meaningfulness offered by this type of religion; the one who flees from modernity into the open arms of the churches has to sacrifice her or his intellect, in some way or another.[83] Christianity, as it is normally practised in the different churches and denominations implies such beliefs of a metaphysical character that cannot be vindicated by normal methods of verification, and in some aspects also beliefs that are absurd from a logical point of view, according to Weber.[84] From his standpoint, modern science and modern philosophy have made traditional Christianity intellectually incredible, and therefore anyone who wants to join a Christian denomination has to sacrifice her or his intellect.

---

[80] Heelas, Paul: *The New Age Movement,* p. 144.

[81] For an account of the different perspectives on secularisation in contemporary sociology of religion, see Repstad, Pål: "Introduction", pp. 1-8.

[82] For a similar argument, see Glebe-Møller, Jens: *Politisk dogmatik,* p. 36.

[83] Weber, Max: "Wissenschaft als Beruf", *MWG I/17,* p. 110.

[84] This is obviously true also of the New Age movement.

One example of Weber's quite overlooked philosophical discussions of the intellectual credibility of religion is his reflections on the problem of *theodicy*. Weber holds that one of the driving forces behind the development of religions was the human need for a meaningful interpretation of suffering.[85] But the failure of the religions to provide a satisfying answer to the question of why there is suffering in the world, is also a major reason for unbelief, according to him. In the history of religious ideas, Weber holds that it is only possible to find three consistent solutions to the problem of theodicy, namely the consequent dualism of zoroastrism, the belief in predestination, and the Hindu teaching of karma.[86]

But the problem with the acceptance of any of these solutions is that they require that some of the traditional predicates ascribed to God have to be tampered with in such a way that the core of the religion in question is changed into unrecognisability in the eyes of the believers. Stewart Sutherland has pointed out that many conventional ways of solving the problem of theodicy has a *procrustean* character. In order to fit the explanation of evil with a traditional theology, the concept of God has to be modified in quite unpleasant ways.[87] Weber primarily discusses the consequences for Christianity, and therefore I shall restrict my discussion to the Christian case, but I think that Weber's view of rationalisation makes it reasonable to infer that his texts would allow the same reasoning about other religions.

According to Weber's understanding, any retreat to dualism would lead to the denial of God's omnipotence. But, on the other hand, if one holds on to omnipotence in combination with the belief in Gods omniscience, this will jeopardise the belief in God's goodness. And the belief in *karma* does more or less exclude the predication of mercy, and perhaps also love to God.[88]

Especially one aspect in Weber's thinking about the problem of theodicy deserves to be emphasised, namely the solutions' relevance in religious life. If Weber is right in saying that one of the main social and psychological functions of religion has been to lend meaning to human suffering, it is problematic if the solutions to the problem themselves are highly problematic. Perhaps some logically acceptable solution of the

---

[85] Weber, Max: "Politik als Beruf", *MWG I/17*, p. 241.
[86] Weber, Max: "Einleitung", *MWG I/19*, p. 95.
[87] Sutherland, Stewart: *God, Jesus and Belief*, p. 25.
[88] Weber, Max: "Zwischenbetrachtung", *MWG I/19*, pp. 520-522.

problem of theodicy can be presented, but this solution will either have to change some central aspect of the traditional belief in such a way that traditional believers will find the solution inauthentic, or it will be so complicated, that it cannot have any impact in the lives of ordinary believers.

Reasons similar to Weber's argument have been given by radical theologians aiming at a reconstruction of Christian faith. Gordon Kaufman has, for example, claimed that the problem of theodicy is one of the main reasons for abandoning traditional metaphysical religious belief. "...if..." Kaufman asks, "...God is an all-powerful, all-knowing, absolutely righteous and merciful Person, why are there such horrible evils – enormous misery, injustice, suffering – in the world? Why would a good God ever have made such an evil order?"[89] And if an omnipotent God really has made this evil order, would he not be an old gangster who is so wicked that his only excuse is that he does not exist, as the Swedish atheist and biologist Georg Klein has put it in an interview.[90]

In Kaufman's view, traditional ways of explaining this problem are *religiously* implausible today. It is not just that there perhaps is no logically acceptable solution, it is also the case that after Auschwitz, such arguments seem "blank and weak" from a religious point of view. The root of the problem for Kaufman is that religious imagery has been reified, so that from the metaphor 'God the Father', people have inferred that God is a person who has control over the world and really exists 'out there'. In Kaufman's view, a religiosity which wants to be intellectually acceptable cannot reify its symbols, because such reification will always create insoluble theoretical problems.[91]

According to Kaufman, the evils of human existence have to be understood as caused by immanent factors, and not by reference to such modes of *explanations* as "original sin",[92] rebellion against God or something of the sort. And if evil has immanent causes, it can be fought against by human means. Therefore we can attack the evils of human existence by first *identifying* evil, and secondly by trying to create a better world to live in by eliminating those evils as good as we can.[93]

---

[89] Kaufman, Gordon: *In Face of Mystery*, p. 335.
[90] In Linton, Magnus: "Gudsförnekarnas innerliga tro", p. 21. In the interview, Klein is reported to have said: *"Min slutreplik i diskussioner med religiösa är att den gamle gangstern, Gud, är så elak att hans enda ursäkt är att han inte finns."*
[91] Kaufman, Gordon: *In Face of Mystery*, p. 335.
[92] This does not exclude the use of the concept *original sin*, which can be religiously relevant, but it excludes it as a genuine *explanation* of human evil.
[93] Kaufman, Gordon: *In Face of Mystery*, p. 336.

A central function for religion, according to Kaufman, is to provide us humans with orientation in the world. Religious faith means many things to people, but, among other things, it gives its adherents an understanding of "what aspirations and hopes men and women may legitimately have..." and "...what humans ought to do here and now...".[94] Religion can give humans instruments for identifying evil and provide visions for a good life, thereby giving orientation and direction to human agency in the world. Such a view of religion may not necessarily come into conflict with intellectual honesty in a rationalised culture.

When one reads Weber's comments on the future of religion in the modern world, it is easy to come to the conclusion that he thought that religion was unable to play any positive role in modern society, except as therapy for those who cannot face the harshness of modernity. Weber's description of himself as religiously unmusical, has not made it easier to see other aspects in his writings, which make another interpretation possible. Perhaps Paul Honigsheim hinted at another possibility in his article *Max Weber: His Religious and Ethical Background and Development*, in which he claimed that Weber thought that it was in the moral decisions of the human consciousness that the divine element in reality was located.[95] Honigsheim's article is perhaps not wholly accurate from a scholarly standpoint, despite its scholarly form; it has too much the character of panegyric. But I think Honigsheim has hinted at a possible interpretation of Weber's texts which have not been much explored. In the next section of this chapter, I shall try to shed some light over this aspect of Weber's texts.

How to Get Out of the Iron Cage

Weber's texts seem to contain the claim that religion cannot have any positive role in modern culture. But such a reading is dependent on the assumption that all religion primarily has to be metaphysical beliefs in a transcendent world and an objective meaning of life. Why should one assume that? Perhaps Weber did, perhaps, as Honigsheim claims, he did not. But, as I shall try to demonstrate, *if* Christian faith is understood in Gordon Kaufman's way, there is a positive role for religion and theology even in Weber's view of modern society.

---

[94] Kaufman, Gordon: "Reconstructing the Concept of God", pp. 98-99.
[95] Honigsheim, *op.cit.*, p. 231.

Faced with the problematic character of modern culture, Weber asks
three questions: 1) How is it at all possible to save some form of individual freedom in a rationalised and bureaucratised society? 2) How can
the power of the indispensable state officialdom be checked and coun-
terbalanced? 3) If there are things that bureaucrats cannot do, and the
role of the politician differs from that of the bureaucrat, what then is the
role of the politician?[96]

In *Parlament und Regierung im neugeordneten Deutschland,* Weber
declares that he will not deal with the first question, but concentrate on
the second and third, of which he regards the third to be the most important. In my opinion it would be totally wrong to infer from this that
Weber did not regard the first question as an important one – rather that
is the question which motivates the two others. But *Parlament und
Regierung* was originally written as a political pamphlet, advocating
constitutional reform in Germany, and was therefore not an adequate
place for the discussion of more philosophical matters – hence Weber's
disregard for his first question. In this section I shall try to answer that
question in a way that is in line with Weber's texts. This, however,
requires that Weber's answers to the second and third questions have
first been explored.

How can the power of the indispensable bureaucracy be checked?
First, it is necessary to note that Weber holds that bureaucratic forms of
organisation cannot be avoided in modern society. For good and bad,
humanity has created a culture with advanced technology and a high
degree of objective rationality which cannot easily be dispensed with. To
take a contemporary example: What would happen if we dispensed with
rational methods of food production and food distribution in an over-
populated world?

But if bureaucracy is indispensable, it becomes the more important to
check its tendency to become all-powerful, according to Weber. One
way to do this is to let competing bureaucracies exist alongside each
other. This is one of Weber's main reasons for advocating a capitalist
form of economy with a high degree of private ownership. In a planned
economy of a socialist kind, the civil service will rule alone, since it has
no competitors, and it will be indispensable because it is necessary for
organising production and distribution. By organising production in the

---

[96] Weber, Max: "Parlament und Regierung", *MWG I/15,* pp. 465-466. For the formulation of the third question, which in Weber's own text is quite dimly expressed, I am
indebted to Slagstad, Rune: "Liberal Constitutionalism and Its Critics", pp. 119-120.

Western capitalist way, the state bureaucracy will be checked by several private bureaucracies, for example the bureaucracies of privately owned companies.[97] In a socialist economy, the worker will be less free than in the capitalist state, since Weber holds that it is impossible to strike against the state.[98]

But it is not enough to create a bureaucratic counterbalance to the civil service; there must also be an effective political control of the official bureaucracy. This is not to say that politics can do without a bureaucratic apparatus – in a modern society it can definitely not. Any political body will be dependent on an administrative apparatus for implementing its policies, collect taxes etc. The same holds for political parties in mass democracies – they are dependent on their own bureaucracies for organising electoral campaigns, recruiting members etc.[99]

As Wolfgang Mommsen has put it, Weber's solution to the problems of modern culture, at least temporarily, is that creative charisma and rationalisation should join forces.[100] True politicians strive to implement their ideas, stemming from their views of life, and bureaucracy should provide the means necessary for this value-implementation. The main problem is how to keep the rational elements of modern culture in its proper place.

In contradistinction to the quite optimistic interpretation of Weber which I put forth it has been claimed that Weber was a fatalist regarding the iron cage of modern society. Bryan Turner can be seen as an exponent of this view. According to Turner, Weber's critique of the iron cage led him to take a nostalgic view of pre-modern times, failing to see the "positive and emancipating element of contemporary culture", such as the low infantile mortality rates.[101] I cannot agree with such an interpretation, even if I acknowledge a strong pessimistic trait in Weber's texts. Weber saw the good sides of rationality very clearly – this can be seen if his analyses of the ideal relationship between the bureaucracy and its

---

[97] Weber, Max: "Parlament und Regierung", *MWG I/15*, pp. 463-464; "Wahlrecht und Demokratie", *MWG I/15*, p. 357.

[98] Weber, Max: "Der Sozialismus", *MWG I/15*, p. 614. It should be noted that later developments have shown that it *is* possible to successfully strike *against* the state, as for example in Communist Poland, where the Solidarity movement succeeded in entirely changing the political system by, among other things, using strikes as a weapon. If one wants to use Weber's argument today, it would have to be modified. Perhaps it is possible to say that it is much more difficult to win a strike against the state than against a private company.

[99] Weber, Max: "Parlament und Regierung", *MWG I/15*, p. 458.

[100] Mommsen, Wolfgang: *The Age of Bureaucracy*, p. 20.

[101] Turner, Bryan: *Max Weber*, pp. 135-136.

political masters are taken into account. A modern politician's wish to lowen mortality rates does not have to remain a *pium desiderium*, but can be realised by, among other things, the operations of a rational bureaucracy. The problem, however – and this is the main basis for Weber's pessimism – is that this means-end relationship between rational instruments and values tends to become blurred, because of the cultural dominance of technical rationality.

A more tangible way to express Weber's problem can be to ask how political bodies can keep control over their own bureaucracy. Weber proposes two solutions to this problem. First, he advocates a strong parliament, that spends much time investigating the activities of the bureaucracy in special committees, in front of which the bureaucrats have to answer. The politicians' problem is mainly that they cannot be other than dilettantes in the areas where the bureaucrats are experts, and therefore it is necessary with a rigorous parliamentary control of civil servants, so that they cannot pursue their own political goals, but, as they should, the goals of their political masters.[102]

But of more importance to the present discussion is the second solution to the problem of how to keep control of the bureaucracy. In some sense the parliamentary control is dependent on this second solution. The bureaucracy should be governed by true *politicians*, and not by persons who see themselves as bureaucrats, which, as I said in chapter two, most of the leading politicians in Imperial Germany did.

A true political character has, according to Weber, three salient features. First, a true politician is characterised by *passion for a cause* (*leidenschaftliche Hingabe an eine Sache*).[103] Weber defined politics as *a struggle for power*.[104] On a superficial reading, this could be interpreted as if he advocated a simple power politics. Nothing could be more wrong, however. The demand for passion for a cause means that true politicians have to be guided by ideals and visions which guide their actions. To have faith in a vision is a necessary element in true political activity, if the activity should not just run out as a natural event without meaning. Political action just for the sake of power in itself, without any vision for the realisation of which power is to be used, is utter vanity and deplorable, according to Weber.[105] A consistent way of political action

[102] Weber, Max: "Parlament und Regierung", *MWG I/15*, pp. 488-489.
[103] Weber, Max: "Politik als Beruf", *MWG I/17*, p. 227.
[104] Weber, Max: "Parlament und Regierung", *MWG I/15*, p. 537.
[105] Weber, Max: "Politik als Beruf", *MWG I/17*, p. 229-230.

demands that it is grounded in the belief in a vision, that perhaps is not fully realisable, but functions as a kind of compass, by the help of which a politician chooses practical goals for her or his activity.[106]

The second feature of a true politician is a sense of *responsibility* to the cause or vision that guides her or his actions. A politician must be able to take the consequences of failure and resign from office, even if no formal mistake has been committed. A politician cannot act in accordance with an ethic of conviction, that is just on the belief in the intrinsic value of the action itself, irrespective of the consequences, and without reflecting much on the possibility of success in reaching the desired goals. Weber's favourite example of such acting is the acting that would follow from a strict application of the Sermon of the Mount:

> The position of the Gospels is absolutely unambiguous on the decisive points. They are in opposition not just to war…but ultimately to each and every law of the social world, if this seeks to be a *place of worldly 'culture'*, one devoted to the beauty, dignity, honour and greatness of man as a creature of this earth. Anyone unwilling to go this far – and Tolstoy only did so as death was approaching – should know that he is bound by the laws of this earthly world, and that these include, for the foreseeable future, the possibility and inevitability of wars fought for power, and that he can only fulfil the 'demand of the day', whatever it may be, *within* the limits of these laws.[107]

A politician has to adhere to the ethics of responsibility. The *political* devotion to a vision implies, according to this ethics, that you accept means-end calculation as a necessary instrument. A true politician has, according to Weber, to be prepared to use the adequate means to realise – at least as far as possible – the vision that is the ground and motive for her or his political activity. A follower of the ethics of the Sermon of the Mount does not resist evil with force, irrespective of what the consequences would be – he leaves the consequences to God, as Weber expresses it. A follower of the ethics of responsibility, on the other hand,

---

[106] Weber, Max: "'Wertfreiheit'", *GAW*, p. 514.

[107] PW p. 78. Weber, Max: "Zwischen zwei Gesetzen", *MWG I/15*, p. 98: "*Die Stellung der Evangelien dazu ist in den entscheidenden Punkten von absoluter Eindeutigkeit. Sie stehen im Gegensatz nicht etwa gerade nur zum Krieg…sondern letzlich zu allen und jeden Gesetzlichkeiten der sozialen Welt, wenn diese* eine Welt der diesseitigen 'Kultur', *also der Schönheit, Würde, Ehre und Größe der 'Kreatur' sein will. Wer die Konsequenzen nicht zieht – und das hat Tolstoi selbst erst getan, als es ans Sterben ging –, der möge wissen, daß er an die Gesetzlichkeiten der diesseitigen Welt gebunden ist, die auf unabsehbare Zeit die Möglichkeit und Unvermeidlichkeit des Machtkrieges einschließen, und daß er nur* innerhalb *dieser Gesetzlichkeiten der jeweiligen 'Forderung des Tages' genügen kann.*"

chooses the most adequate means to implement her or his vision and is even prepared to use violence, if it should be necessary. Politicians are responsible for the failure of their cause. Therefore they cannot afford to abstain from using adequate means to achieve their ends.[108]

This does not imply that politicians, according to Weber, should use violence as soon as they do not get their will through. In most cases, violence would be contrary to values inherent in the political vision itself, and therefore be counterproductive. But a liberal democratic state may have the right to use violence to protect its citizens against criminals, for example. A politician that does not permit the police to use violence even in extreme cases, would be responsible for the consequences, as Weber sees it.

The third feature of true politicians is that they exercise *judgement*. A true politician has to be able to judge reality as it is, to see the facts. It is impossible to pursue goals with responsibility if you do not have knowledge of how reality functions. Therefore a politician has to keep a certain distance to events and persons in the society in which she or he lives. Such judgement implies, for example, that a politician should be ready to listen to the advice of experts, without therefore being subject to their control.[109]

In conclusion, Weber can be understood as saying that a person who wants to avoid the dangers of rationalism and bureaucratisation, has to combine two qualities: a vision that is strong enough to really guide action, and rationality enough to be able to pursue goals with a certain amount of efficiency. What Weber argues for is what Anthony Giddens has called *utopian realism*. Giddens describes modernity as a juggernaut which is extremely difficult to steer. It can, however, be controlled by visions of what would constitute a good society. Such visions set a limit to the totally open character of modernity, and are able to guide action in a specific way. But Giddens also advocates an amount of realism. If politicians just have visions and no sense of measuring causes and effects, the most devastating scenarios can be realised. One might only think of the nuclear powers and what can happen if they are led by irresponsible politicians.[110] Only a person who can let vision and rationality work together, will be able to get out of the iron cage.

---

[108] Weber, Max: "Politik als Beruf", *MWG I/17*, p. 235.
[109] Weber, Max: "Politik als Beruf", *MWG I/17*, p. 227.
[110] Giddens, Anthony: *The Consequences of Modernity*, pp. 154-156, 178.

The Dark Side

There is no doubt that Weber, when it came to constitutional matters, advocated parliamentary democracy, however in different ways according to the political situation of the time.[111] Weber's view of democracy was, however, an elitist one.[112] He thought that just a few people would be able to live up to the three qualities needed for someone to be a true politician, and therefore it was central for him to create a political system that would ensure that only people with excellent leadership qualities reached the heights of political power.

One of the main reasons for Weber to advocate a formally democratic political system, was that he thought it to be the best way to select good political leaders. In a modern mass democracy it is unavoidable that political influence goes hand in hand with demagoguery. In Weber's eyes, the ideal political form in modern societies is a formally democratic system, that puts power in the hands of one person, who then more or less controls political life until next election. Only a person who has won the confidence of the masses in general elections has the power to effectively control bureaucracy, according to Weber. This holds also in parliamentary democracies with a well-developed party system. The most central persons in the electoral campaigns will always be the candidates for the office of prime minister, and the prime minister usually has extensive control of the political agenda.[113]

But this form of democracy, which basically consists in the free election of a 'dictator' for a limited period of time, does not make parliament worthless, according to Weber. Parliament guarantees political stability, it exercises control over the political leader, it functions as a training ground for the formation of leader characters, and it offers a peaceful way of getting rid of a political leader through a vote of no confidence.[114]

---

[111] Weber argues for a democratic form of government in several places. See e.g. "Wahlrecht und Demokratie", *MWG I/15*, pp. 369-370. Before the German revolution in 1918, Weber advocated parliamentary democracy with the preservation of the monarchies in Germany, but after the revolution he preferred a republican constitution. This development can be seen if one compares for example "Parlament und Regierung", written before the revolution, and "Deutschlands künftige Staatsform" *MWG I/16*, written in the end of 1918.

[112] On different models of democracy, see Held, David: *Models of Democracy*. For a discussion of an elitist model of democracy, including Weber's variant, see p. 143-185.

[113] Weber, Max: "Parlament und Regierung", *MWG I/15*, pp. 538-540.

[114] Weber, Max: "Parlament und Regierung", *MWG I/15*, p. 540.

In Weber's eyes, the people may choose the leader, but it should not actively take part in the decision-making since this requires judgement. According to Weber, that quality is something that the masses lack. It is therefore crucial, according to him, to limit real decision-making to as small a group as possible, consisting of politicians with a developed sense of responsibility.[115] In principle, Weber sees a democratic constitution as a matter of expediency – it is the most effective and practical way to provide political leadership in a rationalised culture, not a manifestation of human rights or anything of the sort.[116]

What then was Weber's own central political value? Wolfgang Mommsen has argued that Weber's central political value was his ardent, almost religious, German nationalism.[117] Perhaps the clearest statement of Weber's nationalism can be found in his Inaugural Address at the University of Freiburg im Breisgau, a political statement that most commentators hold as representative of Weber's political thought.[118] In this lecture, Weber discussed the problem of Polish immigration in the Eastern parts of Germany, and the fact that many ethnic Germans moved to the industrial regions in Western Germany, hoping to free themselves from the bond of agricultural labour. For Weber, this was a terrifying development, since it threatened Germany's control of West Prussia. In his view, it was necessary to close the border, and to start a massive re-germanisation of the eastern parts of the empire. It was a primary political goal to enhance Germany's power.[119]

Nationalist ideas can be found almost anywhere in the Weberian *corpus*, and in the German debate after World War II, it is perhaps this line of thought in Weber which has been most heavily criticised, not least by Wolfgang Mommsen. The combination of Weber's elitist and functionalist view of democracy and his ardent nationalism, is in the focus of Mommsen's liberal critique. In Mommsen's eyes, Weber saw democracy only as a means to increase Germany's power, since a successful

[115] Weber, Max: "Parlament und Regierung", *MWG I/15*, p. 549-550.

[116] Weber, Max: "Letter to Hans Ehrenberg 16/4 1917", *GPS*, p. 470. For an interesting comment on how this relates to Weber's view on personality, see Hecht, *op.cit.*, pp. 177-178.

[117] Mommsen, Wolfgang: *Max Weber and German Politics*, p. 49. See also pp. 38 and 67.

[118] see e.g. Beetham, David: *Max Weber and the Theory of Modern Politics*, p. 39. Mommsen agrees with this, see *Max Weber and German Politics*, p. 36.

[119] Weber, Max: "Der Nationalstaat und die Volkswirtschaftspolitik", *MWG I/4*, p. 560. Weber studied the situation of agricultural labourers in his *Die Lage der Landarbeiter im ostelbischen Deutschland*, MWG I/3.

foreign policy with imperialist ambitions could only succeed if it had large popular support.[120] Even if Mommsen does not hold Weber responsible for the tragic development of German history during the Weimar republic and Hitler's reign, he argues that later developments show the dubious character of Weber's thinking:

> ...we have to concede that Weber's theory of charismatic leadership combined with the radical formalization of the meaning of democratic institutions helped, if only marginally, to make the German people receptive to support of a leader, and to that extent to Adolf Hitler.[121]

It is not possible to deny the nationalistic and elitist trait in Weber's writings. Mommsen is surely right in pointing out such morally reprehensive features, and it is a fact that the most famous legal theorist of Nazism, Carl Schmitt, drew heavily upon Weber's thinking when developing his theories about the *Führerstaat*.[122] But it has been questioned if Mommsen is right in claiming that nationalism is the *ultimate* value in Weber's view of life.

David Beetham, for example, claims that there is a genuine tension in Weber's political thinking between liberal and nationalistic values. On the one hand, Mommsen is correct in pointing out Weber's crude nationalism, but he underestimates the liberal values that undergird Weber's discussion of the fate of the individual in modern society.[123] In Beetham's view, Mommsen underestimates the importance of Weber's defence of parliamentarism, for example. For Weber, one of the main tasks of parliament was to control the political leader, and dismiss her or him if she or he threatened the civil rights of the individuals. Therefore, it is unreasonable to hold that the value of individual human beings meant nothing to him, other than as instruments for national power.[124]

In his article *Max Weber's Liberalism for a Nietzschean World*, Mark Warren claims that it is a mistake to believe that Weber's political philosophy is fully reflected in his elitist theory of democracy.[125] In Warren's view, the centre of Weber's thinking is his dedication to the value of the human personality as a free, autonomous and responsible agent. This dignity of human personality is primarily expressed in political activity, where humans strive to realise their values in a rational and

---

[120] Mommsen, Wolfgang: *Max Weber and German Politics*, p. 396.
[121] Mommsen, Wolfgang: *Max Weber and German Politics*, p. 410.
[122] Mommsen, Wolfgang: *Max Weber and German Politics*, p. 410.
[123] Beetham, *op.cit.*, pp. 54-55.
[124] Beetham, *op.cit.*, p. 113.
[125] Warren, Mark: "Max Weber's Liberalism for a Nietzschean World", p. 33.

responsible way.[126] Weber is committed to a broadly Kantian view of humanity. Human dignity is based on the capacity for free and rational agency. What, in Warren's eyes, separates Weber from Kant, is mainly that he does not think it can be rationally argued that the value of humans lie in their potential for rationality, but that such a conviction is a matter of faith.[127] This dignity of the rational agent – the personality – is not relative for Weber, but it is the ultimate value position in his view of life.[128]

The problem for Weber is however – it is this problem that Warren labels *nietzschean* – that rationalised and bureaucratised society leaves less and less room for rational agency in this sense. What makes a life meaningful in Weber's eyes is that the individual can set up goals, the (subjectively) rational pursuing of which gives meaning to life. But because of the threat to independent goal-setting that modern society creates, human dignity is threatened.[129] The basis of Weber's elitist view of democracy is that he thought it more or less impossible to realise his ideals on a broad scale. Under modern conditions, only those with special gifts can ever hope to create a true personality.[130]

For Warren, Weber's elitism is a possible elaboration of his commitment to personality, but elitism is not primary, since it is dependent on Weber's analysis of contemporary society. But Weber is wrong when he holds that only a few are able, or should be allowed to be able, to express their personality politically. There are more aspects of political decision-making than high politics on the national level. Weber's own ethical commitments seem to demand that individuals should have the possibility of realising their goals. But most goals that individuals have are related to their own lives and their own immediate surroundings.

If one accepts that the ultimate value that is expressed in Weber's writings is the value and dignity of the human personality, a *participatory* rather than an elitist model of democracy seems most adequate: people should have the possibility to set goals for their everyday lives and strive for their realisation. This means that every individual does not

[126] Warren, *op.cit.*, pp. 35-36.

[127] Warren, *op.cit.*, p. 39.

[128] Warren, *op.cit.*, p. 40. Hecht, *op.cit.*, basically agrees with Warren's interpretation. See e.g. p. 251.

[129] Warren, *op.cit.*, p. 31. Goldman, *op.cit.,* says that the existence of *ultimate goals* for an individual is a *sine qua non* for labelling her or him a true personality, according to Weber. See p. 165.

[130] Warren, *op.cit.*, p. 42.

have to be able to directly influence *every* decision in a society, but those decisions that most closely affect her or his life.[131]

The value of human personality is in the centre of Weber's thought, and it is his concern for the fate of personality that motivates the discussions of rationalisation in Weber's *oeuvre*. If one strives for an intentional interpretation of Weber's texts, perhaps one cannot do other than conclude that there are two unreconciled traits in his thinking: elitist nationalism and liberalism. But even more constructive approaches have to face severe difficulties when trying to provide interesting and relevant interpretations of Weber's thinking. There is a genuine tension in his texts between nationalism, elitism and gross overestimations of the possibilities of strong leaders on the one hand, and a high evaluation of the dignity of every human being, on the other.

In my opinion, the best way to come to grips with this problem is to make a conscious choice between these lines in Weber's thinking, a choice that has to depend on what purpose motivates the interpretative effort. Since my purpose is to investigate if, and in what way, Weber can be important for Christian theological reflection, this has to guide which traits in his thinking that I emphasise. It seems quite obvious that Weber's nationalism, and most aspects of his elitism, are of no interest for Christian theological reflection. On the other hand, his analysis of the features of modern, rationalised culture, and his emphasis on the need for consistent views of life, seem more promising.

Theological Relevance

There are three traits in Weber's texts, regarding the role of views of life in modern culture, which seem to be of special importance for theological reflection, namely 1) the low credibility of metaphysics, 2) the nietzschean character of the modern world, and 3) the importance of consistent and coherent views of life for human dignity. I shall explore these traits one by one in this last section.

The Low Credibility of Metaphysics

The ultimate justification for a claim that something is the case, is for Weber that it can be scientifically demonstrated, or at least can be well

---

[131] Warren, *op.cit.*, pp. 45-46.

argued for with normal scientific methods. In a contemporary philosophical idiom, one can say that Weber holds that there cannot be any
evidence-transcendent statements. Weber's reasoning about objectivity
in science seems to imply that it does not make sense to consider a sentence as a statement, if there are no relevant evidence which can decide
if it is true or not. As Eberhard Herrmann has pointed out, to claim that
there are no evidence-transcendent statements, is not the same as to say
that there cannot be evidence-transcendent facts. It would be absurd to
claim that nothing can be the case without us knowing it. But it is
equally hard to understand how we can claim that a sentence is a statement about facts, if we cannot point to relevant criteria for judging its
truth-value.[132]

According to Weber, scientific methods are the ways by which statements are judged in modern culture, and scientific methods guarantee
objectivity in a way that other procedures have never been able to do.
The problem with metaphysical claims is that their truth-value cannot be
judged by normal scientific criteria. Theological truth-claims, which can
be regarded as a certain form of metaphysics, are claims to have access
to evidence-transcendent facts.

There is, however, one comment in Weber's texts which says that
metaphysical claims can have some cognitive functions.[133] It does not
seem to be the case, however, that Weber thinks of metaphysical beliefs
as filling other functions than heuristic or evaluative ones. Warren has
suggested that the element of metaphysics in Weber's texts is his view
of what true humanity consists in.[134] Basically, I think Warren is correct.
Weber makes certain assumptions which he does not argue for in a scientific way. One example is his anthropological assumption that humans
are free and rational agents, and another his view of noumenal reality.
These assumptions are not statements in any ordinary sense, however.
Rather they are transcendental prerequisites for certain discourses to be
at all possible. There is, for example, no sense in uttering prescriptions
if we do not assume that people are free to follow them.

This makes theology, as traditionally perceived, to something else
than a science.[135] Because of the claim that statements cannot be evidence-transcendent, and that the paradigm for what counts as evidence

[132] Herrmann, Eberhard: *Meaning and Truth in Religion*, pp. 11-12.
[133] Weber, Max: "'Objektivität'", *GAW*, p. 156.
[134] Warren, *op.cit.*, p. 38.
[135] Weber, Max: "Wissenschaft als Beruf", *MWG I/17*, pp. 107-108.

RELIGION AND MODERNITY   135

in modern culture is – and *should* be – scientific procedures, metaphysical truth-claims have low credibility. There are also logical and religious problems with much of traditional religious metaphysics, as for example Weber's discussion of the problem of theodicy shows. A theology with ambitions to be relevant in a modern context – understood along Weberian lines – should therefore not contain such claims, or at least do so only in a *very* modest way.[136]

A Nietzschean World

Many have studied modern rationalised culture from a critical perspective, similar to that of Weber's. One example is Robert Bellah *et al.*, who in their book *Habits of the Heart* warn us of the modern culture of separation. In their study of modern America, they conclude that today's culture is characterised by a fragmentation of life, that takes away any sense of meaning and purpose. In a culture of separation, people pursue short term individualistic goals, in stead of long term political and communal goals.[137] They find the negative side of modernisation and rationalisation poetically expressed in a poem of the 17th century poet John Donne, that deserves to be cited:

> 'Tis all in peeces, all cohaerence gone;
> All just supply, and all Relation:
> Prince, Subject, Father, Sonne, are things forgot,
> For every man alone thinkes he hath got
> To be a Phoenix, and that then can bee
> Non of that kinde, of which he is, but hee.[138]

In *Habits of the Heart,* the authors argue for a *social ecology.* In their opinion, individualism has to be overcome, however not by returning to an old-fashioned oppressive collectivism. It is, according to them, necessary that people have integrative visions of a common good, that can hold social action together, lest modern society should end up in catastrophe.[139]

Weber's analysis, though performed at the beginning of the 20th century, is strikingly similar to the kind of cultural critique that can be

---

[136] For an interesting discussion of similar questions, see Glebe-Møller, Jens: *Politisk dogmatik,* pp. 52-53.
[137] Bellah, Robert, *et al.*: *Habits of the Heart,* pp. 277-281.
[138] Cited after Bellah *et al.*: *Habits of the Heart.*, p. 276.
[139] Bellah *et al.*: *Habits of the Heart,* pp. 283-286.

found in *Habits of the Heart*. His critique of bureaucracy has also continued to be discussed, as for example by Edward Page in his *Political Authority and Bureaucratic Power*. But there are also dissimilarities. Bellah *et al.* look for a vision which can create integration in the whole society, motivating people to strive for the common good. Weber would have seen their vision as unrealistic, since it, in his view, is impossible to create a unitary vision of what the common good really is in a fragmented culture.

For Weber, the problem of modernity is that people become alienated from their own wishes, and are deprived of the possibility of pursuing their own goals, since technical efficiency demands standardisation. The modern world deprives people of the possibility to create meaning in life through goal-directed actions. Weber would therefore agree with Bellah *et al.* that visions of what a good life is, visions that are strong enough to motivate people to action despite of rationalisation, are necessary. But he would say that in a modern world, there will always be competing and mutually exclusive visions, which should be allowed to fight each other peacefully in a democratic political system.

A Nietzschean world deprives human beings of their worth as rational agents, capable of choosing their own way of life, according to Weber. It makes it impossible to live an autonomous life, and forces people into a heteronomous existence. If one accepts two axioms in Weber's thinking, namely that humans have the capacity to act freely and intentionally, and that a culture which depraves people of that capacity is evil, it becomes morally imperative to try to find a remedy for such a situation.

The Importance of Views of Life

Weber held that it was only possible to be a personality – understood as a person who has organised her or his life around consciously chosen values – if the values were organised in a coherent system (view of life), and if the individual let this value system join forces with rationality. Coherence should not, in this context, be understood as meaning a strict logical relation of entailment (e.g. of the form that for a belief p to cohere with a system of beliefs S, it must entail every other belief in S). Rather, the Weberian demand for coherence should be understood as the demand for an organised system of values, in which some values are basic and 'ultimate' for the person in question. Weber argues in *Wissenschaft als Beruf* that philosophical reflection can show that certain ways of action ought to follow from a certain value-position, if the persons who accept this value-position are to be true to themselves.[140] Weber's demand for coherence is thus not primarily a logical demand, but first and foremost a moral one. In his eyes, a mature personality cannot only acknowledge certain values. She or he ought also to act according to them. In Weber's eyes, a true personality has a view of life strong enough not to be over-taken by rationalisation, and is rational enough to see that it is only through using the means available in modernity that it is possible to realise the visions of a good society which are contained in the view of life.[141]

A reasonable understanding of Honigsheim's claim that for Weber the divine element in human life lay in humans' moral choices, could be to say that it is possible to interpret Weber's texts as I have outlined above. Weber's texts seem to say, that it is through conscious choices of values and constructions of views of life, that humans can transcend everyday reality, and create visions and images of a good human life worth striving for. Such visions are necessary, if life should not just run out into nothingness as a natural event.[142] But it is pointless with visions which are grounded in a religious metaphysics which at any time can be destroyed by science.[143] Therefore a religion which wants to be relevant in the modern context, radically has to abstain from invading the sphere of science.

As Weber aptly puts it, politics is not made with the head alone.[144] Successful politics needs to make use of rational instruments, but it has also to be guided by a political will, which is grounded in a vision of what society should be. A vision may not always be fully realisable, but that is not important. What is important is that it provides a compass which can guide the direction of our acting in the world. Equally important is, of course, that the vision is taken for what it is: a vision, not reality.

But if visions are to be able to fill this function of guiding action, they have to be strong enough to resist rationalisation, at least for a while. Gordon Kaufman claims, that one of the central points with religious views of life is, that they "...are able – with far greater success than

---

[140] Weber, Max: "Wissenschaft als Beruf", *MWG I/17*, p. 104.

[141] Owen, *op.cit.*, has seen the importance of ideals in resisting the alienating forces of modernity in Weber's thought. However, he seems not to make the distinction between the formal value of personality and the substantial requirement that the person should strive towards certain goals, provided by views of life, sufficiently clear. See p. 123.

[142] Weber, Max: "Wertfreiheit", *GAW,* pp. 507-508.

[143] Weber, Max: "Wertfreiheit", *GAW,* p. 504.

[144] Weber, Max: "Politik als Beruf", *MWG I/17*, p. 249.

most metaphysical or scientific theories – to attract the wholehearted allegiance of women and men".[145] This is of course an empirical claim, that can and should be tested. But the point seems to be that religious believers have a primary loyalty to their God, who embodies the values of the faith, and that therefore religious visions are more stable and less prone to be distorted by rationalisation.[146]

A Theological Vision

According to my interpretation of Weber's understanding of modernity, religion can be a part of modernity insofar as it functions as a provider of visions and values, which can help us to orient ourselves in life. This relevance presupposes, that religion does not conflict with the scientific world-view or scientific modes of testing statements.

What would then Christian theology be, given such an understanding of the function of religion? It should be obvious, that theology cannot be a discourse about metaphysics, trying to explore the heavenly secrets. Theology should rather be praxis-oriented, in the way many liberation theologies, feminist theologies and ecological theologies today are. One example of such a theological enterprise is Sallie McFague's *Models of God*. In her book, McFague wants to develop a heuristic and metaphorical theology which views Christian faith as a "destabilizing, inclusive, nonhierarchical vision of fulfillment for all, especially for the outcast and outsider".[147] McFague is well aware of the fictional character of theology, but ventures upon her project because she is convinced that religion without pictures and metaphors cannot provide living visions, but becomes sterile.[148] Another example could be Rosemary Radford Ruether's *Sexism and God-talk*.[149] These two examples are theological projects with radical political implications, but of course it is also possible to create praxis-oriented theologies with other forms of political inclinations.

[145] Kaufman, Gordon: *In Face of Mystery,* p. 228.
[146] Kaufman, Gordon: *In Face of Mystery,* p. 439. A similar point has been made by Bellah *et al.* in *The Good Society,* pp. 181-182, where it is claimed that religious people are primarily loyal to their God, and not to their nation. But it should not be forgotten that this peculiarity of religious visions also can have very destructive consequences, as Kaufman points out, *ibid.*
[147] McFague, Sallie: *Models of God,* p. xii.
[148] McFague, *op.cit.,* pp. xi-xii.
[149] Ruether, Rosemary Radford: *Sexism and God-Talk.* See e.g. chapter 9.

Can then, given the Weberian scheme, reasons be given for choice among different and mutually exclusive theologies? Is there any difference with a praxis-oriented theology in line with that of the *Deutsche Christen* in Germany during the thirties, and that of Dietrich Bonhoeffer? One obvious criterion is of course the degree of respect for science that the theology in question shows. A theology in conflict with scientific truth or logic cannot be acceptable. In my view, it is a logical demand that we should be prepared to universalise our moral statements, and I doubt if any member of the *Deutsche Christen* or other morally deplorable groups would be prepared to do that. Furthermore, the theology of the *Deutsche Christen* is rationally unacceptable, since its racist factual premises obviously were in conflict with truth.[150] But of course, a morally reprehensive theology can be constructed in a way that does not conflict with logic or science.

In a Weberian scheme, there are no absolutely objective values to which we can have access, and by which we can measure the values of theology. But on the other hand, given the Weberian scheme, every theology must be seen as a human construction, and cannot lay claim to absolute authority. And why construct an inhuman and morally reprehensible theology? And if anyone does, any claim to have access to divine truth will be suspect. No one can be stopped from thinking immoral thoughts, but on the other hand, no one can lay claim to *know* God's will, and therefore no one can be obliged to accept a theology which is reprehensible.

Another criterion for choices between views of life is if the visions they provide are viable and adequate visions. Hopelessly unrealistic visions, visions that do not correspond to our experiences, or visions that have no bearing upon our present situation, cannot be said to be adequate, and it would be both meaningless and destructive to adhere to such visions, since they would prevent us from being individuals who actively shape our own future.

But is it not a problem with humanely constructed visions? Can they really have the kind of impact which Weber's thinking demands? Must not the adherents of a view of life believe that their faith in some sense is correct and correspond to how things *really* are? And is not the concept of *revelation* central in many forms of religious thought, and can a theology without a concept of revelation really be said to be a realistic option in today's culture? In the following two chapters I shall turn to such questions.

---

[150] A short overview of the teachings of the *Deutsche Christen* is provided in Schalk, Peter: "Twisted Cross", pp. 73-74.

5. CHALLENGES TO THEOLOGY

Weber held it to be impossible both to live consistently in modernity and embrace traditional religious beliefs. But, as I think I have sufficiently shown, there is no warrant in Weber's texts for saying that all God-talk must be regarded as dead in modernity.[1] Implicit in Weber's text is the claim that views of life have to meet certain challenges, and respect certain criteria if they shall be relevant and adequate in modern culture. Weber's reasoning regarding this matter has been reconstructed in the preceding chapters. Now the time has come to state the criteria and the challenges in a clear and unified manner.

Weber's texts present three basic challenges to theology, namely 1) The primacy of science, 2) The implausibility of traditional understandings of the concept of 'God', and 3) The cultural conditions in modernity. I shall explore these challenges and their implications each in turn.

The Primacy of Science

In sharp competition with other methods, scientific practices have shown their superiority in realising values and explaining phenomena which have caused human wonder. This has given these practices a special authority in judging claims to knowledge, according to Weber.[2] No serious intellectual person would dream of contesting such basic astronomic positions as the fact that the sun and not the earth is the centre of our solar system or that the earth is roughly round and not flat. In a similar manner, scholarly conducted historical investigations are regarded as the best way to gain knowledge of the past. Few educated people would regard a dream as a better way to gain such knowledge, for example. It must be noted that this holds regardless of the fact that science is no unified phenomenon, and employs different methods with sometimes contradictory results; Weber was certainly opposed to any positivistic notion of the unity of science. What is claimed is not that scientifically

---

[1] cf. Turner, Bryan: *Max Weber,* p. 241.
[2] Weber, Max: "Wissenschaft als Beruf", *MWG I/17,* p. 87.

grounded knowledge-claims are *secure* or *absolute,* but only that we know of no other way that gives us more reliable knowledge of reality.[3]

Connected to this methodological claim of the primacy of science is Weber's epistemological view that there can be no evidence-transcendent statements. If we cannot show either how to verify or how to falsify a statement, we cannot really be sure it is a statement at all. This is basically a Kantian view of the *limits* of theoretical knowledge. Since all our experience is structured in time and space, we cannot have any knowledge of what is beyond time and space. All knowledge is structured by the human mind and its conceptualisations, according to Weber. Reality *in se* functions as a kind of check against too fantastic conceptualisations, since it resists certain ways of descriptions. This will be evident to anyone who tries to conceptualise cars as immaterial things and therefore holds that it is safe to walk straight out in the street during rush hours.

The problem with conventional theological claims to knowledge is, in Weber's eyes, that they do not fit in this system. Theological 'knowledge' often has the character of *'Haben'* rather than *'Wissen',* that is, theologians have often claimed to possess evidence-transcendent knowledge.[4] Metaphysical theology has claimed to have access to knowledge of heavenly things which it is beyond ordinary human faculties of knowledge to grasp, located in a space-time continuum as we are. In Weber's eyes, no enlightened person is rationally justified in holding such beliefs in modern culture. However, it should be noted that Weber seldom uses the word 'metaphysics',[5] and he does not define it very well. Here I shall understand 'metaphysics' in an epistemological rather than an ontological way: as propositions which cannot be vindicated either by sense experience or logical reasoning.

The cognitive status of metaphysical propositions is, to say the least, problematical. I propose that three main positions as regards what should be required for a person to be rationally entitled to claim that a metaphysical proposition is true can be identified.

One line of thought could be to say that we are rationally justified in believing anything which does not conflict with what we otherwise have good reasons to think to be true. This is basically what Mikael Stenmark

---

[3] A critique of modern ways of denial of the primacy of science has been provided in Gross, Paul *et al.*(eds.): *The Flight from Science and Reason.*
[4] Weber, Max: "Wissenschaft als Beruf", *MWG I/17*, pp. 107-108.
[5] e.g. in Weber, Max: "'Objektivität'", *GAW*, p. 156.

has labelled a *presumptionist* view of rationality; as long as we do not have contrary evidence, we are justified in holding on to our religious beliefs, for example.[6]

Another line of thought could be to follow Maurice Wiles's *principle of economy* in theology. The principle of economy requires that a theology does not say anything that the evidence does not require it to say. This would mean that theology should only contain such metaphysical propositions that are demanded by the evidence available.[7] This kind of reasoning seems to imply the acceptance of an extended concept of knowledge, meaning, for example, that we should accept at least some forms of religious experiences as ways to theoretical knowledge.[8]

A third position could be to say that all metaphysical propositions should be avoided, since there is no way to judge their truth-value with any intersubjectively acceptable method. This line of thought has at its core the view that scientific procedures are the only legitimate way to justify knowledge-claims. On this view, only science provides us with reliable knowledge. Views of life therefore have other functions than providing knowledge of states of affairs in the world.

Basically, Weber sides with the third position. To know something is, for him, to be able to claim that it is an adequate conception of reality. But such claims can only be justified with scientific procedures, since only they can give a relative security to knowledge-claims. In practice, science has demonstrated its superiority in explaining and mastering the world. Therefore it is unreasonable not to acknowledge its primacy.

But this is not the whole picture. In his article on objectivity Weber expressively denounces the idea that metaphysical propositions *a priori* cannot fulfil *any* cognitive functions:

> We are furthermore completely free of the prejudice which asserts that reflections on culture which go beyond the analysis of empirical data in order to interpret the world metaphysically can, because of their metaphysical character fulfil no useful cognitive tasks.[9]

---

[6] Stenmark, Mikael: *Rationality in Science, Religion, and Everyday Life,* p. 285.

[7] Wiles, Maurice: *The Remaking of Christian Doctrine,* p. 18.

[8] The notion of an 'extended concept of knowledge' is based on Jeffner, Anders: *Vägar till teologi,* p. 48. Accordingly, Jeffner argues that we should accept religious experience as a way to knowledge. See p. 51.

[9] MSS p. 59. Weber, Max: "'Objektivität'", *GAW,* p. 156: "*Ja, noch mehr: es liegt hier das Vorurteil durchaus fern, als ob Betrachtungen des Kulturlebens, die über die denkende Ordnung des empirisch Gegebenen hinausgehend die Welt metaphysisch zu deuten versuchen, etwa schon um dieses ihres Charakters willen keine Aufgabe im Dienste der Erkenntnis erfüllen* könnten."

Given Weber's strong sense of the primacy of science, it is a difficult task to provide an adequate interpretation of this passage. What can reasonably be understood by 'metaphysics' in this context? I would like to propose, that it can be understood as certain *heuristic assumptions* or *regulative ideas*, necessary for both science and the formation of views of life in modern culture. I understand 'heuristic' as implying that something, for example an assumption or a method, which in itself is not or cannot be proven to be true, still can lead to the discovery of, or be the necessary prerequisite for, the discovery of facts. In a wider sense, heuristic assumptions can also be assumptions of a kind which resemble statements about facts and which are necessary for our orientation in the world, but which are impossible to falsify or verify.

The most obvious assumption of this kind in Weber's own texts, is, as I have said in previous chapters, the assumption that humans are free agents. His own method of interpretative sociology and his view on the importance of personality in modern culture are based on this assumption. But certainly it cannot be proven or made probable by scientific inquiry alone. And formally speaking, the claim that humans are free agents is not a proposition of the same logical order as statements of what is the case in the world. Rather, it is a transcendental claim which is necessary for certain discourses to be at all possible, for example the ethical discourse or Weber's discussion about personalities. The claim that humans are free is also a necessary presupposition for scholarly work. If determinism was the case, scholarly activity would be quite pointless. We would not hold something to be true because we found it intellectually convincing, but because we were *caused* to believe so or so by factors beyond our control.[10]

In the same category can be put Weber's realist assumption of a noumenal reality. Since this reality never can be perceived without our conceptualisations, we cannot have any direct experience of it. But still it is a prerequisite for Weber's epistemological position to assume the existence of an independent reality. This assumption, however, cannot be anything more than a formal, transcendental assumption, and as such it is not a metaphysical statement in the same sense as claims to have *knowledge* about facts beyond experience.

In this very limited sense, then, Weber does not exclude metaphysics. This must not be seen as a deviance from the third line of thought sketched above, since a *heuristic assumption* is a transcendental requisite

---

[10] For this argument, see Macquarrie, John: *In Search of Humanity,* p. 17.

for certain kinds of statements, rather than a statement in itself.[11] Heuristic assumptions are such assumptions which must be made if a certain way of reasoning shall be possible at all. It is not possible to *prove* that humans have a free will, because the procedure of proving presupposes that we have the capacity to accept reasonable arguments freely. If knowledge or ethical reasoning at all should be possible, we have to accept certain such presuppositions. They turn into 'bad' metaphysics, however, when we forget that they are heuristic *assumptions* rather than statements. To heuristically assume a noumenal, ontic reality is not the same as claiming that there is one to which we can have access and truthfully describe in our language. But if we do not make the assumption, it seems impossible to uphold the distinction between knowledge and illusion, and that would cause an intellectual chaos with which we would not be able to live.

More precisely, Weber's first challenge to theology can be formulated in the following way.

1) One shall not believe anything which there are good reasons not to believe.[12]

2) There are good reasons not to believe in metaphysical theological statements.

3) Therefore one shall not believe in metaphysical theological statements.

I do not think that it is possible to prove the correctness of the premises in this argument. Many theologians and philosophers would at least contest the second premise, and argue for the possibility of an extended concept of knowledge. Others would say that there is no difference in principle between religious experiences and sense experience, and that we therefore are rationally entitled to believe that God exists, if we have an experience of the presence of God, for example. William Alston is a good exponent of this view, when he concludes that "one to whom God is apparently presenting Himself as ϕ is thereby prima facie justified in believing God to be ϕ".[13]

---

[11] I use the concept 'transcendental' in a bit looser sense than Kant did. In my usage, a 'transcendental' assumption is such an assumption which provides a framework for a certain way of thought. In this I follow Daphne Hampson's usage. See her *After Christianity*, p. 244.

[12] Note that this basically is a presumptionist view. The main difference between this position and Mikael Stenmark's is located in the second premise, and not the first.

[13] Alston, William: *Perceiving God*, p. 279.

᾽ As I see it, we have to make an unguarded choice between these different positions.[14] Weber urges us to follow a restrictive line of thought, in which only scientific procedures are acceptable when it comes to *judging* the correctness of knowledge-claims. To me this seems as the best way if we want to be able to distinguish knowledge from illusion. There is of course a risk that we by applying scientific standards come to regard a statement of the form "There is an X" as false or meaningless, when it in fact is the case that X, but this seems to me a lesser evil than the opposite possibility.

This is not to say that scientific procedures are unproblematic and gives us a true picture of reality. Weber's epistemological position excludes such an optimistic view of science, and he reminds us that no scientific result is stable. Rather, scholarly work is an endless process of change.[15] Since we do not have access to noumenal reality, but only to our conceptualisations of it, scientific results are always to some extent dependent on the value-position which constitutes the objects of research. But having said this, I for myself cannot see that this state of affairs radically undermines the priority of science. For if this is the case with scientific practices, is it not much more so with other conceivable ways to knowledge, and must not such ways if they claim to provide knowledge of a transcendent reality be regarded with much more suspicion than scientific procedures?

The Problematic Concept 'God'

One of the main reasons behind the development of religions has, according to Weber, been the desire to find meaning in the world, and especially in suffering.[16] But there are few, if any, acceptable solutions to the problem of theodicy in the history of religious thought, and this constitutes the major threat to religious faith in modern culture. As Weber sees it, the problem of theodicy is a more serious threat to the future of religion than any other single factor, even if social or economic factors must not be disregarded. In his opinion, there are only three consistent solutions to the problem, namely 1) a consequent *dualism*, 2) belief in *predestination* and *determinism*, and 3) the Hindu teaching

---

[14] For the notion of 'unguarded choice' see my discussion in chapter 1.
[15] Weber, Max: "Wissenschaft als Beruf", *MWG I/17*, p. 85.
[16] Weber, Max: "Politik als Beruf", *MWG I/17*, p. 241.

of *karma*.[17] But all these three solutions are connected to severe religious and/or philosophical problems.

Weber points out some such problems related to theistic concepts of God. Dualism requires that the belief in divine omnipotence is abandoned. This is of course a possible way of solving the problem of theodicy within a theistic belief system, but, as Weber hints at, it is difficult to bear such a limitation of God's capacities.[18] And the idea of *predestination* and determinism seems to require an abandoning of belief in God's love, if we by love should understand anything similar to normal usages of the word:

> The more modern eschatological hope, however, makes the god of purity and benevolence triumph, just as Christianity makes the Savior triumph over the devil. This less consistent form of dualism is the popular, worldwide conception of heaven and hell, which restores God's sovereignty over the evil spirit who is His creature, and thereby believes that divine omnipotence is saved. But, willy-nilly, it must then, overtly or covertly, sacrifice some of the divine love. For if omniscience is maintained, the creation of a power of radical evil and the admission of sin, especially in communion with the enternity [sic!, misprint in the translation, TE] of hell's punishments for one of God's own and finite creatures and for finite sins, simply does not correspond to divine love. In that case, only a renunciation of benevolence is consistent.[19]

If Weber's argument is elaborated, one could say that it perhaps is possible to solve the problem of theodicy in a consistent way, but that such solutions risk being *religiously* irrelevant.[20] A religiously irrelevant solution should in this context be understood as a proposal which is intellectually satisfying but which cannot fulfil the spiritual and psychological function which it was intended to fill. In order to explicate my

---

[17] Weber, Max: "Einleitung", *MWG I/19*, p. 95.

[18] Weber, Max: "Zwischenbetrachtung", *MWG I/19*, p. 521.

[19] FMW pp. 358-359. Weber, Max: "Zwischenbetrachtung", *MWG I/19*, p. 521: *"...läßt die modernere Endhoffnung den Gott der Reinheit und Güte ebenso siegen, wie das Christentum den Heiland über den Teufel. Diese inkonsequentere Form des Dualismus ist die volkstümliche über die ganze Erde hin verbreitete Vorstellung von Himmel und Hölle. Sie stellt die Souveränität Gottes über den bösen Geist, der sein Geschöpf ist, wieder her, glaubt dadurch die göttliche Allmacht gerettet, muß dann aber, wohl oder übel, eingestandener- oder verhülltermaßen, etwas von der göttlichen Liebe opfern, der, wenn die Allwissenheit festgehalten wird, die Schaffung einer Macht des radikal Bösen und die Zulassung der Sünde, zumal in Gemeinschaft mit der Ewigkeit der Höllenstrafen an einem eigenen endlichen Geschöpf und für endliche Sünden, schlechterdings nicht entspricht. Konsequent ist alsdann nur ein Verzicht auf die Güte."*

[20] This line of reasoning bears some similarities with John Hick's case against Chalcedonian christology in *The Metaphor of God Incarnate*. See e.g. p. 45.

point, I shall briefly refer to a debate between William L. Rowe and Stephen J. Wykstra on the implications of the problem of theodicy for the reasonableness of classical theism.[21]

Rowe's argument against classical theism runs in the following way:

1. There exist instances of intense suffering which an omnipotent, omniscient being could have prevented without thereby losing some greater good or permitting some evil equally bad or worse.

2. An omniscient, wholly good being would prevent the occurrence of any intense suffering it could, unless it could not do so without thereby losing some greater good or permitting some evil equally bad or worse.

3. There does not exist an omnipotent, omniscient, wholly good being.[22]

Rowe acknowledges that the first premise in his argument is impossible to prove, but he claims that we can have some good reasons for holding it to be true. It is very unlikely that *all* instances of suffering are such that the first premise in his argument is false.[23]

Wykstra responds to this argument by proposing the principle of CORNEA (Condition of Reasonable Epistemic Access):

> On the basis of cognized situation s, human H is entitled to claim "It appears that p" only if it is reasonable for H to believe that, given her cognitive faculties and the use she has made of them, if p were not the case, s would likely be different than it is in some way discernible by her.[24]

Wykstra's point is, that Rowe's critique of classical theism does not satisfy CORNEA, since it is implicit in classical theism that humans can have no real, or at least *very* limited, access to the purposes of God. God's wisdom "is to ours, roughly as an adult human's is to a one-month old infant's", according to Wykstra.[25] Therefore classical theism can not reasonably be rebutted by the argument from suffering, since it is immanent in theistic belief to hold that God is good and that we cannot know God's ways. So the theist is justified in saying that it *appears* that there is suffering which is meaningless, and still hold on to belief in an omnipotent, omniscient and supremely good God, since he can say

[21] The notion 'classical theism' is suggested by John Macquarrie in his book *In Search of Deity*, p. 30. I take it to mean the belief that there is an omnipotent, all-loving, omnipresent, omniscient and timeless or eternal personal Being, who has created the universe.

[22] Rowe, William L: "The Problem of Evil and Some Varieties of Atheism", p. 336.

[23] Rowe, *op.cit.*, p. 337.

[24] Wykstra, Stephen J: "The Humean Obstacle to Evidential Arguments from Suffering", p. 85.

[25] Wykstra, *op.cit.*, p. 88.

that this good Being certainly must be believed to have good reasons for permitting suffering, even if we can know nothing about them.

I admit that Wykstra has a case. Theism can be construed in such a way as his, with an almost unbridgeable gap between our cognitive faculties and God's wisdom. But is such a faith really plausible? If I am to God as a one-month old baby, can I really know that I have a relation to God? Without pressing the analogy *in absurdum*, is it not still legitimate to ask if the baby really has a *personal* relation to the parent? Does the baby know that the person (if it has any idea of what a person is) is a *parent*? And can God reveal Godself to humans who have so limited cognitive powers?

It seems to me that Wykstra's case is dependent on believing that there must be an unbridgeable cognitive gap between us and God. But if so, are not much of the religious advantages with theism lost? Is not one of the main points with theism that we can have a personal *relation* to God? And is it possible to talk about a relation between two persons, if one of them is cognitively absolutely inferior to the other? And is it not reasonable to believe that it is this experience of relation with God that has made classical theism able to provide believers with the sense of meaning that Weber holds to be one of the central components in traditional religion?

Another argument against Wykstra's position is, that it threatens human freedom and autonomy. Wykstra's position implies that human beings should put their trust in a person whose ways and activities they cannot understand, and whose activities or lack of activity *prima facie* seems to be morally questionable, to say the least. It can certainly be asked, if it would be regarded to be wise or morally acceptable to put such trust in any other person than God.[26]

Just as in the case of the primacy of science, we stand in a situation where we have to make an unguarded choice. To some of us, CORNEA is a sufficient reason for saying that classical theism can be defended when confronted with the problem of theodicy. Others would side with Gordon Kaufman when he concludes that after Auschwitz, all such arguments are "blank and weak" – that is, that they are not really helpful when we try to orient ourselves in life – and that the root of the problem is the reification of the concept of God.[27]

---

[26] For a similar point, se Glebe-Møller, Jens: *Politisk dogmatik*, p. 125.
[27] Kaufman, Gordon: *In Face of Mystery*, p. 335.

The problems connected to theistic beliefs are of course manifold, and the problem of theodicy is but one of them. Weber holds that views of life, if they shall be able to promote the full humanity of human beings, must have the capacity to resist the alienating aspects of the process of rationalisation. One can certainly ask, if a belief which raises so many intellectual and moral problems as classical theism really has such a capacity. Weber, as I have shown, does not think so. Given this problematic character, it seems reasonable to ask if theology should not try to formulate alternatives to classical theism which does not fall prey to these difficulties. My answer is in the affirmative, and I will try to indicate at least one possible way in the final chapter.

The Cultural Condition of Modernity

Modern culture in the West is, according to Weber, a product of a universal historical process of rationalisation, where ends-rationality (*Zweckrationalität*) becomes more and more dominating, and threatens to make calculability and effectiveness to ultimate values and goals for social acting.

Connected to this process is the fragmentation of life, which Weber describes as the development of the autonomy of different spheres of life. One example, which sometimes evokes public discontent, is the separation of jurisprudence from ethics. A modern legal system strives to operate *sine ira et studio* in a way that is formally calculable. From the perspective of jurists, moral considerations threatens to undermine the effectiveness of the legal apparatus. From a moral point of view, a court order to evict a person from her or his home, even if it is based on law, established through formal democratic procedures, can be judged as very immoral in certain cases. However, if courts should try to take ethics into account, the judicial process would be impossible to calculate. The formal rationality which is a characteristic feature of modernity thus seems to demand that different value spheres are separated from each other.

The instrumentalisation of reason, and the tremendous development of technical efficiency which have been salient features of modern society are for both good and bad. On the good side can be listed the extended technical possibility for value realisation. Infant mortality could be one example. It is reasonable to assume that the death of small children was regarded as something evil in, say, the 17th century. But the technical possibilities to prevent it were small: there were, if Weber's analysis is applied, too little objective rationality in the science of medicine to make this possible. The organisation of society in general also was a major hindrance to the realisation of the wish to lowen the mortality rate among infants; for example, the allocation and distribution of economic resources in a regular manner presupposes an effective bureaucracy. Modern bureaucracy, technology and medicine has made it possible to realise such and other values.[28]

But, on the other hand, rationalisation can create *alienation*, which should be seen as a condition where human beings no longer are in control of their own situation, and regard this undesirable state of affairs as unavoidable. Modern culture risks to become an *iron cage,* in which humanity is trapped. When efficiency becomes one of the main ends, instead of being a means to other ends, rationalisation is complete. The only way to break this situation, is, according to Weber, as I have shown, to let rationality and charisma join forces. When values are independent and "strong" enough to motivate action, it may be possible to set viable goals for political activity, and keep rationality in check. When bureaucracy is controlled by a true *political* will, it can be made to serve ultimate values rather than itself. But the process cannot be reversed – we cannot return to pre-modernity. Modern culture is for Weber, to borrow a metaphor from Anthony Giddens, a juggernaut; it crushes those who try to resist it.[29]

Rationalised culture is an austere milieu to live in, according to Weber. Therefore many people (and to some extent all of us), try to escape from this situation. It is here that religion becomes a risk. Traditional Christianity, where people can orient their life towards a transcendent reality and look for their own personal salvation beyond the earthly life, risks making people uninterested and unengaged in the struggles of this life.[30] Religion can foster the feeling that it is no idea to try to change the earthly life-conditions (You will have pie in the sky when you die). This is, as I have pointed out, one of Weber's main criticisms of traditional Lutheranism: it fosters quietism.

Another aspect of modern culture is what Weber labels *polytheism*. In modern culture, the meaning of world and life is not self-evident, since different views of life exist alongside each other and compete with each

---

[28] This example is inspired by Turner, Bryan: *Max Weber,* p. 136.
[29] Giddens, Anthony: *The Consequences of Modernity,* p. 139.
[30] Weber, Max: "Politik als Beruf", *MWG I/17,* p. 251.

other. It is no longer self evident in Western Europe, for example, that Christian belief has any priority among different views of life. There exists an intense awareness that world and life can be interpreted in different ways, and that there are very different values in society, and no obvious criteria by means of which these can be evaluated.[31]

In such a cultural situation, it must be seen as extremely anachronistic and arrogant to claim to have found the *true* meaning of life, a meaning which is better and more in agreement with how reality *really* is. In this modern condition, no one can claim to have access to the true meaning without denying modernity, and the insight that *my* perspective is only *one* perspective among other equally reasonable perspectives is a fundamental blow to traditional Christian theology. Jesus can no longer be said to be *the* way, *the* truth and *the* life. He can be all these things for some, but others will deny his relevance, and there will be no overarching cultural support for the claims to Christian exclusivity.[32]

In a rationalised culture, there will always be an element of irrationalism, in the sense of the unsystematised, the aesthetic and erotic. The irrational side of aesthetics can have the function of providing a possible way of escape from the austere and pressing reality. Music, film and literature offer ways of getting out, at least temporarily, of the iron cage.[33]

This puts traditional Christianity under cross-fire. On the one hand, it is subject to severe criticism from scientific and philosophical reason for being intellectually problematic. On the other hand, it stands in conflict with the irrational sphere of modern life, because it is too systematised and institutionalised. Most people who want to get out of the iron cage do not turn to traditional religion, because it too is too rationalised. Rather escape options are looked for in popular music, sports or erotics. As Randall Collins aptly has put it, Weber's analysis anticipates the conditions of the concluding 20th century.[34]

There is, according to Weber, a deep gulf between the cultural condition of modernity and traditional Christianity. Modernity is fragmented – Christianity claims to grasp the meaning of the universe. Modernity is pluralist – traditional Christianity claims to be in possession of the final truth. Modernity is an austere milieu to live in, and people try to escape into the irrational – but traditional Christian theology

---

[31] Weber, Max: "Wissenschaft als Beruf", *MWG I/17*, pp. 99-100.
[32] Jens Glebe-Møller has developed this idea in *Politisk dogmatik*, pp. 38-56.
[33] Weber, Max: "Zwischenbetrachtung", *MWG I/19*, p. 500.
[34] Collins, *op.cit.*, p. 78.

is extremely systematised, and *in that sense* far too rational. Weber thus seems to confront us with an either-or. *Either* we adhere to traditional faith of some kind, and opt out from modernity, *or* we live in modernity, and renounce faith. Weber can surely be interpreted in this way,[35] but the most reasonable reading, as I have argued all along, is different: *tertium datur*.

An Adequate View of Life

Weber challenges theology and faith, but a close reading of his texts also points to the need of views of life in modern culture. For a view of life to be adequate, however, it must satisfy certain criteria. Adequacy in this context should be understood as meaning that the view of life helps its adherents to orient themselves in life in such a way that they can live in modernity without being alienated. Such a view of life enables people to create and shape their own lives, that is, it contributes to their development into true personalities.

On the basis of Weber's texts, five criteria for an adequate view of life can be formulated.

1) An adequate view of life should promote the full humanity of all human beings.

2) An adequate view of life should provide us with values so that we can orient ourselves in life. This orientation has a twofold character: a) We need values in scholarly work in order to form the research object; b) We need values in order to be able to identify problems of political and moral character and apply our technical skills to solve such problems.

3) To provide orientation in life, a view of life must be consistent and coherent.

4) An adequate view of life should respect the primacy of science.

5) An adequate view of life should provide us with resources to handle the contingencies of life, without therefore leading us to believe that we have grasped the true meaning of life and world.

---

[35] e.g. in Tyrrell, Hartmann: "'Das Religiöse' in Max Webers Religionssoziologie", p. 223.

Full Humanisation

What makes a human being truly *human*, is for Weber that her or his life transcends nature, by being a consciously chosen way of life. Natural events are such events that have no meaning – they are determined happenings in a causal chain. Meaningful events, on the other hand, are intentional and based on values. What separates humanity from nature is the capacity for intentional acting on the basis of consciously constructed and chosen values.[36]

Weber's fourfold typology of action is central in this respect. Strictly speaking, only value-rational and ends-rational acting are truly *human* ways of acting, since only they are consciously chosen.[37] But, as Brubaker has pointed out, the distinction is not easy to make, since a person can act according to tradition in a reflective way, and thereby act value-rationally.[38]

Weber's notion of the truly human is of course a normative standpoint, and, as such, not incontestable. But it is quite attractive, as I see it. For what he says, basically, is that a good human life is a life formed according to our own wishes. And, as a normative concept, it is in no way intended to be a description of what humans *are,* but of what they can and should become. Elaborating on Weber's thought in the spirit of Mark Warren's reconstruction of Weber's ethics, one could say that human dignity requires that every person should be allowed to develop into an autonomous personality in accordance with his or her capacities.[39]

This concept of the human does not imply that oppressed people really are autonomous. Rather it can be an instrument for identifying oppression. Some feminists, as for example Daphne Hampson, have used the concepts of autonomy and freedom as critical devices. For Hampson, the real problem with patriarchy is that it has not allowed women to form their own lives autonomously, but forced them to live in an heteronomous existence.[40] Feminism is, understood in this way, the struggle for the recognition of the full humanity of women.[41]

---

[36] Weber, Max: "Wertfreiheit", *GAW,* p. 507-508. To separate truly human acts from natural events by the quality of *intentionality* is often done in theology. See e.g. Kaufman, Gordon: *In Face of Mystery,* p. 142. Kaufman's model of human acting on p. 145 is very instructive, and can be applied also to Weber's reasoning.

[37] Weber, Max: *Wirtschaft und Gesellschaft,* p. 12.

[38] Brubaker, *op.cit.,* p. 93.

[39] Warren, Mark: "Max Weber's Liberalism for a Nitzschean World".

[40] Hampson, Daphne: "On Autonomy and Heteronomy", p. 1.

[41] Ruether, *op.cit.,* p. 18.

If Weber's basic assumption that what constitutes a desirable form of human existence is freedom and rational action – rational in the widest sense possible – is accepted, it seems reasonable to demand that views of life should promote this good state of affairs, both theoretically and practically. An adequate view of life should, accordingly, contain a central value: it is good that human beings are free and autonomous and have the possibility to shape their own existence. But mere lip-service to such a value is not enough. A view of life should also be judged according to its practical consequences: *does adherence to the faith in question actually promote the full humanisation of all?* This is a heavy demand. It demands, first, that the adherents themselves should be made into more autonomous and rational agents by their adherence to the view of life in question, and, also, that the view of life should promote humanisation among other members of society, who are not adherents to the view of life themselves.

A *caveat* is necessary here. This criterion does not exclude conflicts between views of life, since views of life can contain very different sorts of substantial values. The criterion of humanisation is a *formal* criterion, demanding respect for other people's choices, and an appreciation of their freedom to choose and form their own lives accordingly.[42] It does not imply, however, that one has to like what they in fact choose. Such a demand would be in blatant conflict with Weber's view of the polytheism of modern culture. Believers of different sorts, such as Christians, Buddhists, Marxists, neo-liberals or whatever, will oppose each other's values and views of life and the struggle can sometimes be very serious. But the criterion of full humanisation demands that the struggle is fought in a non-coercive way, in a democratic fashion and within democratic institutions.

Value-orientation

If the primary function of views of life is to provide us with values by the help of which we can orient our acting, both in scholarly research and in society at large, then it seems to be self-evident to say that an adequate view of life should fulfil this task. The matter is not that simple, however. Human existence is, to put it frankly, *political*. Society develops through human agency, and therefore we have to decide in what

---

[42] Weber's position is thus of a typical liberal character, as this is understood by e.g. Will Kymlicka in *Contemporary Political Philosophy*, p. 200.

direction we want it to develop. Of course, people want different things, and this is to quite an extent due to the fact that they have different views of life. But politics is also the art of the possible, and unrealisable values will be of very little help in the shaping of society, if they are not conjoined with a sense of realism.

Basically, then, an adequate view of life should provide us with a vision of human life at its best, to borrow an expression from Eberhard Herrmann. Such a vision will, however, be a utopia, which never can be completely realised. One reason for the unrealisability of such a utopia is that other views of life will contain other utopias, and if views of life are allowed to compete with each other in a democratic society, it is extremely unlikely that any single utopia can be realised. Another reason is that a utopia seldom is stable. A Christian view of life, for example, changes with theological trends, social change and other factors. The point with the utopia is thus not that it provides us with an *unchanging* vision. Rather it should provide us with a *viable* one, and this seems to demand readiness for change when the societal conditions change.

We need utopias to know in what direction we should strive, but we also need concrete, realisable values. An adequate view of life, therefore, should provide us with a vision of such a character that it allows us to derive practical values from it. A view of life should be compatible with the conditions of politics, and should allow responsible political action. Politics implies means-end calculating, and a view of life which does not allow such calculating does not seem adequate.

This can be illustrated by the problem of the Sermon of the Mount. The Sermon of the Mount puts us in front of a radical demand: do not resist an evildoer (Mt 5:39). But such a demand is politically impracticable: it would for example demand the abolition of the police and the whole judicial system. Sometimes Weber seems to hold that such consequences makes the ethics of the Sermon of the Mount completely irrelevant for political acting.[43] But such an interpretation should be restricted to instances when the Sermon of the Mount is put forward as a set of practical values. As is clear from a passage in *Politik als Beruf*, Weber does not exclude the possibility that religious ideals can provide visions for political acting:

> The *nature* of the cause the politician seeks to serve by striving for and using power is a question of faith. He can serve a national goal or the

---

[43] E.g. in Weber, Max: "Zwischen zwei Gesetzen", *MWG I/15*, p. 97.

whole of humanity, or social and ethical goals, or goals which are cultural, inner-worldly or religious...[44]

Adherence to religious goals is not impossible even for genuine political acting. But perhaps the specific ethic of the Sermon of the Mount is? This depends, I contend, on how the Sermon of the Mount is understood. If it is seen as a set of practical recommendations it is irrelevant, but if it is seen as a vision of a just order of things, from which more practical goals can be derived, this must not be the case. To return to the example above: the police, or, for that matter, peace-keeping military operations, can then be seen as grounded on practical values of the desirability of peace derived from the vision provided by the Sermon of the Mount.

The conclusion is, that an adequate view of life must allow for the distinction between *visions* of human life when it is at its best, and *practical* goals for political acting, which are *derived* from the vision. Only if such a distinction is possible without internal tensions and contradictions, a view of life can provide adequate value-orientation.[45]

Consistency and Coherence

A view of life must be free from internal contradictions if it is to give orientation in life. According to Weber, the test of consistency is one of the most important ways to test a system of values.[46] This test of consistency must be applied on several levels. First, it must be applied on the 'utopian' level. If a view of life provides us with a 'picture' of human life at its best, this picture cannot contain contradictory visions. If it does, it cannot guide our practical acting, since contradictory principles of action can be derived from it. Secondly, the relation between the 'utopian' values and the practical values must be consistent. The utopian vision is the transcendent goal of acting, and has the function of directing our acts. Acting in a concrete social milieu as we are, our actions cannot be directly governed by a utopia. An intermediary stage of more practical values has to be formed. But this intermediary stage cannot be in logical conflict with the utopia, if the utopia really should have the

---

[44] PW p. 355. Weber, Max: "Politik als Beruf", *MWG I/17*, p. 230: "Wie *die Sache auszusehen hat, in deren Dienst der Politiker Macht erstrebt und Macht verwendet, ist Glaubenssache. Er kan nationalen oder menschheitlichen, sozialen und ethischen oder kulturlichen, innerweltlichen oder religiösen Zielen dienen...*"

[45] This criterion has some affinities with Anthony Giddens's concept of *utopian realism*. See his *The Consequences of Modernity*, pp. 154-158.

[46] Weber, Max: "Wertfreiheit", *GAW*, p. 510.

function of directing our lives. The example of the relation between the love of peace and support of military operations can illustrate my point.

Suppose a Christian believer who holds that the 'kingdom of God' is the ultimate vision of the just order of things. In God's kingdom oppression and violence will not exist, and hence peace and just relations between human beings is an ultimate value for her or him. But the world here and now is not a place of just relations and peace. Our Christian believer may then think that under certain conditions it may be permissible to use military force to prevent worse evils, say genocide. The practical value in question then can be formulated as "It is permissible to use military force to prevent worse evils from happening, on the condition that no other realistic and less violent way can be found". This practical value can be consistent with the utopia, if the utopia does not exclude all means-end calculating. If the view of life of our Christian believer is to be adequate, it must be able to contain both her or his vision of the kingdom of God, and her or his practical support for peace-keeping military operations.

The capacity for orienting people in life will be severely damaged if there are in-built conflicts between utopian and practical values. Therefore, it is desirable that views of life are formed as coherent wholes, providing both transcendent utopian models of human life at its best, long-term practical goals and short-term practical goals, which form a coherent system of values, by the help of which its adherents can orient their acting in the world. As was pointed out in chapter four, coherence should not, in this context, be understood as a strict logical relation of entailment. What Weber demands is rather a kind of moral coherence within a personality. On his view, philosophical analysis can show that the acknowledgement of a certain utopian value should lead to actions in accordance with the acknowledged value, if the person in question wants to lead an organised and structured life. One possible way of understanding this demand would be to regard acknowledgements of value as prescriptions. If you for example claim that human beings are equal irrespective of their skin-colour, you have uttered a prescription by which you have bound yourself to treat them equally. If you do not do that in your day-to-day practice, Weber, on this account, would say that you have an incoherent perspective on life.

The Primacy of Science

If views of life are to be able to orient our action in the world, it is necessary that they respect the role of science to provide us with knowledge of facts. As scholarly methods, on good grounds, are regarded as the best way available to justify knowledge-claims, an adequate view of life should not conflict with established scholarly results. This prescription is made on the basis of several circumstances. First, as has been presented at length above, it is questionable if we are rationally entitled to claim that metaphysical propositions are true, and this of course makes it desirable that an adequate view of life avoids making such claims. This argument will not be further explored here.

Second, if views of life are to be able to orient us in the world, we have to have the best conception possible of the world, and for this purpose, science is required.[47] Any attempt from the side of views of life to prescribe what the results of scholarly investigations should be, will diminish our capacity to orient ourselves in the world. Faiths simply cannot compete with scientific procedures when it comes to producing knowledge, and therefore does not give us as good a conception of reality as science does. If we shall be able to realise our values and strive for a better world to live in, we have to have knowledge of the world and its operations. If views of life try to prescribe what the results of our investigation ought to be, intellectual and practical chaos will follow.[48]

Third, a person who lives in a culture where scholarly procedures are widely known and available to almost everyone, cannot be seen as rationally justified in believing propositions contrary to evidence, or propositions highly incredible from a scholarly point of view. I shall give two examples of problematical attempts to question the primacy of science. As soon as conventional Christian apologists want to defend faith against the challenge of of secular thinking, they seem to have to accept the principle of the primacy of science. But traditional Christianity cannot survive such a principle, and therefore it has to be denied, one way or another. This procedure can often be observed in efforts to defend the claim that the narratives about miracles in the New Testament, especially the resurrection narratives, give us information about historical events.

In the discussion about the historicity of the empty tomb-traditions concerning Jesus' resurrection, apologists for a traditional Christian interpretation – understood as the claim that Jesus rose from the dead in a bodily (even if his body in some sense was spiritual) way – often try

---

[47] Weber, Max: "Wissenschaft als Beruf", *MWG I/17*, p. 103.
[48] This is of course not a denial of the importance of views of life in the formation of scientific problems.

to question the principles of secular historical scholarship. Two examples of this procedure are William P. Alston's article *Biblical Criticism
and the Resurrection* and the Swedish New Testament scholar Bengt
Holmberg's article *Den historiske Jesus – nutida diskussionsläge och
bedömning.*

In my opinion, their arguments are not very convincing, since they
lead to contradictions or paradoxes which do not seem to fulfil any positive functions. It would, in my opinion, be more reasonable to follow
Weber's recommendation and return to the open arms of the church and
put *all* faith in its teachings, and retreat from modernity and its reason.[49]
For a faith that wants to exist *within* and in positive relation to modern
Western culture, no other option seems to be open than the full acceptance of the criterion of the primacy of science.

Alston begins with acknowledging that "it is certainly not irrelevant
to Christian concerns to do the best we can to determine what we can
reasonably believe about Jesus' return to life after his death and bur-
ial".[50] But, according to Alston, a Christian believer does not accept the
primacy of science when it comes to determine such matters. A Christian believer has a basic *trust* in the church's teaching, and therefore she
or he can only allow historical results to have a limited role of "shore up
or weaken parts of the Christian belief system, without being allowed
the presumption of completely determining even the historical parts
thereof by themselves".[51]

One can certainly ask what should be understood by Alston's claim
that it is not irrelevant for Christian theology to try to determine what
reasonably can be believed about Jesus' resurrection, when the basic
epistemic category in the effort is the trust in Christian theology.[52] If
Christians are rationally entitled to trust the church's teachings and do
not have to revise their faith in the light of the severe intellectual difficulties it implies to claim that the resurrection is an historical event, I
cannot see the point in giving historical scholarship *any* role when it

---

[49] As I understand him, this is what John Milbank recommends in the final words of
his book *Theology and Social Theory.* Milbank writes on p. 434: "Even today, in the
midst of the self-torturing circle of secular reason, there can open to view again a series
with which it is in no continuity: the emanation of harmonius difference, the exodus of
new generations, the path of peaceful flight."

[50] Alston, William: "Biblical Criticism and the Resurrection", pp. 148-149.

[51] Alston, William: "Biblical Criticism and the Resurrection", p. 150.

[52] This argument is inspired by Sarah Coakley's response to Alston's article in the
same volume. See Coakley, Sarah: "Response", p. 186.

comes to theologically exploring the resurrection narratives. Alston tries to rescue the acceptability of traditional Christian dogma. But he realises that he would not convince anyone outside the group of people who already believe that Jesus rose in bodily form from the dead, if he did not try to use the criteria of secular scholarship. In my opinion, such a procedure of paying lip-service to historical scholarship is not very attractive, since it both accepts and denies the methods of historical scholarship at the same time.

My other example is Bengt Holmberg. In his article, he presents three stages in the Life of Jesus-research, namely the Liberal or First Quest, the Second Quest and the Third quest. The Third Quest, with which Holmberg associates himself, operates with social scientific theories in trying to understand Jesus and his contemporaries, and has, according to Holmberg, liberated itself from reductionist approaches in methodology.[53] Therefore, many of its representatives are willing to recognise a supernatural element in history.[54]

The main target for Holmberg is Troeltsch's criterion of analogy in historical research (implying that historical events in the past should be assumed to be mainly similar to what happens today), since it means that it is quite unreasonable to regard the miracle stories of the New Testament as records of supernatural events which have occurred in history.[55] Holmberg discards the principle of analogy. But what happens with the possibility of using social scientific methods in New Testament scholarship, if the principle of analogy is not accepted? Has not social science been developed during the 20th century, and is not then its usefulness in historical New Testament research dependent on the basic analogy between human and social life in the 20th century and the first? On the basis of this, the conclusion that Holmberg's refusal to accept the primacy of science causes a fundamental blow to his own theological and exegetical agenda seems to be quite reasonable.

Capacity to Handle the Contingencies of Life

According to Weber, one of the main factors behind the development of religions was the human need to come to grips with the problem of

---

[53] Holmberg, Bengt: "Den historiske Jesus", p. 29.
[54] Holmberg, *op.cit.*, pp. 30, 42.
[55] Holmberg, *op.cit.*, p. 37. Troeltsch's formulation of the principle can be found in his "Ueber historische und dogmatische Methode in der Theologie", p. 732.

suffering.[56] As a hypothesis regarding why religions developed, this claim might be questionable. But it is indisputable that the world religions have tried to give answers to questions about the meaning with suffering, and such answers often seem to have a central place in the religious system as a whole, as for example in Buddhism.[57] But if metaphysical systems and beliefs are dubious in a modern context – Weber claims, as I have shown, that it is impossible to find the *true* meaning of the world and human life – what happens to this central function of views of life?

It is clear from Weber's argument, that any claim to be able to give an *answer* to the meaning of suffering will be futile and senseless. But does this exclude the possibility of providing resources for *handling* suffering, and, for that matter, joy? I do not think so. What matters is the kind of metaphysical claims which are conjoined with such expressions. If views of life are seen as providing visions of human life at its best, they should also help us to express the fact that often our lives fall short of the vision, and, on the other hand, sometimes come close to the vision in certain respects.

A view of life that contains symbolic expressions for suffering and joy, love and fear, the feeling of moral responsibility and the feeling of guilt seems to be able to help the individual to lead an organised and structured life. A view of life which, on the other hand, is nothing more than a political or moral teaching, is, at least for many persons, I suspect, not very attractive. We adhere to views of life because we think that they help us to orient ourselves in the world, and we need to handle not only questions about how to act, but also situations where no action is possible or relevant.

Weber notices that humans have sought meaning in life for as long as we can know, and he seems to think that it is a *sine qua non* for being able to lead a truly human life that we live in a structured way, having a view of life or a value-system which allows us to act responsibly and in a coherent manner. But I think that he does not give proper attention to the fact that his stoic ideal is totally unrealistic. Without any 'spiritual' resources to handle the contingencies of life, any value-system risks to be seen as futile in the face of death and suffering. I would say that not

---

[56] Weber, Max: "Politik als Beruf", *MWG I/17*, p. 241.

[57] For an overview of the discussion of the problem of suffering in the world religions, see Bowker, John: *Problems of Suffering in Religions of the World*. For the central place of reflection on suffering in Buddhism, see p. 237.

even his famous example about the meaningful death of soldiers can serve as a rebuttal of this argument.

Weber claims that only the warrior in battle can have a sense of a real meaning of death, because he can be sure he dies *for* something, for example his fatherland.[58] It is hardly conceivable that this sense of the fatherland – if the soldiers of World War I really had such a sense – can be upheld without the symbolisms of the nation state: banners, military colours, the rhetoric of Empire etc. The sense of meaning which Weber finds in modern warfare is dependent on nationalism's capacity to provide resources for handling contingencies of life, resources which are related to its providing of values for action. And in Wilhelmine Germany, these resources could not be separated from religion, at least not the official version practised in Prussia.

In his *The Christian Faith,* Schleiermacher defines piety as "the consciousness of being absolutely dependent",[59] and in *On Religion,* he claims that religion is the "sensibility and taste for the infinite".[60] In modern theology, this thought has been expressed in various ways. For Gordon Kaufman, modern human beings are well aware of their absolute dependence on the whole of cosmos for their sustenance.[61] For Kaufman, the symbol 'God' can function as a kind of focus in which our sense of being dependent on and created by something greater than ourselves and our visions for a just order of things can be held together.[62] Thus, God-language enables us to hold our visions and our need to come to grips with the contingencies of life together. Perhaps this could be seen as what makes the difference between religious and non-religious views of life: religious views of life direct believers to a transcendent absolute, upon which they in some sense feel themselves dependent.[63]

---

[58] Weber, Max: "Zwischenbetrachtung", *MWG I/19,* pp. 492-493. Of course, this quite distasteful reasoning should be seen in the light of the political context in which Weber wrote this text: World War I.

[59] English quote from Schleiermacher, Friedrich: *The Christian Faith,* §4. Schleiermacher, Friedrich: *Der christliche Glaube,* §4. Schleiermacher's German expression for being absolutely dependent is that a pious person is conscious of being *schlecthin abhängig.*

[60] Schleiermacher, Friedrich: *On Religion,* p. 23. *Über Religion,* p. 80: "*Religion ist Sinn und Geschmak*[sic, TE] *fürs Unendliche"*.

[61] Kaufman, Gordon: "The Epic of Evolution as a Framework For Human Orientation in Life", p. 178.

[62] Kaufman, Gordon: *In Face of Mystery,* p. 354.

[63] This is similar to Eberhard Herrmann's hint about differences between religious and other views of life. See his *Scientific Theory and Religious Belief,* p. 126.

How does this relate to Weber? This fifth criterion is based on Weber's reflections on the role of the human need of meaning in suffering in the development of religious systems. But it is also a critique of Weber's lack of understanding of the necessity to handle this need even in modern culture. So the fifth criterion is basically an effort to ameliorate Weber's thought about these matters, but it is an amelioration which tries to be true to his central views on the fate of humanity in the modern world.

Religion and Science Once Again

In his book on the reception of Karl Barth's thinking in the Swedish theological context, Ola Sigurdson dissociates himself from a Christian theology that too easily succumbs to the demands of secular rationality, or, to speak with Niebuhr, chooses Culture rather than Christ.[64] In Sigurdson's eyes, Swedish academic theology has tended to universalise science and culture at the cost of theology, since philosophy and science has got the role of delineating what theology properly can say. However, it has not been as generous when it comes to allowing for a theological critique of science and culture.[65]

Sigurdson is no advocate of fideism. Rather he proposes a kind of dialogical tension between Christian theology and science, based on the insight that every perspective, be it Christian or scientific, is particular, albeit often with universal claims. In a dialogical relation between Christian theology and science, each should be allowed to criticise the other.[66]

It might seem that the perspective which I have developed on the basis of Weber's texts, is totally opposed to Sigurdson's view. Given Weber's view, science has a monopoly when it comes to the justification of knowledge-claims. But there is also a point of contact between my perspective and Sigurdson's. Scientific work is not made in a vacuum, and Weber reminds us that scientific work is always based on a value relevance. To *a certain extent*, then, scientific results are value-dependent. This does not pertain to the results as such, at least not ideally, since the method of investigation should be value-free. But it does pertain to the formulation of scientific questions. The values of the individual scholar

---

[64] Sigurdson, Ola: *Karl Barth som den andre,* pp. 294-296.
[65] Sigurdson, *op.cit.*, pp. 216, 295-296.
[66] Sigurdson, *op.cit.*, p. 296.

and her or his community decide which questions that are asked. In that way all scientific work is an expression of a view of life, and can be criticised both from the perspective of academic theology and from the perspective of other views of life.

One example of this could be the science of biology. Perhaps biology, with its evolutionary paradigm, is the dominating science in contemporary Western culture. This in itself does not have to be problematic, but it might become so if the view of life motivating biological research of a certain kind contends that there is no difference in value whatsoever between human beings and animals. At least such a value is problematic from, say, most Christian views of life. Christian theologians are, given this perspective, fully entitled to criticise and oppose the view of life underlying and motivating this kind of research. But they have to stay clear of the temptation to criticise reasonable scientific results on the basis that these do not correspond with the Christian worldview.[67]

There is, if Weber's idea of the value-relevance of scientific work is taken seriously, nothing illegitimate with a religious critique of the values establishing value-relevance in scholarly work, and thereby to *some extent* religious critique of scientific activities. This possibility of a mutual dialogue between views of life and science was not discussed by Weber, however. As far as I can see, it has not been very much discussed in the literature on Weber either.[68] Academic theology, as I understand it, has as one of its main tasks to analyse such conflicts, and to point out hidden value conflicts in scientific work. As a scholarly activity, academic theology should make clear to its sisters in the academic community the importance and problematic nature of the value relevance of the objects of research, and facilitate and provide tools for a mutual critique between views of life and science, and between different views of life. Summarily stated, a view of life can criticise a scientific activity for its value assumptions, and science can criticise a view of life for its (illegitimate) metaphysical claims. If this limitation is respected, a fruitful dialogue between science and, say, Christian theology can be established.

---

[67] A critical discussion of a 'biological world view' can be found in Jeffner, Anders: *Biology and Religion as Interpreting Patterns of Human Life*, pp. 10-20. For the question of ideology in natural science, see Stenmark, Mikael: "Science and Ideology".

[68] Not even Bruun, whose work on Webers methodology, *Science, Values and Politics in Max Weber's Methodology*, still is one of the best in the field, discusses this aspect of Weber's thinking at any length.

But Christian theology cannot come about without some form of revelation. Christianity has its ground in the carpenter from Nazareth, Jesus, whom Christians regard as God's Son, the Revealer of God. But is there any room for a concept of revelation in Weber's understanding of modernity? Is it not rather reasonable to assume that any appeal to revelation will imply that Christian theology claims to be in possession of some sort of secret knowledge not accessible to all? In the following chapter I shall develop a model of revelation that is compatible with the criteria for an adequate view of life put forward in this chapter.

6. CHARISMA AND REVELATION

Charisma as a Creative Force

In *Wirtschaft und Gesellschaft,* Weber defines charismatic phenomena as a type of phenomena which have a special creative force in human history. According to Weber, charisma is the truly revolutionary force and the only effective impetus for change in traditionalistic epochs.[1] The evolution of jurisprudence began, for example, according to Weber, with charismatic revelation through what he calls 'legal prophets',[2] who often received their 'revelations' without this always being caused by any knowable external social factor.[3]

Weber understands 'charisma' as an extraordinary (*außeralltäglich*) quality of a person, because of which he or she is regarded as empowered with supernatural or at least very rare capacities. These qualities are so exceptional, that the bearer of charisma is regarded, by her or his followers, as being of divine origin or at least as embodying a very important value or ideal. According to Weber, this makes the charismatic person a 'leader' in the eyes of her or his disciples.[4]

Weber's theory of charisma was developed on the basis of the writings of the theologian and jurist Rudolph Sohm.[5] However, Weber's understanding differed from Sohm's in a crucial aspect. The notion 'charisma' was for Weber an analytical concept, designating certain phenomena that could be found in different epochs, cultures, religions and ideological systems. Weber wanted his notion of charisma to be value neutral in the sense that it should be possible to apply it to both 'good' and 'bad' phenomena, judged by the standards of the scholar.[6] When the

---

[1] Weber, Max: *Wirtschaft und Gesellschaft,* p. 142. Weber distinguishes between three types of authority *(Herrschaft)*: charismatic authority, traditional authority, and legal authority. Legal authority is rationally motivated and based on the assumption that the person who exercises authority has been given that authority for rational reasons. Traditional authority is based on the fact that the leaders by tradition are seen as invested with the right to lead. On the types of authority, see Weber, Max: *Wirtschaft und Gesellschaft,* p. 124.

[2] Weber, Max: *Wirtschaft und Gesellschaft,* p. 504.

[3] Weber, Max: *Wirtschaft und Gesellschaft,* p. 446.

[4] Weber, Max: *Wirtschaft und Gesellschaft,* p. 140.

[5] See Weber, Max: *Wirtschaft und Gesellschaft,* pp. 124, 655.

[6] Weber, Max: *Wirtschaft und Gesellschaft,* p. 654.

concept is used in accordance with Weber's intentions, both Jesus and Hitler can be said to be bearers of charisma.[7]

When Sohm spoke about charisma, however, he had the Christian theological understanding of gifts of grace from God in mind. According to him, charisma is a gift from the Holy Spirit, and the charismatic leaders of the church have got this gift, which enables them to govern the church. The Christian church, according to him, is a charismatically governed organisation.[8]

Weber has been accused of not connecting his concept of charisma to any moral or religious ideal. For example, Peter Haley concludes that Weber by constructing the concept of charisma in this value neutral way, emptied it of all religious content. In Haley's eyes, Weber's usage is shocking to "anyone viewing Jesus through the eye of faith",[9] since it implies that there may be no reason to regard Jesus as more of an ideal and a leader than the Homeric hero Achilles.[10] According to Haley, Sohm's idea of a charismatic organisation as a gift from God is a religious view sharply in contrast with Weber's reductive approach.[11] According to Haley's dichotomising argument, either you have a Christian view of charisma, and then you cannot accept Weber's view, or you have a Weberian view, and then you cannot be a Christian.

Another example of this kind of critique is Alan L. Berger's article *Hasidism and Moonism: Charisma in the Counterculture.* Berger concludes that the lack of clarity concerning a transcendent reality as the origin of charisma has created a distorted form of religiosity. According to Berger, the leader of Moonism seems to be the object of worship for his followers, while the Hasidic leader, the zaddik, points beyond himself, his charisma being restrained both by a transcendent reality and tradition in the Jewish community.[12] For Berger, Hasidic charisma is genuine, because it refers to the transcendent, while Moonism is idolatrous,

---

[7] For a discussion of Hitler's charisma, see Schweitzer, Arthur: "Hitler's Dictatorial Charisma".

[8] Sohm, Rudolph: *Kirchenrecht,* pp. 26-28.

[9] Haley, Peter: "Rudolph Sohm on Charisma", p. 196.

[10] Haley, *op.cit.*, p. 196. The example of Achilles is taken from Weber, *Wirtschaft und Gesellschaft,* p. 654. In this passage, Weber concludes that the concept of 'charisma' can be applied to inspired warrior heroes as Achilles or the Irish legendary hero Cúchulainn (Weber spells *Cuculain*). The charismatic quality in Cúchulainn was his battle frenzy, making him an ideal Celtic warrior, as is pointed out in MacCulloch, John A.: *The Religion of the Ancient Celts,* p. 132. Weber's examples should be seen as ideal-typical; they do not necessarily imply that he thought that Achilles or Cúchulainn actually had existed.

[11] Haley, *op.cit.*, p. 197.

[12] Berger, Alan L.: "Hasidism and Moonism", pp. 308-309.

because the charisma of the leader makes the followers worship him instead of worshipping God. The criterion for distinguishing between genuine charisma and false, idolatrous charisma is the religious tradition,[13] and therefore Berger criticises Weber for drawing too sharp a line between charisma and tradition.[14]

Neither Haley nor Berger denies that the notion of charisma can be used as a sociological concept even if it lacks religious content. What their critique seems to imply is that only if charisma is assumed to have a direct link to God as transcendent being, can it be useful for religious thought. It is one of my aims in this chapter to propose a constructive theological use of Weber's concept of charisma which does not presuppose this. A theology which accepts the primacy of science cannot overlook secular understandings of the concept of charisma. In my opinion, theology may benefit more from Weber's usage than from Sohm's.

Weber's value neutral concept of charisma can also be criticised for its lack of moral content. The Swedish sociologist and interpreter of Weber, Kerstin Lindskoug, has argued that it is the content of the charisma which decides if it is for good or bad. Depending on what kind of message the charismatic leader proclaims, charisma can bring us to heaven or hell, as Lindskoug puts it. Her own examples of good charismatic leadership are the political leadership in revolutionary China and Cuba.[15]

Weber would agree with Lindskoug that charismatic phenomena can be for good or bad. But his theory precludes him from saying that this decision can be made on scientific grounds. *That* a phenomenon can be labelled charismatic is a scientific question, but judging its moral value is not. Lindskoug's own examples of good charisma are obviously not self evident, and this, I think, is a sufficient reason for concluding that judging charisma is a matter of values more than a matter of scholarly reasoning, *aiming* at producing intersubjectively valid results. As has been, I believe, sufficiently argued in previous chapters, what Weber's thinking does *not* imply, however, is that there are *no* rationally grounded criteria by the help of which we can decide if, and which, charismatic leader we should follow.

Not everyone becomes a charismatic person, so the first question to Weber's texts will be: What makes a person a bearer of charisma?

---

[13] Berger, *op.cit.*, p. 381.
[14] Berger, *op.cit.*, p. 378.
[15] Lindskoug, Kerstin: *Hänförelse och förnuft*, p. 153.

Further, if charisma is revolutionary, it cannot be wholly determined by the cultural context. So the second question, or set of questions, will be: To what extent is charisma an irreducible phenomenon, and in what ways does it relate to the context in which it occurs? A third question, related to the second set of questions is of course what makes people followers of charismatic phenomena. Why do people give up certain aspects of their individuality and follow Jesus, chairman Mao or Mohammed? And, fourth, are there different forms of charisma? Is not Haley saying something important when he finds problems with grouping Jesus with warrior heroes and political leaders?

The analytical scheme by the help of which I shall analyse Weber's view of charisma contains the following components. 1) The characteristics of a person capable of becoming the bearer of charisma; 2) The degree of social determination of charisma and its overall relation to the social context; 3) The characteristics of the followers of a charismatic leader; and 4) The different forms of charisma.

The Charismatic

Weber's most elaborate analysis of charismatic leaders and their characteristics can be found in his study of ancient Judaism. The prophets of the Old Testament function for Weber as a model of charismatic leadership.[16] As was stated in chapter two, Weber made a distinction between an older and a younger type of Old Testament prophecy. The older type of prophets were prophets of good fortune, organised in guilds, and bringing about their charismatic qualities with certain techniques, such as dance and music. The younger type of prophets – the scriptural prophets – were prophets of doom and ardent critics of the kingdom and its rulers.

In chapter two, I analysed Weber's discussion of these scriptural prophets, and showed that it is very similar to the kind of understanding of the prophets that was common in the History of religions school, and especially in the writings of Hermann Gunkel. For the sake of convenience, I shall briefly recapitulate my findings.

Weber thought of the prophets as solitary ecstatics who had some sort of religious experience to which we cannot have any real access. However, he repeatedly stressed that this experience has to be regarded as at least partly autonomous. It cannot be explained only by reference to the

---

[16] Zingerle, Arnold: *Max Webers historische Soziologie,* p. 131.

social context, because the message of the prophets did not really benefit anyone, unless one was willing to change one's whole attitude to life.
And even then the benefit was spiritual, not material. The political
power, as portrayed in the Old Testament, certainly had nothing to gain
from it.

On the other hand, the message of the prophets was dressed up in the
current religious language, and was therefore not totally original. But the
preaching of the prophets had a content which cannot be explained
exclusively by reference to tradition, and it was characterised by a
tremendous *élan,* for which the best explanation, according to Weber, is
that it originated in a transforming religious experience.

A genuine, religious charismatic would, according to Weber, seem to
have some sort of exceptional experience, insight or what else we may
call it, to which not everyone has access. What signifies this experience
is that it is socially and sometimes psychologically underdetermined, as
far as we can judge.[17] However, there are no compelling reasons to conclude that these insights are *caused by* or *referring to* a transcendent
reality. The only scholarly attitude to these insights, according to Weber,
is to acknowledge their existence, and to analyse their effects. Their
causes are, at least to a certain extent, hidden and will remain so.

Charisma and the Social Context

In *Wirtschaft und Gesellschaft,* Weber holds that charismatic authority only exists as a social fact when it is accepted by a group of followers, and it may cease to exist if the charismatic leader fails to prove her
or his gifts. Charismatic leaders are accepted as long as their charisma is
visible to their followers. According to Weber, charisma has traditionally been proven by miracles.[18] A modern analogy could be charismatic
political leaders who for a long time fail to fulfil their promises to the
electorate. Sooner or later people will abandon them and vote for someone else.

Charismatic leadership, according to Weber, often occurs in times of
need or enthusiasm *(Begeisterung)*.[19] In extraordinary times, when peo-

---

[17] Weber discusses the possibility that charismatic phenomena depends on psychic ill-
ness, and concludes that at least not all phenomena can be sufficiently explained by taking recourse to clinical psychology. See Weber, Max: *Wirtschaft und Gesellschaft,*
p. 188.

[18] Weber, Max: *Wirtschaft und Gesellschaft,* p. 140.

[19] Weber, Max: *Wirtschaft und Gesellschaft,* pp. 142, 657, 661.

ple's normal life-conditions are radically changed, there arises a need to
find the meaning in what happens. In such a period people become more
prone to listen to and accept a charismatic message and the authority of
a charismatic leader, claiming to have a special mission. As I showed in
chapter two, the authority of the Old Testament prophets of doom, as
understood by Weber, was an example of this mechanism. By preaching
a message that could explain the misfortunes of Israel (thereby providing
a kind of theodicy), the prophets could help to heal the lack of meaning
which was felt because of the political catastrophes that the nation experienced. But Weber also held that the prophets' religious experiences
could not easily be seen as a function of the social situation or their psychological dispositions. Rather, the view expressed in his texts is that the
prophetic message has its ground in an interaction between the prophets'
ecstatic experiences and their social milieu.[20]

In the modern discussion, the question of whether charismatic phenomena could be said to have some grounding in the charismatic
leader's personal experiences has been widely debated. In his article *The
Social Construction of Charisma*, Roy Wallis argues that charisma "is
essentially a relationship born out of interaction between a leader and his
followers".[21] Wallis studies the sect *The Children of God* and its founder
and charismatic leader Moses David and shows that the charismatic
authority of Moses David is constructed by him and his followers
because it gives advantages to both parties. The leader is recognised as
God's representative, and the followers' self-esteem is heightened by the
fact that they have contact with the divine leader.[22] According to Wallis,
charismatic phenomena are best explained as a rational exchange
between charismatic leaders and their followings.[23]

At the beginning of his article Wallis discusses a certain ambiguity in
Weber's understanding of charisma. According to Wallis's understanding, Weber often seems to hold that charisma is a *personal* quality of an
individual, but at the same time he says that it only exists when it is
recognised by a group of followers. On the basis of his empirical study
of *The Children of God,* Wallis opts for an understanding of charisma
which does not imply that the charismatic leader is seen as having any

[20] In his discussion of the social determination of theology, Pål Repstad has argued for
a similar position. See e.g. his article "Between Idealism and Reductionism", p. 96.
[21] Wallis, Roy: "The Social Construction of Charisma", p. 26.
[22] Wallis, *op.cit.*, p. 35.
[23] Wallis, *op.cit.*, p. 27.

extraordinary personal qualities and claims that such a view makes best sense also of Weber's writings.[24]

A somewhat different view has been taken by, for example, Robin Theobald. Theobald argues that the charisma of the Seventh-Day Adventist prophet Ellen G. White is an important causal factor in the explanation of how a part of the Millerite movement could overcome the cognitive dissonance arising from the fact that Jesus did not return to earth in October 1844, as the prophet William Miller had foretold.[25] According to Theobald, Mrs White often did *not* get anything in exchange for her prophetism, but she continued to be a religious visionary.[26] Theobald's study shows that Mrs White was regarded as a charismatic authority for Seventh-Day Adventism when her prophetic gifts had any relevance for the solution of the movement's problems, and that her charisma was not recognised when it did not have such relevance.[27]

It should be noted that Theobald does not in any way deny that charismatic authority is socially constructed. What separates his view from Wallis's is primarily that he does not understand charisma as a rational exchange. Rather, his view implies that the personal qualities and experiences of the charismatic leader is one important component among others for explaining at least religious charismatic authority. As I see it, Wallis's theory of mutual exchanges does not hold as a clarification of Weber's theory of charisma. It cannot, for example, explain Weber's discussion of genuine prophecy (*echte Prophetie*),[28] or his designation of the founder of Mormonism as a swindler.[29] If Joseph Smith was a swindler, he must be understood as someone who *pretended* to have charisma. But, given the mutual exchange view, this would not be a problem. And what would discriminate between genuine and false prophecy, (in Weber's phenomenological view, not in a substantial theological view), if not that genuine prophets have certain extraordinary experiences which false prophets only pretend to have? Moreover, Wallis's suggestion cannot incorporate Weber's view of the Old Testament prophets as *solitary* ecstatics.

---

[24] Wallis, *op.cit.*, p. 26.

[25] Theobald, Robin: "The Role of Charisma in the Development of Social Movements", p. 95.

[26] Theobald, *op.cit.*, pp. 92-95.

[27] Theobald, *op.cit.*, p. 96.

[28] Weber, Max: "Wissenschaft als Beruf", *MWG I/17*, p. 110.

[29] Weber, Max: *Wirtschaft und Gesellschaft*, p. 140. Strangely, Wallis mentions this passage, but chooses not to take it into serious account. See Wallis, *op.cit.*, p. 26.

It might be that Wallis's theory of charisma is better than Weber's original one, at least as an explanation of *The Children of God*, but it cannot be said that Wallis clarifies *Weber's* texts. Neither can it be said that Wallis's understanding of charisma as a mutual exchange can be applied to all charismatic phenomena, as Theobald's study shows.

In my opinion, Theobald has caught something essential in Weber's view of how charisma relates to the social context. Ellen G. White had certain religious experiences of an extraordinary kind, but she only had charismatic authority when her message was relevant in the context in which her followers lived. Only when charisma helps people to orient themselves in their own social setting, will it be listened to and recognised.

Another way to express this is to say that the content of a charismatic message to quite an extent is formed by the social carriers of the charismatic movement.[30] Different groups have different problems, and will be attracted to different teachings, and inclined to formulate religious teachings as an answer to their own needs. The religious life of a medieval nobleman and crusader was in certain respects very different from the religion of a peasant working on his estate, even if both in some sense related to Jesus and his charisma.[31] In this sense, then, the same (nominally) religion can satisfy different needs.[32]

Batson, Schoenrade and Ventis have in their book *Religion and the Individual* pointed to the relation between social context and religious relevance in a way reminiscent of Weber's. According to them, religion can be seen as a leader of people's lives, but only if it speaks to "problems that are our problems, and speak to them in a style that is our style".[33] The social milieu will thus be the factor which determines what is *recognised* as charisma, but it must not necessarily be the origin and operative cause of the charismatic *phenomenon* as such. This is, I think, the essence of Weber's view.

The Followers

In *Escape from Freedom*, Erich Fromm pointed out that people tend to give up their freedom in exchange for safety and stability provided by a

---

[30] Weber, Max: "Einleitung", *MWG I/19*, pp. 100-101. Bryan Turner has stressed the importance of the carriers for the formation of the charismatic message and critically discussed Weber's view in his *Max Weber,* pp. 58-61.

[31] Weber, Max: *Wirtschaft und Gesellschaft,* pp. 285-290.

[32] See Turner, Bryan: *Max Weber,* p. 62.

[33] Batson, C. Daniel *et al.*: *Religion and the Individual,* p. 372.

strong leader.[34] This kind of leader functions, according to Fromm, as a kind of *magic helper*, who provides protection, help and development for the individual.[35] Perhaps charismatic authority depends on people's need to escape from freedom and individuality? Is charisma necessarily wedded to authoritarian personalities and authoritarian organisations?

In Weber's analysis of charismatic authority, the relation between charisma and authoritarianism does not escape unobserved. In a charismatically founded community, the acceptance of the leader's authority normally is conceived as a duty. Genuine prophets do not ask their disciples to vote on the prophetic mission, but demands obedience.[36] And the disciples obey because the charismatic message provides them with meaning and orientation in life. As I have discussed previously, Weber's own political ideal had some affinities with his scholarly theory of charisma, since Weber advocated a parliamentary democratic system dominated by strong charismatic leaders. *Prima facie,* it would thus not seem as if charisma and charismatic authority is a very attractive phenomenon, because of the link with authoritarianism.

However, modern culture is a culture of polytheism, according to Weber. This implies that there will be several charismatic movements and claims to authority existing alongside each other and competing with each other.[37] This pluralism leads to a process of *democratisation* of charisma. When different charismatic claims compete with each other, it is inevitable that in this process the foundation of the legitimacy of charismatic authority gradually shifts from being *ex sese* to the acceptance of the followers. In the pure type of charisma, the leader is accepted as legitimate *because of* his charisma, but in the democratised version, the leader's charisma is legitimate because it is accepted.[38]

The democratic forms of charisma presuppose that individuals are able to choose among charismatic leaders. In a democratic political milieu, for example, there will be several charismatic politicians, and ultimately it will be up to the electorate who will be elected. A theological interpretation of Weber can, I hold, relate to, and has to elaborate, his theory of the democratisation of charismatic phenomena. Religious founder figures, like Jesus or Mohammed, certainly can be described as charismatic leaders, whose charisma is the ultimate ground for religious

---

[34] Fromm, Erich: *Escape from Freedom,* p. 256.
[35] Fromm, *op.cit.,* p. 174.
[36] Weber, Max: *Wirtschaft und Gesellschaft,* p. 141.
[37] Weber, Max: "Wissenschaft als Beruf", *MWG I/17,* pp. 99-100.
[38] Weber, Max: *Wirtschaft und Gesellschaft,* p. 156.

and theological systems. But their authority, and the interpretation of what it means for today, cannot be established without concern for what is relevant in the modern situation.

Weber's ideas about the role of scientific and scholarly reasoning when judging between views of life can, as I see it, be applied to charismatic phenomena as well as ideological systems. If one should regard the stories about Jesus the charismatic as important in one's life must not be a matter of obedience, but should be a matter of choice, guided at least partly by rational deliberations.

This is not to say, however, that people normally choose if and what charismatic leader they should follow. People who claim to be disciples of Jesus, for example, have not normally made a conscious choice to be his followers, but has been brought up as Christians, been overwhelmed by a religious experience, has a psychological need of a magic helper, or has been forced by political circumstances to accept a Christian world-view. What Weber's texts say is only that it is *in principle* possible to make a choice.

Different Forms of Charisma

Even if Weber did not want to make a *scholarly* distinction between good and bad charisma, and thought that charismatic phenomena had a core of common characteristics, his texts actually imply some distinctions between different forms of charisma. The charisma of an ancient warrior hero, of a founder of a world religion, or a modern politician is not just the same phenomenon. I shall try to spell out some similarities and differences between two major forms of charisma, namely political charisma and religious charisma.[39]

What unites political and religious charisma, ideal-typically, is the strong sense of mission which the charismatic person, be it a religious prophet or a politician, has. The followers normally regard the mission as embodied in the leader's person.[40] Jesus was the embodiment of his mission, and so was Mahatma Gandhi or is Nelson Mandela. But there is also a difference between political charismatic leaders and religious charismatics. Weber and Gunkel saw the charisma of the Old Testament

---

[39] It is important to remember that this discussion centers around *types*, and is not a historical comparative effort. From a strict and limited historical perspective, it might seem anachronistic to compare Old Testament prophets with modern politicians.

[40] Weber, Max: *Wirtschaft und Gesellschaft*, p. 658.

prophets as related to the feeling that they had been standing "in Yahwe's council".[41] The Old Testament prophets saw themselves as sent by God, only preaching what God told them to say (even if Weber points out that there was a state of reflection between religious experience and prophetic preaching). The prophets claimed authority out of religious motives, and were opposed to political control over religion. Political leaders normally are critical of religion claiming to have an authority different from their own, and therefore tend to limit the influence of religion.[42] However, this does not exclude political charismatics from deriving their authority from the Deity, either for pragmatic reasons, or out of true conviction.[43]

Political and religious charisma thus cannot be totally separated, since religious charisma – like the charisma of the Old Testament prophets, can have political consequences, and political charisma can refer to the Deity as its source – as Hitler did – but neither can they be said to be totally similar phenomena. Religious charisma primarily tries to reform or create a spiritual life, directed towards some sort of ultimate reality, while political charisma normally has only a limited goal, like changing the political life of a community, state or region.

In the following, I shall limit my discussion of charisma to the religious type, since Christian theological reflection *prima facie* seems to benefit most from a type of charisma which is oriented towards the ultimate mystery – God, in Christian terms – and not to penultimate things as the political life of a nation. This is not to say that religion and politics has nothing with each other to do. One of the central tenets in this investigation is that they have, but it is equally essential to uphold the distinction between religiously constructed visions of a good life and political action.

Prophets as Carriers of Charisma

In his analyses of prophetism, Weber makes a distinction between *exemplary* and *ethical* prophetism. Ethical prophetism regards the

---

[41] AJ, p. 291. Weber, Max: *Das antike Judentum,* p. 305: *"Jahwes Ratsversammlung"*.

[42] Weber, Max: *Wirtschaft und Gesellschaft,* p. 271.

[43] This was for example the case with Hitler. He sometimes referred to his own political activity as a divine mission. See Schweitzer, Arthur: "Hitler's Dictatorial Charisma", pp. 149-151.

prophet as a means by the help of which a transcendent, personal Deity communicates his will to humanity. The listeners to the prophetic message have, in this type of prophecy, a duty to obey, since the message is from God. Examples of ethical prophets, are, according to Weber, Mohammed or Zarathustra. In exemplary prophetism, the prophet is not seen as the carrier of a divine message, but as a person who by her or his own life conduct shows a way to salvation. There is no *duty* to follow the prophet, but every person has a rational interest to do so, since the prophet shows the true way to salvation. Weber regards the Buddha as an example of an exemplary prophet.[44] Despite the difference between these forms of prophecy, the prophetic revelation provides the prophet and the disciples with a view of life, which makes it possible for them to orient themselves in life in a meaningful and coherent way.[45]

Prophetic revelation, either of an exemplary or an ethical kind, is an important factor in the development of religious views of life, according to Weber, even if he does not hold that every religion has its roots in prophetic revelation.[46] Different kinds of prophetism are, according to Weber, major factors in the development of the world religions, as we meet them today. The Buddha, Mohammed or Jesus were founding figures, whose religious insights and prophetic message were accepted by a group of disciples because they experienced that the message could help them to orient themselves in life. Jesus, the Buddha or Mohammed had answers to questions which were asked in the cultural milieu in which they lived.[47]

If prophecy is an important factor in religion, Weber's distinction between genuine and false prophecy becomes interesting. In *Wissenschaft als Beruf* Weber says that there is no point in trying to establish new religions, if they are not founded on "genuine prophecy" (*echte Prophetie*).[48]

What Weber seems to say is, that it is, from a spiritual point of view, impossible to construct a new religion at the desk in one's study. Religions

---

[44] Weber, Max: *Wirtschaft und Gesellschaft*, p. 273.

[45] Weber, Max: *Wirtschaft und Gesellschaft*, p. 275.

[46] See for example Weber, Max: "Zwischenbetrachtung", *MWG I/19*, pp. 483-484.

[47] Weber's reasoning has an ideal-typical character. Basically it does not matter if Siddharta Gautama really existed, for example. The point is that the insights and message of religious "geniuses", to use Söderblom's expression in *The Nature of Revelation* (e.g. pp. 34, 152), is one of the main causal factors behind religious views of life.

[48] Weber, Max: "Wissenschaft als Beruf", *MWG I/17*, p. 110. See also Weber, Max: "Wahlrecht und Demokratie in Deutschland", *MWG I/15*, p. 375.

can only come about by – phenomenologically speaking – revelation. Without a genuine charismatic message, there is no point in religion. This idea can be understood as having two components: First, the 'prophet' has to be genuine, that is, she or he must have had some sort of experience which can be understood as autonomous. Secondly, people will hardly try to put their faith in what they see as *only* a construction. Such an intellectually constructed view of life cannot function as something which strengthens personality in modern society.

Admittedly, this second component is quite far from what directly can be read from Weber's text, but it seems to me as a reasonable interpretation of what Weber means when he speaks of the bad effects of such constructions. Purely intellectual views of life have not got the same spiritual force as religious views founded in genuine prophecy, and cannot withstand the threat against personality from modern rationalised culture. They thus promote alienation.

But also religious faith grounded in prophetic revelation, such as traditional Christian faith, can promote alienation. In *Wissenschaft als Beruf*, Weber discusses the possibility of the return to the old churches for those who cannot bear the fate of living in modernity. They might escape from modernity into traditional religion, and become alienated in rationalised culture. So religion is no easy way out from the modern dilemma. What seems to be needed is a form of religiosity which is not alienating, but functions as a true leader of people's lives *in*, and not *outside*, modernity.

To make better sense of what it is in genuine prophecy that can provide this spiritual strength, I suggest that we should look back to the sketch of Wilhelm Windelband's philosophy of religion.[49] Windelband describes religion as *transcendent life*, understood as the feeling of belonging to a world of eternal spiritual values. What we call the *holy*, is for Windelband the consciousness of norms, which we experience as making an absolute claim on us. In Windelband's philosophy, the concept of God is a way to express belief in these norms; God is the personalisation of our ultimate values and concerns. Religion is for Windelband a way to see life *sub specie aeternitatis*.[50] In a well-found

---

[49] See chapter two.

[50] This is the title of a philosophical meditation printed in Windelband, Wilhelm: *Präludien*, pp. 333-345. It should be noted that the concept of *'sub specie aeternitatis'* has been used in a similar, albeit not identical, way by Stewart Sutherland, *op.cit*. For a way of reasoning which has much affinity with Windelband's, see especially p. 88: "...the language of theism embodies, offers and protects the possibility of a view of human affairs *sub specie aeternitatis*".

expression, Windelband states that "the light of eternity does not shine in my knowing, but in my conscience".[51] It is impossible to have knowledge – in an ordinary sense – of a transcendent order, but in religion we experience trans-individual life when we have insights concerning how we ought to live our lives.[52]

The prophets in various religious traditions can, if Weber's and Windelband's texts are read together, be understood as persons who have made such insights which, through their teachings, enable us to view our life *sub specie aeternitatis*. This makes them relevant in our lives, but it does not automatically make every prophet equally relevant in every context. For a charismatic message to have authority, it has to answer questions which are asked; it has to be experienced as relevant by the listener. This means that a Christian is entitled to understand her or his religion as laying an absolute claim on her, but it does not make claims to Christian exclusivity trustworthy. Christianity can be seen as the only true religion only if by this is meant *the only true religion for those who are Christians.*

However, it might be asked if it is not probable that charismatic prophets like Jesus or Mohammed thought very differently of their own missions than what this interpretation of the texts of two German professors from the beginning of the 20th century seems to imply. And if the answer is yes, is it really reasonable to understand their religious significance in this way? In discussing this topic, I shall limit my examples to the Christian theological field, since it is in focus in this book.

There is a vast collection of books discussing what Jesus thought of his own mission, and the opinions vary from those who think that he claimed to be the long awaited Messiah or at least had claims of enormous proportions,[53] while others claim that he had quite modest claims for himself,[54] and yet others have thought that we cannot really know anything about what he thought of himself. During the last 20 years, some agreement upon what minimally can be said of Jesus' life and activity has developed. One major scholar in this field of Jesus-research is E. P. Sanders. In the following, I shall build on Sanders's results in my discussion of the historical figure of Jesus, since he seems to provide

---

[51] Windelband, Wilhelm: *Präludien*, p. 342: *"Das Licht der Ewigkeit leuchtet mir nicht im Wissen, sondern im Gewissen."*

[52] Windelband, Wilhelm: *Präludien*, pp. 344-345.

[53] For example Holmberg, *op.cit.*, p. 42.

[54] E.g. Macquarrie, John: *Jesus Christ in Modern Thought*, pp. 38-43; Dunn, James: *Christology in the Making*, p. 60.

a balanced and widely recognised account on what can be seen as *relatively* safe knowledge of Jesus. I do recognise, however, that it is always risky to build on just one scholar. My point is not, however, to hold forth *the* historical Jesus as presented by Sanders, but to engage in a very tentative and hypothetical discussion between academic and Christian theology on the one hand, and New Testament scholarship on the other in order to show how historical scholarship can enrich Christian theology.[55]

Sanders describes Jesus as "a *charismatic and autonomous prophet* [Sanders's italics]; that is, his authority (in his own view and that of his followers) was not mediated by any human organisation, not even by scripture".[56] According to Sanders, Jesus saw himself as God's representative on earth, and in the coming kingdom of God. In Sanders' words, Jesus saw himself as God's "viceroy".[57] Jesus preached the coming of the kingdom of God, which would bring about a fundamental change of values.[58]

Jesus did of course not understand himself and his mission in Weberian terms. His beliefs were deeply embedded in his own cultural milieu. But the Weberian conceptual scheme helps us to interpret him and his activity. The narratives of him and his mission have continued to inspire people ever since. There is something in his life and teachings which has a continuing value for people in their struggle to come to grips with the contingencies of life.

Why does Jesus have this prevailing power, when so many other religious leaders and innovators of his time have not? And why did Christianity prevail, while so many other new religious movements in the first centuries a.D. did not? Of course these are questions which cannot be answered in any compelling way, and such a phenomenon as Christianity has a vast number of causes. It is my belief, however, that one of these causes is that Jesus must have had genuine charisma, in Weber's sense. I agree with John Hick when he concludes that Jesus had a "firm prophetic assurance and charismatic power", grounded in an extraordinary experience of being close to God.[59]

---

[55] For an overview of modern life-of-Jesus research see Evans, Craig A: "Life-of-Jesus Research and the Eclipse of Mythology". Evans points out Sanders as a representative of the contemporary life-of-Jesus research, p. 14. Evans discussion of the miracles of Jesus in the same article are, one might note, highly problematic from a philosophical point of view.

[56] Sanders, Ed Parish: *The Historical Figure of Jesus*, p. 238.

[57] Sanders, *op.cit.*, p. 248.

[58] Sanders, *op.cit.*, p. 196.

[59] Hick, *op.cit.*, p. 18.

Jesus had charisma, and preached a message which seemed to be relevant in the lives of his disciples. Parts of that message are still believed
to be relevant for orientation in life by many. I say parts, because there
are also much in the traditions stemming from Jesus that have lost their
relevance for us, living in other contexts than he did. But, I suggest,
those parts which are held to be relevant, are somehow dependent on the
conviction that they have their ground in autonomous insights. If Christians did not believe that, for example, the insight that God is love somehow 'came' to Jesus, but was invented by him, or by the writers of the
biblical texts, it would loose much of its force.

But Jesus lived a long time ago, and we have not met him. So how
can we be influenced by his charisma and his message? Weber thought
that a genuine charismatic movement, centred around a charismatic
leader, cannot last for a very long time. Charisma is hostile to the everyday world, just because of its 'extraordinary' character. Sooner or later,
economic and social needs will force the charismatically founded community to create a more stable organisation. Not least the death of the
charismatic founder will enhance this development. In Weber's terminology, charisma will inevitably undergo a process of *routinisation*
(*Veralltäglichung*). Genuine charisma is the founding force of many religious and political movements, but when the movement has been established, and especially when it has developed into a mass movement, it
will be transformed into other forms of social organisation, better
equipped to handle everyday affairs.[60]

Since the movement originally rested on a charismatically formed
message, it will develop social forms to remember, transmit and preserve the charisma of the founder. Generally speaking, Weber says that
charisma gets objectified. Objectified charisma is a quality which can be
transferred to other persons or institutions, like the church, or the
ordained ministry.[61] This can be done in several ways, depending on the
character of the movement, and I shall not discuss all the forms that
Weber mentions. Some forms are of special interest, though.

One such form is the charisma of office (*Amtscharisma*). In its ecclesiastical form, this type of charisma is what constitutes the ordained
ministry, and in its most typical form, it is expressed in the doctrine of
the necessity of the *apostolic succession*. By the laying on of hands in
a chain which is assumed (unhistorically, I believe) to go back to the

---

[60] Weber, Max: *Wirtschaft und Gesellschaft*, pp. 142-148.
[61] Weber, Max: *Wirtschaft und Gesellschaft*, p. 671.

historical Jesus' election of the apostles, Jesus' charisma is transferred in an objectified way within the ministry.[62]

Of course, the objectification of charisma can take place in various other ways. Charisma can be objectified as belonging to a certain family,[63] as for example in the Shi'ite idea that the true imams have to belong to the Prophet's family.[64] A Western example is the case of hereditary monarchies, where the charisma is transmitted by primogeniture. Monarchies in modern Europe are of course a mix of legal, traditional and charismatic forms. In some sense, though, the Sovereign has a charismatic quality which is used (except in Sweden) for giving legality to the government's decisions: *le roi règne, mais il ne gouverne pas*, as Weber expresses this phenomenon.[65]

By analogy, one can say that the charisma of Jesus is made present by elements of the Christian traditions, such as the Bible, the sacraments and other religious objects and practices. Jesus' charisma has become routinised and objectified, but it seems reasonable to say that his charisma is the *core* of all these things.[66] By celebrating the eucharist, for example, Christians recall the founder of the religion, and make his charisma present, and in that way Jesus' charisma enables them to view life *sub specie aeternitatis*. The routinisation of charisma should therefore not be lamented *tout court* by religious people; it is because of this process that they still have access to the founder of their faith.[67]

In a religious movement, there are normally more charismatics than the original one. Christianity, for example, has produced charismatics ever since its beginning. The long tradition of mystics, saints and reformers have in different degrees and different forms provided Christians with charismatic resources, sometimes claiming authority for new interpretations of the original charismatic phenomenon. But all these different forms of charisma are to some extent derived from Jesus' charismatic authority. One could say, with Paul Tillich, that the charismatic message and activity of Jesus is an *original revelation,* and the messages

---

[62] Weber, Max: *Wirtschaft und Gesellschaft,* p. 674.

[63] Weber, Max: *Wirtschaft und Gesellschaft,* p. 671.

[64] Esposito, John: *Islam,* p. 43.

[65] Weber, Max: *Wirtschaft und Gesellschaft,* p. 680.

[66] On the concept of a 'charismatic core' see Schluchter, Wolfgang: *Rationalism, Religion and Domination,* p. 405.

[67] Martin Hecht has pointed to the positive effects of routinisation. See his *op.cit.,* p. 231.

of other Christian charismatics are instances of *dependent revelations,* whose authority and religious relevance are dependent on the original.[68]

The existence of dependent revelations and their role as transmitters of the original revelatory events makes it possible to avoid a one-sided accentuation of one person as the fountain of revelation. Given the view presented here, the entire Christian tradition, in all its diversities, can function as revelation. This does not diminish the fact that it is dependent on the original revelation in Jesus for its authority.

A Theological Model of Revelation

The American Catholic theologian Avery Dulles has presented a profound analysis of five different models of revelation in 20th century Christian theology. Dulles's models are ideal-typical constructions of different possible views of revelation in theology, and he never claims to directly describe what any single one theologian thinks. Rather, his ambition is to provide a conceptual apparatus for describing and classifying different views.[69] In applying such a typological model, Dulles has no ambition to do justice to any single theologian; for example, it might seem as a gross simplification of the thinking of Barth and Bultmann to put them together in one model of revelation, if that model was intended to *describe* their positions. What Dulles tries to do, on the other hand, is to formulate a model *on the basis of* certain affinities between various theologians.

On the basis of his classification, Dulles tries to judge the reasonableness of the different models with the help of certain criteria. In this part of the present chapter, I shall present a model of revelation which combines certain features from three of Dulles's models, and argue that this suggestion is compatible with my construction of Weber's view of views of life, modernity and charisma. Before doing this, however, it is necessary to present Dulles's analysis at some length.

Dulles's first model is called *Revelation as Doctrine,* represented in modern theology foremost by Conservative Evangelicalism and Roman Catholic neo-Scholasticism.[70] In this model, revelation is seen as propositional, consisting in clear words proclaimed by God through Scripture,

---

[68] Tillich, Paul: *Systematic Theology I,* p. 126.
[69] Dulles, Avery: *Models of Revelation,* pp. 24-26.
[70] Dulles, *op.cit.,* p. 37.

or in the case of the Roman Catholic variant, through Scripture and tradition.[71]

The second model implies that revelation is seen as *history*, and its main representatives, according to Dulles, are Oscar Cullmann and Wolfhart Pannenberg. According to this view, God reveals himself through his salvific deeds in history, like the resurrection of Jesus, rather than in verbal propositions. The Bible or the church's declarations can then be seen as revelatory only in a derivative sense, as trying to explain what is conveyed in the salvational deeds of God in history.[72]

In the third model, revelation is understood as an *inner awareness* of the Deity. Under this heading, Dulles groups theologians like Schleiermacher, Wilhelm Herrmann, Nathan Söderblom and John Hick.[73] In this model, the distinction between natural and revealed religion becomes blurred, since religion "always arises out of some particular experience of the divine".[74]

For the sake of my argument later on, it might be convenient to look upon the understanding of revelation in Schleiermacher's *On Religion: Speeches to its Cultured Despisers* where he defines 'revelation' in a quite open way:

> What is revelation? Every original and new intuition of the universe is one, and yet all individuals must know best what is original and new for them. And if something of what was original in them is still new for you, then their revelation is also one for you, and I advise you to ponder it well.[75]

According to Schleiermacher, every original insight might be understood as a kind of revelation, and if this insight is relevant in the lives of others, it can be a revelation also for them. To speak of revelation as inner experience does not, if it is done in Schleiermacher's way, necessarily imply the assumption that this experience is caused by or referring to an individual cosmic agent called God. For Schleiermacher, *every*

---

[71] Dulles, *op.cit.*, p. 45. This model has some affinities with what George Lindbeck has called a propositional understanding of religion. See his *The Nature of Doctrine*, p. 16.

[72] Dulles, *op.cit.*, pp. 53, 60-61.

[73] Dulles, *op.cit.*, pp. 69-70.

[74] Dulles, *op.cit.*, pp. 70-71. This model has some affinities with Lindbeck's experiential-expressive way of understanding religion. See *The Nature of Doctrine*, pp. 16-17.

[75] *On Religion*, p. 49. Schleiermacher, Friedrich: *Über Religion*, p. 108: "Was heißt Offenbarung? jede ursprüngliche und neue Anschauung des Universums ist eine, und Jeder muß doch wohl am besten wißen was ihm ursprünglich und neu ist, und wenn etwas von dem, was in ihm ursprünglich war, für Euch noch neu ist, so ist seine Offenbarung auch für Euch eine, und ich will Euch rathen sie wohl zu erwägen." This understanding of revelation has some similarities with Nietzsche's in *Ecce Homo*, p. 72.

new insight is revelatory. This way of understanding revelation is obviously close to Weber's understanding of prophetic charisma. The prophet has, according to Weber, an overwhelming experience, which, when communicated, is received as revelatory by the disciples. Therefore it seems reasonable to conclude that Schleiermacher's view of revelation can be read together with Weber's view on charisma in an effort to develop a model of revelation in modern theology.

Dulles labels the fourth model *Revelation as Dialectical Presence*. In this model, the content of revelation is not located in Scripture or experience, but in God himself, when he speaks forgiveness and judgement to humans. Ultimately Jesus as Judge and Redeemer is the content of revelation. Revelation takes place whenever we encounter God, but Scripture is seen as a witness to revelation, and a vehicle of it. Leading representatives of this model are – despite many and important differences between them – Karl Barth and Rudolf Bultmann.[76]

The fifth and last model understands revelation as a *new awareness*. Revelation according to this model does not give us any new knowledge, but provides us with a new perspective on our life and the world. God, in this model, can be described as "the transcendent dimension of human engagement in creative tasks".[77] One representative of this model is, according to Dulles, Paul Tillich. In his *Systematic Theology*, Tillich understands revelation as "the manifestation of what concerns us ultimately".[78] Revelation, according to Tillich, has two sides, one subjective side and one objective. The subjective side means that revelation takes place in a state of *ecstasy*, understood as an extraordinary state of mind, where the mind "transcends its ordinary situation".[79]

What Tillich seems to mean by this understanding of ecstasy is that the ecstatic person in this state is able to go out of her or his ordinary life-conditions and view life *sub specie aeternitatis*. In an ecstatic revelatory experience the individual is able to go out of the own self, and look upon reality from a new perspective. It should be noted that Tillich warns us from associating the word 'ecstasy' solely with religious sects of dubious character – self-transcendence does not necessarily have to mean psychological overexcitement.[80]

---

[76] Dulles, *op.cit.,* p. 85-88.
[77] Dulles, *op.cit.,* p. 28.
[78] Tillich, Paul: *Systematic Theology I*, p. 110.
[79] Tillich, Paul: *Systematic Theology I*, pp. 111-112, quotation from p. 112.
[80] Tillich, Paul: *Systematic Theology I*, p. 112.

The objective side of revelation is for Tillich *miracle*, or as he prefers to say, *sign-events*. A miracle is an astonishing event which points to the mystery of being and is received in an ecstatic experience. In ecstasy, we can experience certain happenings as happenings which enable us to understand what is of ultimate value and interest for us. The stories about Jesus' healing miracles are examples of witnesses of such happenings, according to Tillich.[81]

In Tillich's view, revelation does not provide us with facts about nature, history or human beings. Revelation gives us a new perspective on reality, it reveals "the mystery of being" to us.[82] Therefore, science and revelation can never conflict, if both are properly understood. Revelation cannot, for example, be the object of historical research, and can therefore not be seriously threatened by history.[83] On this point I will part company with Tillich, as will be evident further on. For the moment, I shall return to Dulles, and his evaluation of the models.

Dulles suggests seven criteria for evaluating different views on revelation:

1. *Faithfulness to the Bible and Christian tradition.* Any view on revelation should be faithful to the biblical witnesses and to what Christians in general have believed.

2. *Internal coherence.* Any theory on revelation must be free from self-contradiction.

3. *Plausibility.* A theory of revelation has to be able to be integrated with what we know about the world apart from revelation, unless it is capable of providing a better explanation than science.

4. *Adequacy to experience.* Any acceptable theory of revelation must be able to provide secular and religious experience with a depth dimension.

5. *Practical fruitfulness.* A view on revelation should produce good fruits, as for example by enhancing moral effort, contribute to the mental health of the believers or strengthen the life of the church.

6. *Theoretical fruitfulness.* Any theory of revelation should be of value for theological reflection and promote the understanding of faith.

---

[81] Tillich, Paul: *Systematic Theology I*, pp. 115-117.
[82] Tillich, Paul: *Systematic Theology I*, p. 129.
[83] Tillich, Paul: *Systematic Theology I*, p. 130.

7. *Value for dialogue*. In a world with so many religious conflicts, a theory of revelation should make dialogue easier, and lessen the potential for conflict.[84]

Judged by these criteria, Dulles finds strengths and weaknesses in every model. The propositional model has some basis in tradition, is internally coherent and is fruitful for the unity of the church. But it can also be judged to be unfaithful to tradition – the Church Fathers were not so 'propositional' in their views –, it ranks low on plausibility, adequacy to experience and fruitfulness for dialogue, for evident reasons.[85]

The second model preserves the church's sense of continuity with the past, and is less authoritarian than the propositional model, according to Dulles. It is also a defence against relativism, since it anchors faith in history and to events which really have occurred. But Dulles finds fault with this model because it fails to do justice to much of the biblical material. What happens to Wisdom literature, for example? And much of the New Testament material is so laden with post-resurrection doctrinal assumptions that it cannot in any direct way be said to be a witness to what 'objectively' has happened in history.[86]

The third model, understanding revelation as an *inner awareness* of the Deity, has one major advantage, according to Dulles. Since revelation is an inner experience of God, and does not contain propositions, it cannot conflict with ordinary knowledge. It thus ranks high on the plausibility scale. But this strength is also a weakness, since this theory implies that there are no religious answers to questions about the origin and final destiny of humanity and the world. There is also a risk that proponents of this model does not take seriously the fact that experience does not occur in a soul which is like a *tabula rasa*, but is formed by the cultural milieu in which it lives.[87]

The *dialectical model* of revelation must be credited for the fact that it renewed revelation as a theological category in a period when it was under severe attack, but it is also very problematic, according to Dulles. The main problem is that if God is utterly transcendent and his revelation can only be accepted in obedient faith, it becomes impossible to distinguish faith from mere fanaticism.[88]

---

[84] The discussion of criteria can be found in Dulles, *op.cit.,* pp. 16-17.
[85] Dulles, *op.cit.,* pp. 46-52.
[86] Dulles, *op.cit.,* pp. 61-63.
[87] Dulles, *op.cit.,* pp. 77-81.
[88] Dulles, *op.cit.,* p. 95.

The last model, understanding revelation as the acquisition of a *new awareness*, ranks high on the scales of plausibility and practical fruitfulness, according to Dulles. This model makes it easier to see the Christian revelation as an imaginative vision for acting towards a more humane world. Seeing revelation as a new awareness, it also avoids conflict with scientific propositions. But the model is also subject to severe criticism by Dulles. His major objection is that it seems to imply a very untraditional understanding of God. Many theologians of this model do not see revelation as coming about by divine intervention, but rather view revelation as an immanent phenomenon in human life.[89] In so doing it risks to lead theology towards relativism.[90]

My own model of revelation will draw upon certain features of Dulles's second, third and fifth models. The first and fourth models does not seem promising, since they easily risk to come into conflict with ordinary knowledge and reason. If the Bible and church traditions necessarily have to be regarded as at least approaching infallibility, or if revelation is just an authoritative word spoken by God, it seems to me difficult to separate true knowledge from illusion, a capacity that is a *sine qua non* for any critical theology.

My suggestion is, that Christian theology can view revelation as *taking place in history, being mediated through inner experience* and *providing a new awareness* or *perspective*. I shall discuss each of these aspects in turn. First, however, I have to say something about Dulles's own perspective on revelation.

Dulles does not want to propose an own, sixth model, but he offers a perspective on all the five models, aiming at preserving what is good in all of them. Revelation, according to him, is always *symbolic mediation*. Dulles holds that revelation always comes to us through symbols. A symbol is a sign which "works mysteriously on the human consciousness so as to suggest more than it can clearly describe or define".[91] One example of such a symbol is the symbol of the *kingdom of God*. This symbol cannot be given any univocal meaning. Rather it is capable of arising in us a vast number of associations and ideas. By so doing, this symbol can bring "the hearer into the very reality borne by the preaching of Jesus".[92]

---

[89] Dulles, *op.cit.,* pp. 110-112.
[90] Dulles, *op.cit.,* p. 123.
[91] Dulles, *op.cit.,* p. 131.
[92] Dulles, *op.cit.,* p. 135.

To a very large extent, I share Dulles's view of revelation as symbolic. To take the above example – the symbol of *the kingdom of God* – symbolism gives us rich opportunities to relate the Christian traditions to our own situations and problems. The symbol 'kingdom of God' has shown its potential to communicate something important to feminist theologians such as for example Elisabeth Schüssler Fiorenza, to classical liberal theologians as Harnack, or to philosophers like Kant.[93] In a Weberian idiom one could say that symbolism is a way to routinise and preserve the religious relevance of charisma.

I cannot follow Dulles, however, when he criticises what he calls a one-sided, projective view of religious symbols. A projective view, according to Dulles, holds that symbols, for example the Christ-symbol, comes not from above through the self-communication of God, but are products of the "creative powers of human religiosity in a particular sociocultural situation".[94] Such a view, according to Dulles, stands in sharp contradiction to Scripture and tradition, and must therefore be discarded by a theologian who wants to take seriously the "distinctive witness...to the God 'who so loved the world that he gave his only Son'".[95]

I can see no compelling reason for giving priority to Dulles's first criterion in evaluating positions on revelation theology. To hold that it is necessary to hold on to belief in God as a transcendent cosmic person because believing otherwise would be contrary to the witness of Scripture, is a possible view, but not necessary. There are at least as good reasons for giving priority to the *plausibility* and *practical fruitfulness* criteria. The problem of theodicy threatens the plausibility of classical theism, as theologians such as Gordon Kaufman and Stewart Sutherland have pointed out. When deciding if one should give priority to Scripture or to the principles of plausibility and practical fruitfulness in theology, it is unavoidable to make a choice which in certain respects can be described as theoretically unguarded. If Scripture is more important than plausibility is a matter of preference, but I would say that a theological enterprise that purports to justify itself in front of the bar of reason and modernity, has to choose plausibility over scripture. Within the frame of

---

[93] Fiorenza, Elisabeth Schüssler: *Jesus: Miriam's Child, Sophia's Prophet*, p. 89. Fiorenza prefers to speak of the *basileia* of God, because she thinks that the word "kingdom" has far too kyriarchal connotations. See her discussion on p. 92, *op.cit.*; Harnack, *op.cit.*, pp. 34-36; Kant, Immanuel: *Religion within the Boundaries of Mere Reason*, p. 128. See also Habichler, Alfred: *Reich Gottes als Thema des Denkens bei Kant*.

[94] Dulles, *op.cit.*, p. 172.

[95] Dulles, *op.cit.*, p. 173.

options that Weber offers, no other alternative is open for a theology which wants to provide orientation in *this* life, rather than in the next.

Scripture and tradition are not fixed entities. What should count as authentic tradition is and has always been widely contested. If tradition would be defined according to the famous dictum of Vincent of Lérins, saying that tradition is that *quod ubique, quod semper et ab omnibus creditum est*, Christianity would be without authentic tradition, since Christianity *never* has been a unified phenomenon. Rather, I would say that Christian tradition and dogma consist of many fragments which can be put together in a vast number of ways. Therefore I would like to suggest a reformulation of Dulles's first criterion:

1_2) A reasonable Christian theological view of revelation should use material from the Christian traditions in such a way that this material in the best way possible fulfil criteria 2-7.

As the observant reader notices, this gives the first criterion a quite different character than Dulles's original one. Instead of saying that a view of revelation should be *true* to a fixed *depositum fidei*, it says that the function of a theory of revelation is to make elements of the Christian tradition *revelatory* in the present context. This could also be expressed in the following way: A reasonable view of revelation should try to order the different fragments in the Christian tradition in a maximally meaningful and relevant manner.

Jesus and Revelation

Finally, the time is ripe for me to present a model of revelation which can be integrated with Weber's thought, as interpreted in this book. As I said, my model will draw upon certain features of Dulles's models two, three and five. Revelation occurs in history, is mediated through religious experience and provides a new perspective on life. I shall try to spell out these three components of my suggestion in turn.

Revelation in History

Christian faith has at its core the charisma of Jesus. It presupposes that Jesus had revelatory insights of a very special kind, and that his insights, or some of them, still can be revelation for us. Jesus is the original revelation of Christian faith. This revelation is passed on to new

generations in different ways, which can be understood as the routinisation of Jesus' charisma. The revelation thus can be said to occur in history, through certain individuals and events. To that extent I am in line
with the theologians of Dulles's second model.

If revelation takes place in history, it is also vulnerable to historical
criticism. Given the acceptance of my model, it would be fatal for Christian faith if Jesus had not existed, for example. In the words of Stewart
Sutherland, some historical beliefs are *internally* related to Christian
faith, and if these beliefs are changed, Christian faith will also change.[96]
This is so because Jesus' charisma is the core of Christianity. Without
the charismatic authority of Jesus, there would be no Christianity. By
connecting itself to history, Christian theology can acquire a certain connection to reality, and the vulnerability of historicity can function as a
check against a false security in theological thinking. The relation
between revelation and history also functions as a guard against a total
theological relativism – there is a limit to what can be said about history.

But, on the other hand, theology and faith are not totally subject to the
whims of historical research. Jesus' charisma has been routinised and
objectified in the Scriptures, prayers and liturgies of the Christian communities, and it has been interpreted through and elaborated by dependent revelations mediated through other charismatic figures during the
history of Christianity. Religious symbols have several layers of meaning which can be interpreted on their own terms, and not only with reference to the historical teachings of Jesus.[97] Their ultimate *authority*,
though, rests with Jesus as the founding figure of Christianity. The symbolic heritage of Christianity thus can be said to establish a *religious*
contact between Jesus and his contemporary disciples.

It is important to note the consequences of this perspective. The view
of Jesus and his ministry presented by historical scholarship can never be
a carrier of religious charisma. The routinisation of charisma takes place
within the religious community, through its rituals, texts and offices. It is
thus not by studying Jesus as a historical phenomenon that the *essence of
Christianity* (cf. Harnack) can be discovered. Rather, it is in the Bible and
in the Christian traditions that Jesus' charismatic authority is located.
This means that the theological use of the Bible, for example, ought to be
directed more to the biblical *text* than to the Bible as a historical source

---

[96] Sutherland, Stewart, *op.cit.*, p. 144.
[97] One such symbol with many layers of meaning is the *eucharist*. See Neville,
Robert: *The Truth of Broken Symbols,* pp. 77-88.

to Jesus' life, since it is the text as we have it that has become the carrier
of charisma. But, at the same time, Christian theology cannot forego of
its connection to the historical figure of Jesus. Most Christians do in fact
regard it as central to their faith to believe in the human being who actually walked around Palestine around the year 30 a. D. Historical scholarship can thus anchor Christian faith in history by providing a corrective
to theological thought, and inspiring it by investigating the origins of
Christian faith. There is thus no need for an either-or perspective; theology can be oriented *both* to the biblical texts *and* to the Bible as historical source within the Weberian scheme as interpreted here.

Revelation through Experience

Sometimes it happens that people have insights which help them to
see what an ideal human life might be. Some of these insights are more
influential than others, and becomes paradigmatic for a view of life.
Christian faith ascribes to the insights of Jesus such a paradigmatic role.
For Christians, it is Jesus who shows that God is love, and that therefore
love and compassion are central organising values in a Christian view of
life. But of course Jesus' insights were formed by his cultural milieu and
therefore many of them have lost their paradigmatic significance, or
acquired meanings which were not intended by him. That must not be
understood as a problem, however. It is not necessary that everything in
Christianity can be attributed to Jesus. Rather, Jesus' charisma is what
enables Christians to view their life *sub specie aeternitatis*. It is by relating their life to God, through Jesus, that Christians can feel themselves
to be subject to an absolute moral obligation.

Christian tradition has been elaborated by various charismatic
insights. Francis of Assisi, Martin Luther or Bridget of Sweden have, for
example, in different ways provided the community of Christians with
revelatory insights, sometimes with a content which hardly can be said
to have been present in the teachings of Jesus. But their insights have
always been *dependent* on the original charismatic authority of Jesus.

But religious experience is not confined to those who Nathan
Söderblom called *geniuses*.[98] Ordinary believers also have religious
experiences. How do they fit into this view of revelation? I would say
that religious experience can be *theologically* understood as being of two

---

[98] Söderblom, Nathan: *The Nature of Revelation,* p. 152.

types: creative experiences and re-creative experiences. A paradigmatic creative experience would be experiences like Jesus' insights, or such revelatory insights like those of the Christian mystics. Re-creative experience would be experiences when people find the accounts of original revelatory insights adequate in their own life. A person who comes to believe in Jesus as God's Son, whose authority anchors her or his life in ultimate reality, has such a re-creative experience of Jesus' charisma. At this point Schleiermacher's definition of revelation should be recalled: Every *new and original intuition of the universe* is revelation, and if you find that this insight provides you with a fresh perspective on your life, it will be revelation also for you.

Revelation and New Awareness

Windelband thought that the concept 'God' is a way to express our feeling of being bound by norms which make an absolute claim on us – God is a personalisation of ultimate values. In a similar manner, Sutherland holds that theistic language enables us to view life *sub specie aeternitatis*. If Jesus is seen as the charismatic prophet who is authoritative for Christian faith, it is Jesus who, in Christianity, shows and symbolises this possibility of a view *sub specie aeternitatis*. The new awareness given in Christian revelation thus can be said to be the sense of being subject to something ultimate, called God.

But many theologies imply that faith can provide Christians with something more than a view *sub specie aeternitatis*, such as ethical or political insights of various kinds. Not the least in liberationist and feminist theologies is this the case. One example of this way of reasoning is Rosemary Radford Ruether's Christology as formulated in *Sexism and God-Talk*. Jesus, although not a feminist, "renews the prophetic vision whereby the Word of God does not validate the existing social and religious hierarchy but speaks on behalf of the marginalised and despised groups of society".[99] According to Ruether, a feminist Christianity has this prophetic character of taking sides with the marginalised and oppressed. Thus Christian revelation can be said to provide a new perspective on reality: The last shall be first and the first last. The prophetic message, according to Ruether, "...aims at a new reality in which hierarchy and dominance are overcome as principles of social relations".[100]

---

[99] Ruether, *op.cit.*, pp. 135-136.
[100] Ruether, *op.cit.*, p. 136.

Christian revelation thus can give believers a new awareness in life in different ways. Basically, this new awareness can be of a *formal* or a *substantial* character. Nothing prevents the new awareness given to be both formal and substantial, but for the sake of clarity I shall distinguish the two types from each other.

A new awareness of formal character would be what Sutherland calls a view *sub specie aeternitatis*. Christian revelation, given this understanding, provides believers with a sense of being under obligation.[101] When we view our life *sub specie aeternitatis,* we see that we ought to seek spiritual ends rather than material ones. Sutherland's primary example of this is a conversation between Thomas More and the young courtier Rich in Robert Bolt's play *A Man for all Seasons.* Rich asks More for advancement, but More suggests that he instead should become a teacher, telling him that "if he becomes a teacher and teaches well, 'You will [k]now it, your pupils will know it, and God will know it'".[102] By adding "and God will know it", no claim about a celestial Being knowing everything that happens is made. Rather, More tries to enable Rich to view his life *sub specie aeternitatis*. Revelation in this formal sense then, is providing us with a perspective which relativises our own ambitions and strivings.

Ruether, on the other hand, sees Jesus as one of many revelators of a prophetic radicalism which enables us to see the hierarchies of our social life in a radically new perspective. For Ruether, Jesus tries to embody a "new humanity of service and mutual empowerment".[103] For her, Jesus does not only provide us with a perspective which relativises our positions, he also offers a substantial value according to which we can orient our action. Revelation thus becomes the offer of accepting new values of a substantial character. Jesus saw in a revelatory manner that the outcast and lowly have the right to be seen as full humans, and if his insight is new and relevant in our context, it is revelation also for us.

Ultimately, revelation gives us an awareness of our finitude and interconnectedness with the much larger web of reality. This holds for both substantial and formal ways of understanding this new awareness. God becomes, in the words of Gordon Kaufman, *a limiting idea.* God relativises us, our ideas and cherished beliefs, and makes us relate to

---

[101] It should be noted that Sutherland discards the concept 'revelation'.

[102] Sutherland, Stewart, *op.cit.,* p. 83. It seems to be a misprint in Sutherlands quote – a 'k' is missing.

[103] Ruether, *op.cit.,* p. 137.

others.[104] God enables us, through Jesus, to see life *sub specie aeterni-tatis,* and God can, through Jesus, make us see caring love for others as an absolute and ultimate ideal for human life. To be bold, I would say that revelation, understood in this way, makes humans to see them-selves as creatures, dependent of the universe for their sustenance, and subject to an absolute moral obligation under God.

It remains to show a bit more fully what consequences for Christian theology a serious dialogue with Weber's texts can have. What will be the consequences for anthropology, for a view of the world, for the understanding of the concept of God and of Christ? And what about the church? Is it possible to construct an ecclesiology which does not fall prey to Weber's assumption that the churches more or less by necessity stand outside modernity? In the next and final chapter I shall address these more substantial theological questions. Of course, it is not possible to construct a full-fledged systematic theology on such a limited space. I restrict myself to sketch the contours of a Christian theology which takes Weber's challenges to theology seriously.

---

[104] Kaufman, Gordon: *In Face of Mystery,* p. 369.

7. CHRISTIAN UTOPIAN REALISM

In the previous chapters I have shown that Weber argues that we need views of life to provide us with values by the help of which we can orient our action in the world. Science gives us knowledge about the world, and our views of life provide us with values which give direction both to scientific work and political acting. If views of life should be able to fulfil these functions without aggravating our possibilities to form our own lives, they must not be in conflict with modern culture and science. Views of life must allow us to accept the world in which we in fact live. At the same time they must show us the directions in which the world might be changed for the better. With a concept borrowed from Anthony Giddens, I have claimed that Weber points out the need for *utopian realism*. Utopian realism implies that we have visions of how a good life would be, but at the same time a good sense of realism so that we are able to distinguish ends from adequate means.[1] Most obviously this can be seen when Weber discusses what characterises a true politician. Weber reminds us that

> Politics is an activity conducted with the head, not with other parts of the body or soul. Yet if politics is to be genuinely human action, rather than some frivolous intellectual game, dedication to it can only be generated and sustained by passion.[2]

Passion is for Weber, in this context, the same as devotion to an ideal. True political acting has, as I have pointed out previously, to be characterised by a combination of charisma and reason. If we want to create a good life, we have to have some idea of what would constitute such a life, and we must be prepared to use the most adequate means we know of to attain our goals, lest our actions will be futile and we be the most to be pitied, to allude on the apostle Paul.

In this chapter I shall sketch the contours of one way of formulating Christian theology in such a way that it can function as an adequate view

---

[1] Giddens, Anthony: *The Consequences of Modernity,* p. 155.
[2] PW p. 353. Weber, Max: "Politik als Beruf", *MWG I/17,* p. 228: "*Politik wird mit dem Kopfe gemacht, nicht mit anderen Teilen des Körpers oder der Seele. Und doch kann die Hingabe an sie, wenn sie nicht ein frivoles intellektuelles Spiel, sondern menschlich echtes Handeln sein soll, nur aus Leidenschaft geboren und gespeist werden.*"

of life in modernity as Weber understands it. I develop a model of a realist utopia which can be tested against the criteria formulated in chapter
five. Of course, this can only be a sketch, and must not be taken as a full
account of a Christian theological system. Central elements within the
Christian doctrinal tradition is therefore absent here. For example, I say
almost nothing about the doctrines of justification or creation. This does
not imply that I think that these topics are uninteresting or irrelevant for
a modern Christian theology. On the contrary, I am, as a Christian, convinced that Christian theology would loose a great deal of its freshness
and importance if it did not reflect upon the topics of reconciliation and
forgiveness, for example. By having faith in a forgiving and merciful
God, Christianity upholds and presents a way of life which is centered
around compassion and love. When I abstain from commenting upon
those topics here, it is because of my limited purpose in this chapter.

Basically, any theology which should be able to be integrated with
Weber's neo-Kantian thought, has to be non-metaphysical and praxis-
oriented in character. A Christian theology of such a kind can, however,
be constructed in various ways. It is, of course, not my task as a scholar
to prescribe how Christians ought to construct their faith, and I do not
claim to have presented *the way* in which Christian theology *ought* to be
formulated. Instead, I have selected four topics which are central in
Christian theological reflection and at the same time in need of revision
if they should be compatible with the non-metaphysical and praxis-oriented kind of theology which Weber's thinking seems to allow for.
These topics are 1) The idea of God, 2) The Son of God, 3) Humanity
and 4) The kingdom of God.

Already the ethymology of the word *theology* gives at hand that
Christian theological reflection cannot dispense with thinking about its
understanding of God. And if a theology purports to the name *Christian*,
it cannot avoid to reflect on the person which Scripture and tradition call
Jesus Christ. The view on humanity also seems to be a central topic for
any Christian theology, since human beings in various ways, according
to most Christian theologies, are the counterparts of God in God's
salvific work. The most controversial topic is, I believe, the concept of
the *kingdom of God*. Since Johannes Weiß criticised the unhistorical use
of the concept in Ritschlian theology, it has been a risky business to
introduce it in theological thinking. It does not become less risky in this
investigation, since the theological model I am proposing has some quite
obvious similarities with the theology of Ritschl. However, I still think
that the use of the concept of the kingdom of God is justified, on the

condition that Weiß recommendation that a proper distinction between the original meanings of the concept and my constructive use of it is upheld.[3]

I have two reasons for discussing the idea of the kingdom of God. First, it seems to be one of the central concepts in the teachings of Jesus as presented by the New Testament, even if it is very difficult to understand exactly what it meant in its original context.[4] Second, it is a concept which is widely used in contemporary praxis-oriented Christian theologies, such as for example in Elisabeth Schüssler Fiorenzas book *Jesus: Miriam's Child, Sophia's Prophet*, where it is argued that the kingdom of God is an emancipatory vision for the well-being of all.[5] Further, in his nowadays classic book *A Theology of Liberation*, Gustavo Gutiérrez described liberation theology as a theology which is especially open to the gift of the kingdom of God.[6] Leonard Hell has argued for the fruitfulness of employing the idea of the kingdom of God as a central theme in modern Roman Catholic theology,[7] and in the Swedish context the theologians Jarl Hemberg, Ragnar Holte and Anders Jeffner have put forth it as one important topic in Christian theology.[8]

More recently, the Norwegian theologian Jan-Olav Henriksen has argued that the concept of the kingdom of God can be seen as pointing out – from a Christian perspective – what is the highest good in human life. According to Henriksen, the eschatological character of the concept does not therefore have to be denied. The idea of God's kingdom is a teleological concept, referring to the Christian hope for a future good order. As such it can also function as a standard against which human actions can be measured.[9] From these deliberations, it seems to me that the concept of the kingdom of God is a rather central concept in Christian theology, used to unify and symbolise the Christian vision of a just

---

[3] Weiß, *op.cit.*, p. 7.

[4] Sanders, *op.cit.*, p. 169.

[5] Fiorenza, *op.cit.*, pp. 89-96. Fiorenza avoids speaking about 'kingdom' beacause of its hierarchical connotations, and recommends the Greek word *basileia* instead. A similar understanding of the kingdom of God can be found in Hopkins, Julie: *Towards a Feminist Christology*, pp. 34-47.

[6] Gutiérrez, Gustavo: *A Theology of Liberation*, p. 15.

[7] Hell, Leonard: *Reich Gottes als Systemidee der Theologie*, pp. 216-226.

[8] Hemberg, Jarl *et al.*: *Människan och Gud*, pp. 154-159. The discussion on the kingdom of God in *Människan och Gud* has been criticised in, for example, Skogar, Björn: "Teologins språk – och livets", p. 47.

[9] Henriksen, Jan-Olav: "Guds rike og etikken – uten sammenheng?", p. 60. Another interesting discussion of the concept of the kingdom of God can be found in Jeanrond, Werner: *Call and Response*, pp. 1-23.

order of things, whatever it may have originally meant in the teachings of Jesus.

A few words should be said about the concepts 'symbol' and 'metaphor', which I use in this chapter. A symbol is, on my usage, a sign which has a vast range of possible meanings. By using a symbol, we suggest something more than what can be said in plain language. The meaning of a symbol cannot, on this usage, be exhausted by just one referent. I use 'metaphor' in a more narrow sense. Metaphor should be understood as a word or an expression which is used unconventionally in order to express something which is not easy or possible to express in plain language. 'God' is, in my usage here, a symbol. It is a word which suggests a wide range of meanings but it has no obvious referent which exhausts all these meanings. Metaphorical talk of God can then be seen as a way to express and point to some of the meanings of the symbol. The metaphor 'father' for God highlights certain aspects of the symbol. When God is called 'The Lord of Hosts', other layers of meaning in the symbol are emphasised. But of course, it is difficult to draw any strict line between symbols and metaphors. A word like God can also be used metaphorically, as when a human being is said to be 'God' for someone. If an expression is a symbol or a metaphor thus depends on the context of use.[10]

The Idea of God

Classical theism claims that God is a person, who is omnipotent, omniscient and wholly good, and who exists externally to the world. This person is assumed to have created the world out of nothing and to still intervene in the course of events when he finds it necessary.[11] This view of God falls prey to several difficulties. Any such theology would be at great risks to fall under the type of theology which Weber says has a *Haben*-character, that is, it claims to have access to evidence-transcendent knowledge.[12]

One problem which any such theology has to handle is of course the problem of theodicy, as I have argued in previous chapters. Classical

---

[10] Basically, I follow Dulles in my use of the concept 'symbol'. I am not as optimistic as he is about the cognitive capacities of Christian theology, however. See his *op.cit.*, pp.131-134.

[11] Macquarrie, John: *In Search of Deity*, pp. 30-42.

[12] Weber, Max: "Wissenschaft als Beruf", *MWG I/17*, pp. 107-108.

theism can also be subjected to the critique of Tillich: does it not reduce God to an object within the world? In his *Systematic Theology*, Paul Tillich argues that it is problematic to say that God exists. If God is said to be a cosmic person who exists in the same way as other objects exist, God is reduced to an object alongside other objects of the world. Such an object can hardly be said to be God, who is supposed to be something else than a part of the universe.[13]

Further, classical theism has been vividly criticised by feminist theologians who have claimed that it reinforces patriarchy.[14] Daphne Hampson has formulated this feminist critique in a very lucid and convincing way:

> It would...seem to be the case that a transcendent monotheism comports ill with the society which feminists seek to create. 'He' [i.e. the God of classical theism, TE] is singularly undemocratic. He is one and alone, separate from the rest of reality. Moreover...the male God appears to reflect something about the male psyche. He is self-sufficient. He allows no competition. (...) He has the first word and the last. Everything is ultimately under 'his' control.[15]

For someone who wants to promote human autonomy and prosperity, the image of God provided by classical theism does not seem very attractive. If God is an agent above the world, who is in charge of history in some way or another, humans cannot be anything else than heteronomous. Respect for human dignity seems, on Hampson's account, to require a thorough revision of the idea of God.

A basic trait in Weber's analysis of the cultural condition of modernity is what he called *polytheism*. Modern Western culture is pluralistic and fragmented, and people tend, metaphorically speaking, to follow

---

[13] Tillich, Paul: *Systematic Theology I*, pp. 235-237. A similar point has been made by John Macquarrie in *In Search of Deity*, pp. 172-173. It might also be possible to interpret §4.4 in Schleiermacher's *Der christliche Glaube* in this direction. Schleiermacher points out that if God exists like an object exists, God would be affected by our doings, since every object is influenced, however slightly, by anything else that happens in the world. This interpretation of Schleiermacher is advocated by Daphne Hampson in her *After Christianity*, pp. 218-219.

[14] E.g. Ruether, *op.cit.*, pp. 70-71. From the perspective of the psychology of religion it has been claimed that the hierarchical model of God in classical theism is an unhealthy form of religion, not least for women. See e.g. Junus, Petra: *Den levande gudinnan*, p. 234.

[15] Hampson, Daphne: *After Christianity*, pp. 128-129. A few pages later, Hampson argues that certain modifications of classical theism, such as process theology, are not much better, because they still leave God pretty much in charge of the world. See p. 134. I would contend that this is likely to hold for any theology which reifies the concept of God.

very different gods. In such a situation, claims to have privileged access
to the creator of the world – a claim that Christians often rise in one
form or another – can be seen as extremely arrogant and unreasonable.
It does certainly not speak in favour of classical theism. In connection to
this it is interesting to note that in Sweden only 15 % and in Europe
taken as a whole only about one third of the population believes in a personal God.[16] Perhaps, one might speculate, the inherent arrogance of
classical theism should be allowed to play some role in the causal explanation of its low plausibility in people's eyes.

It seems safe to say that classical theism is a very problematic position
to hold, even if it might always be possible to solve some of the problems connected to classical theism in a philosophically plausible way.
One example could be Wykstra's principle of CORNEA in regard to the
problem of theodicy. Arguments for a revision of classical theism cannot, in my opinion, be conclusive in character, but are rather based on an
overarching perspective, which finds the problems connected to classical
theism *taken together* as a strong reason for suggesting alternative ways
of talking about God.

A *caveat* is necessary here. The conception of God can be revised in
several ways. Further, these revisions can be justified and argued for in
at least as many ways. I do not here intend to present *one* revisionary
conception and present compelling reasons for my proposal. Rather I
hint at a *direction* in which I think such revisions should go, if they
should be compatible with Weber's understanding of modernity. The
full argument for any such proposal must be presented by the theologian
who wants to put forth a concrete suggestion.

In my view, Gordon Kaufman's constructive theology is a good guide
to how a constructive reinterpretation of the idea of God could be formulated. For Kaufman, Christian theology has as its main task to
explore and interpret the symbol of God. But, due to the modern situation, 'God' cannot be understood along the lines of classical theism.
However, the symbol still has features which a Christian theology cannot dispense with. In Christian faith, according to Kaufman, God is the
object of devotion and loyalty. 'God' is a symbol which presents "us
with a norm or criterion or reality…'an ultimate point of reference'…in
terms of which all else may be assessed and understood".[17] When the
word 'God' is used, it is, according to Kaufman, a way to express "one's

[16] Kallenberg, Kjell *et al.*: *Tro och värderingar i 90-talets Sverige,* p. 60.
[17] Kaufman, Gordon: *In Face of Mystery,* p. 28.

basic commitment in life", rather than a cognitive claim about a transcendent being existing outside the empirical world.[18] To believe in God is thus primarily to commit oneself to a way of life and trust that it has the capacity to handle the contingencies of life, such as death and suffering. The symbol 'God' functions, in Kaufman's opinion, as a unifying element in the Christian view of life:

> ...the symbol "God" presents a focus for orientation which claims to bring true fulfilment and meaning to human life. It sums up, unifies, and represents in a personification what are taken to be the highest and most indispensable human ideals and values, setting these before the minds of men and women in what seems an almost visible standard for measuring human realization, an image/concept capable of attracting devotion and loyalty which can order and continuously transform individuals and societies toward fuller realization of their humanity. To love God is to be wholly devoted to the meanings and values mediated through this image; to serve God's will is to attempt to realize in life and action all that is required by such devotion and love.[19]

Christian faith can be understood as a view of life which, among other things, contains a set of values. These values are organised in a system which is united by the symbol of God. This means that God can be seen, in the Christian context, as the one who represents these values' claim on us. God wants us to be good, just and loving. For Kaufman, the idea of God has, as no other symbol, such a position in Western culture that it is capable of empowering Christian believers to act for the realisation of the ideals contained in Christianity.

To serve God's will is to realise Christian values, according to Kaufman. This implies that Christians ought to try to put their values into concrete existence. Christians cannot be satisfied with invoking God. They also have to strive for the realisation of the kingdom of God. It does not seem unreasonable to interpret Jesus' saying in Mt 7:21 along such lines: "Not everyone who says to me 'Lord, Lord' will enter the kingdom of heaven, but only one who does the will of my Father in heaven".[20] In such a perspective a conflict with the Christian value of love and the necessity of means-end calculating in political action does not have to occur. God wants Christian believers to strive for the realisation of the kingdom of God. This cannot be done by prayer alone, but demands wise political actions. Thus, it has not to be any opposition between Christian faith and rational action.

---

[18] Kaufman, Gordon: *In Face of Mystery,* p. 346.
[19] Kaufman, Gordon: *In Face of Mystery,* pp. 310-311.
[20] Sanders, *op.cit.,* p. 202.

If 'God' is the symbol that holds the Christian view of life together, does not that imply that – ordinarily speaking – God does not exist? I, for my sake, cannot accept such an interpretation. What it implies is rather that Christian theology ought to be exclusively interested in God's revealed activity – the God *pro nobis* – and forego of any speculation concerning the aseity of God. A Christian theology capable of being integrated with Weber's thought can thus heuristically assume God as a kind of *focus imaginarius*, a unifying symbol for the religious concern, as Don Cupitt has put it.[21]

A central question in regard to this approach to the idea of God is how the *reference* of the word 'God' should be understood. The problem of the reference of religious language is the subject of a never-ending debate within the philosophy of religion. I shall not here indulge in an argument for *one* position in that debate, but try to point out what kind of positions that are possible to integrate with Weber's thought. A *conditio sine qua non* for any such position is that it accepts Weber's epistemological restrictionism. For Weber, it is impossible to have any direct access to reality. Reality is always a conceptually and culturally constructed reality. Accordingly, 'God' can not be conceived as a *name* which, so to say, *belongs* to an object or a person. Rather, 'God' must be seen as a conceptual construct which is employed in human discourse in order to organise certain ideas and experiences.

The idea of God must thus be conceived as a *regulative* idea.[22] It can provide a framework for a Christian way of life, understood as a view *sub specie aeternitatis*. In employing God-language, Christian theology says that it conceives of its ideas as expressing something ultimate, which can provide human life with meaning.[23] It might perhaps be possible to envisage this 'ultimate' as somehow existing independently from how humans think of it. It seems, however, impossible to say, in positive terms, what this 'ultimate' would be. A more radical approach could be to say that when theology uses God-language, it expresses the conviction that the values of a Christian view of life are worth striving for, since they *for Christians* express what a true human life is. When, for example, Ritschl defined God as "the will to love" (*Liebeswille*) it can be understood as a way to claim love as the basic and most fundamental value in

---

[21] Cupitt, Don: *Taking Leave of God,* pp. 9-10.

[22] Following Hampson's usage, this can also be said to be a *transcendental idea*. For the concept 'transcendental', se my discussion in chapter five.

[23] For a similar, although not Christian, argument, see Hampson, Daphne: *After Christianity,* pp. 244-253.

human life.[24] 'God', as a regulative idea, provides the framework *sub specie aeternitatis* for such a claim.

Gordon Kaufman has pointed out that God relativises all human ambitions and strivings. This is, I contend, one of the most important functions of a view *sub specie aeternitatis*. In Christian faith, God is absolute and transcendent. Put in front of God, human ambition and human claims must be seen as provisional. By using the concept of God, humans can express a sense of being dependent on something greater than themselves for their sustenance. Devotion to God thus helps humans to find their proper place in creation. God puts our ideologies, our ambitions and strivings in their proper place, as human and temporary.[25]

This is not least important for a praxis-oriented Christian theology, which may risk falling prey to a narrow moralism and self-righteousness. When one understands Christianity as primarily a view of life which provides its adherents with values, it may happen that those who seem to be more successful than others in realising those values are regarded as both better Christians and better human beings. But from a perspective *sub specie aeternitatis* any such glorification of the seemingly virtuous is inadequate, since only God is perfect. Theistic language can, I believe, enable Christianity to uphold the Lutheran insight that a human being who has faith in Christ is *simul iustus et peccator*.[26]

The notion of 'idolatry' is a critical device related to this understanding of God. Our god is, in Tillich's words, that which concerns us ultimately.[27] Whenever something else than the God revealed by Jesus is the ultimate concern of humans who call themselves Christians, they are worshipping an idol. If good reputation is more important than God, it is an idol, and if one's own moral perfection is more important than God, then morality has become an idol too. The symbol of God thus can help Christians to pay attention to the central values of Christianity and function as a kind of limiting idea which, so to say, keeps Christians on the track.[28]

---

[24] Ritschl, Albrecht: *Die christliche Lehre von der Rechtfertigung und Versöhnung III*, p. 260.

[25] Kaufman, Gordon: *In Face of Mystery*, p. 78.

[26] By suggesting this I am not indulging in any speculative niceties about the Christian doctrine of justification. I just want to point out that, for most Christian thinking, no human being can claim to be morally perfect. In my usage here, the formulation 'simul iustus et peccator' should be acceptable to most Christian theologians, irrespective of denominational belongings.

[27] Tillich, *Systematic Theology I*, p. 211.

[28] Kaufman, Gordon: *In Face of Mystery*, p. 369.

What does all this mean for metaphorical talk of God? If God is to be seen as a heuristic assumption or a regulative idea in Christian faith, can we metaphorically say something about God, and how should such God-talk be understood? I would propose that metaphorical talk about God can be understood as the enhancing of certain values. When Sallie McFague wants to remytologise our notion of God by describing God as mother, lover and friend, she points to values in the Christian faith as she understands it.

The form of love connected with God as Mother is, according to McFague, *agapeic*. To talk about God as Mother then becomes to advocate agapeic love, which is a central feature in McFague's understanding of distributive justice.[29] When God is seen as lover, it expresses an erotic form of love which desires its object. McFague, by using the metaphor of God as lover, wants to say that she believes that the world is valuable and deserves our best efforts.[30] And when God is understood as the friend of the world, we are invited to work together for the life of the world.[31] With her metaphors, McFague thus manages to express values which she believes are basic in a Christian view of life. Her metaphors express a vision of destabilising, inclusive and non-hierarchical love in an empowering way that the expressions of such values in plain language could never do, according to her.[32]

Perhaps the above reasoning can provide some clues to how Christian theology ought to handle the doctrine of the Trinity. Trinitarian dogma, implying that God is three persons in one divine essence, is metaphysical speculation without much credibility. As metaphysics, it amounts to little more than a "glorification of an absurdity in numbers", as Tillich has put it.[33] This has, I believe, been shown lucidly by Schleiermacher in his *The Christian Faith*. The problem in the doctrine of the Trinity can be seen in the claim that the three persons are equally divine but at the same time distinct persons. Since Christianity excludes tritheism, the divinity of the persons must consist in their partaking in the one divine essence. Thus what distinguishes them must be something else than the divine essence, as for example their relations.

Now, if the Father begets the Son from eternity, and the Son is eternally begotten, this accounts for the necessary distinction between them.

---

[29] McFague, *op.cit.*, pp. 106-107.
[30] McFague, *op.cit.*, p. 132.
[31] McFague, *op.cit.*, p. 165.
[32] McFague, *op.cit.*, pp. 168-169.
[33] Tillich, Paul: *Systematic Theology III*, p. 291.

But it then follows that the Father eternally has the power to beget the Son, while the Son has no such power. This also holds for the much disputed question on the *filioque*. If the Spirit proceeds from the Father alone, Son and Spirit may be equal, but in a dependent relation to the Father. If the Spirit proceeds from the Father and the Son, the Father and the Son are equal in this respect, but the Son still is not equal to the Father when it comes to begetting. If equality within the Deity also implies equality in power, which at least the *Quiquncue vult* seems to imply, it follows that the Father must be seen as superior to the two other persons.[34] The three persons are thus not equal in traditional Christian doctrine. From these deliberations Schleiermacher concludes that Christian theology has to choose between stressing the unity of God or sincerely face the danger of tritheism.[35]

McFague shows a pragmatic way to conceive of the divine Trinity. Instead of talking about Trinity in an ontological fashion as being a description of the being of God, Trinity can be seen as a way of organising Christian talk of God. McFague's proposal is one example of how Trinitarian language can be useful in theological imaginations. Another, more speculative, way can be that of Kaufman, who sees the doctrine of the three persons as expressing different motifs in the Christian idea of God. The Father thus represents God's transcendence, and the Spirit God's immanence.[36] Trinitarian formulations can be seen as historically given resources which help Christian theologians to express what they conceive as various aspects of God's relation to the world. But as soon as theology conceives of the Trinity as a metaphysical evidence-transcendent claim to know someting about the internal relations within the Deity, it will put itself outside the cultural conditions of modernity, as Weber understood them to be.

The Son of God

Jesus is the founder figure of Christian faith. This can safely be said to be a historical fact, even if scholars endlessly debate exactly how

---

[34] *in hac Trinitate nihil prius aut posterius, nihil maius aut minus, sed totae tres personae coaeternae sibi sunt et coaequales, ita ut per omnia, sicut iam supra dictum est, et unitas in Trinitate, et Trinitas in unitate veneranda sit.* Cited after Persson, Per-Erik: *Kyrkornas bekännelser*, p. 59.
[35] Schleiermacher, Friedrich: *Der christliche Glaube*, §171.
[36] Kaufman, Gordon: *In Face of Mystery*, p. 418.

much of the New Testament material that can be traced back to Jesus, and how much that must be attributed to the theological reflection of the early churches. From a Weberian point of view it is obvious that Jesus was a charismatic leader and a religious prophet who taught with authority. A prophet can, according to Weber, be defined as an individual bearer of charisma who teaches a religious message.[37] If the prophets are successful, they will gather a group of disciples around their teachings. The disciples will, typically, be of different kinds. Some will be more close 'assistants', other more distant followers, which provide the prophet and his assistants with material help, lodging etc.[38] When the prophet dies, the group of followers can be organised in some sort of congregation, which in a routinised way carries the charisma of the prophet. The prophetic movement will then be transformed into a permanent institution.[39]

It seems as Jesus as a prophet follows this typical pattern. According to Sanders, it is fairly safe to say that Jesus in the beginning of his ministry called a small number of disciples. After a while, when his preaching of the kingdom of God got more widely known, a large group of people listened to his message and became followers or at least sympathetic to him.[40] After Jesus' death, his disciples started to organise the followers into congregations and initiated an enormous missionary work. Eventually, the various Christian churches stood forth as institutionalised carriers of Jesus' routinised charisma.

A Christian theology which wants to avoid getting into metaphysics cannot speculate about the eternal Logos sent down from heaven by God the Father and incarnated in Jesus. Such metaphysical speculations demand in one way or another a *sacrificium intellectus*, which would place Christian believers outside the cultural conditions of modernity.[41] Christian faith would be better off discarding such speculation and instead be content with the belief *that* Jesus is the one who originally has revealed the Christian understanding of God. This must not be taken to imply that I think that Jesus got his understanding of God out of nothing. Clearly he was deeply imbedded in Israel's religion. This can account for the continuing importance of the Hebrew Bible in Christianity. If Jesus, the Son of God, regarded for example the prophets of the Hebrew

---

[37] Weber, Max: *Wirtschaft und Gesellschaft*, p. 268.
[38] Weber, Max: *Wirtschaft und Gesellschaft*, p. 275.
[39] Weber, Max: *Wirtschaft und Gesellschaft*, pp. 275-276.
[40] Sanders, *op.cit.*, p. 13.
[41] Weber, Max: "Wissenschaft als Beruf", *MWG I/17*, p. 108.

Bible as revealers of God's will, it seems quite reasonable for Christians to do the same.

Christians know God and God's will through Jesus. Almost all Christians would agree to such an assertion, and it must be the basis for the building of any Christology. But how do Christians know Jesus? That is not a simple matter, and my answer can only be sketchy. Weber points out that when a charismatic prophet dies, her or his charisma, typically, is transferred to other persons, to objects and institutions. This is what has happened with the charisma of Jesus. Christians get to know Jesus through the various institutions of Christianity. They meet Jesus through their upbringing, through worship or through reading the Bible. Jesus' charisma, in routinised form, continues to gather followers. In this perspective, it seems fully adequate to say with the apostle Paul that the church is Christ's body (1 Cor 12:27).

At this point it can be useful to look back to the model of revelation which I suggested in the previous chapter. A central feature of that model is that revelation should be seen as taking place *in history*. Jesus is the founder of Christian faith, and faith is ultimately based on his charismatic authority. But Christians living after his death have not met Jesus in person, but only his charisma in routinised form. The 'Son of God' is present for Christians through the biblical texts and the various Christian traditions, and he cannot be separated from these. The so-called *historical Jesus* will always be a product of historical scholarship, and can hardly be seen as a carrier of religious charisma. But this does not exclude that historical scholarship can function as a *corrective* to the picture of Jesus presented by Christian traditions. Even if we cannot know much about Jesus as a historical person, modern New Testament scholarship as represented by for example Sanders, seems to hold that we at least can know something about him. If Christian faith has some connections with what the historical figure called Jesus from Nazareth said and did, it seems reasonable that Christian theology should listen to and let itself be corrected by what scholars believe they can safely say about him.

But historical scholarship also points out to Christians that there is a deep cultural *and* theological gulf separating them from Jesus. Many things have happened since Jesus wandered around Palestine, and Christian theology has developed on the basis of intellectual reflection and new charismatic revelations. Jesus is the fountain of Christian faith, but his original teaching surely cannot be seen as its total content. As routinised charisma, the church is the body of Jesus Christ and shares in his charismatic authority. Therefore the body of believers must be seen as having the right to develop Christianity so that it can be revelation also for them.

It is in this perspective that different motifs in the Christian churches should be seen. Weber points out that one way to routinise charisma is to transfer it to certain offices (*Amt*). In the churches, this has been done by the institution of holy orders. Priests, pastors, bishops and deacons are, through ordination, bearers of an institutionalised form of charisma.[42] The Bible, as a holy object, is also a bearer of Jesus' charisma, as are various saints and teachers in the churches. S:t Bridget of Sweden or Martin Luther, for example, can be understood as dependent revelators within Christian tradition, depending on the original charisma of Jesus.

Christianity has also developed rites to remember its founding figure. Absolutely central in this respect is Holy Communion. In some form this ritual is based on Jesus' own actions. He did probably have a symbolical last supper with his disciples and perhaps also commanded them to continue to have such ritual meals in remembrance of him (Lk 22:19, 1 Cor 11:25).[43] Holy Communion has, in various ways, been the ritual event in which the charisma of Jesus has been made present to his followers in later days than his own. And as a symbolic act, it also contains some motifs present in Jesus' own teachings.

Robert Cummings Neville claims that the eucharistic symbol contains several layers of meaning. I shall not comment on all these layers, but point out those that relate most clearly to my analysis of the charisma of Jesus. According to Neville, the first level of meaning in the eucharist is that it involves food. The bread and wine points to the crucifixion and resurrection of Jesus. The broken bread and the wine represents the broken body of Jesus on the cross, and in consuming them Christians acknowledge that they are prepared to follow Jesus even when belief in him leads to suffering and death. But food also is nourishment, and thus the eucharistic meal stands for the spiritual nourishment that Jesus provides for his followers. Another layer of meaning in the eucharist is, according to Neville, its character of being a common meal. This signifies that Christians are each others fellows. It also represents Jesus' inclusive table fellowship and thus expresses a basic value of love. The

---

[42] Weber, Max: *Wirtschaft und Gesellschaft*, p. 674. Note that it is the following of the prophet which institutionalises charisma, not the prophet himself. The charisma of office in the Christian church is thus not dependent on the claim that the so called *apostolic succession* can be traced back to Jesus.

[43] Sanders, *op.cit.*, pp. 263-264.

eucharist is further an act of remembrance. According to Neville, everyone who participates in the eucharistic meal "locate themselves in their own particularity as disciples of Jesus".[44]

Basically, the routinisation of charisma is a good thing. If a view of life generated by a charismatic revelation should be able to provide orientation in life to later generations than the one which followed the original prophet, routinisation is inevitable. Charisma is, when it bursts forth, a destabilising and revolutionary phenomenon. As such, it creates new values. But if these values should have any long-term influence on the course of events, they have to be institutionalised.[45] This does not diminish the importance of the charismatic founder of the faith. It is her or his legitimacy which is the base for the institutional forms of charisma, and it can be made tangibly present by dependent charismatic revelations.

In various Christian confessions and creeds, Jesus is called the Son of God. As John Macquarrie aptly states, it is common to regard the confession that one believes that Jesus is God's Son as a *conditio sine qua non* for being a Christian.[46] Since the council of Chalcedon at least, this confession has been connected to metaphysical claims about Jesus having two natures, one human and one divine, which are united in one person. As is the case with the idea of God, so here it is impossible to integrate any metaphysical Christology with Weber's thinking. Accordingly, any theology which purports to be compatible with his thought has to understand Jesus' divine sonship in a revised way.

It might then be good to note that it seems probable that not even the early Christians associated any strong metaphysics with the belief that Jesus was God's Son. It is probable that the title 'Son of God' was used by the early Christians in an adoptionist sense, as God giving Jesus the status of son at his baptism or at the resurrection. In any case, they did not refer to the way Jesus was conceived in his mother's womb.[47] Sanders writes:

---

[44] Neville, *op.cit.*, pp. 78-84. From this overview over Neville's analysis I have excluded symbolic layers which connect the eucharist to the idea of the sacrificial lamb, creation, the idea of an axial age and to cannibalism. This is not done because of any disagreement with Neville on these points, but because those layers of meaning do not seem relevant in this context.

[45] Hecht, *op.cit.*, p. 231.

[46] Macquarrie, John: *Jesus Christ in Modern Thought*, p. 42.

The first followers of Jesus, however, when they started calling him 'Son of God', would have meant something much vaguer: a person standing in a special relationship to God, who chose him to accomplish a task of great importance.[48]

Modern Christian theology could relate to early Christian usages of the title 'Son of God' and use it as a symbolic device for expressing the fundamental importance of Jesus in Christian faith. Being a symbol, 'Son of God' cannot be fully spelled out in plain language. Rather, it sums up all feelings, loyalties, respect, obedience, love etc. that Christians have in regard to Jesus. A Christian theology that follows such a path would both be in reasonable continuity with early Christianity and be more capable of avoiding the *sacrificium intellectus* which threats to undermine the intellectual acceptability of any metaphysical theology.

Humanity

According to Ernst Troeltsch, one of the basic features in the ethics of the gospels is the stress on individualism. For Christianity every individual is a child of God, and as such infinitely valuable. In Jesus' teaching the social belongings of a person have no bearing on her or his relation to God. It is not by being born into a specific social setting that one acquires community with God, according to Jesus as interpreted by Troeltsch, but by a personal decision to respond to God's calling.[49] In phrases reminiscent of Harnack, Troeltsch claims that

> the only distinctions which remain are those which characterize creative personalities of infinite worth, each one of whom must trade with his "pound" to the best of his ability, and in no way whatever may make compromise with the differences and interests of the world. Whether, indeed, in practice this ideal will be generally accepted is another question.[50]

---

[47] Sanders, *op.cit.*, p. 244.

[48] Sanders, *op.cit.*, p. 245. For a similar point, se Dunn, James: *Christology in the Making*, p. 22.

[49] Troeltsch, Ernst: *Die Soziallehren der christlichen Kirchen und Gruppen*, pp. 39-40.

[50] *Social Teachings*, p. 55. Troeltsch, Ernst: *Die Soziallehren der christlichen Kirchen und Gruppen*, pp. 39-40: "*[sind] alle sonstigen Unterschiede ausgelöscht und besteht nurmehr die Differenzierung in die unendlichen Wert besitzenden und ihn durch sittliches Handeln in sich schaffenden Individuen überhaubt, deren jedes mit seinem Pfund nach bestem Vermögen zu wuchern hat und mit den Interessen und Unterschieden der Welt schlechterdings keine Kompromisse schließen darf. Ob freilich bei allen dieses Ideal auch wirklich Platz greifen wird, ist eine andere Frage.*" See Harnack, *op.cit.*, p. 43-45, who speaks of the infinite value of the human soul as one of the central tenets in Jesus' teaching.

This stress on the individual, so characteristic for liberal theology, seems to have some backing by modern New Testament scholarship. Despite the fact that Jesus' message about the kingdom of God was oriented towards the future, he continuously pointed out that the individual's relation to God here and now was very important. Jesus' parenetic teaching, for example, is clearly oriented towards individual behaviour, and not to groups. And when he comforts, he focuses on the feelings of individuals, such as when he tells about the good shepherd who goes looking for one lost sheep and leaves the other ninety-nine behind (Lk 15:3-10).[51]

Weber understood a true human personality as someone who has organised her or his life around a system of consciously chosen values. It is this consciously chosen way of life which principally separates humanity from the animal world, as Weber sees it.[52] This understanding of true humanity is, of course, a normative one, and it is not without its difficulties, since it might lead to an understanding of human dignity which is dependent on the capacity for free and rational action, which not every human being has.[53] But, as Mark Warren's interpretation of Weber's view of democracy has shown, it is not necessary to interpret Weber in this elitistic fashion. Weber's discourse on personality could be understood as saying that every human being *ought* to become an autonomous and rational person to the best of her or his abilities, rather than that the essence of humanity lies in such a capacity. In my view, such an interpretation seems to be easier to accomodate for Christian theology.

If Christianity is to be acceptable with respect to the criterion of full humanisation, it has to embrace human freedom and cultural, ideological and religious pluralism. In this perspective, it is better that a person is a non-Christian by virtue of free choice, than a Christian by unreflected tradition. If Troeltsch, Harnack and Sanders are right in their interpretation of the teachings of Jesus, there seems to be some basis in his teaching for forming a Christian theology which assents to the basic value of the autonomous human personality. But there are strong elements in the Christian tradition which point in the opposite direction. The Christian churches have not – seen in a historical perspective – shown much

---

[51] Sanders, *op.cit.,* p. 193.

[52] Weber, Max: "Roscher und Knies", *GAW,* p. 132, "'Objektivität'", *GAW,* p. 152.

[53] For a developed argument of this kind, directed against Kantian understandings of human dignity, see Sundman, Per: *Human Rights, Justification and Christian Ethics,* pp. 62-63.

appreciation of political liberty or religious pluralism. I cannot dwell upon such topics at any length here, and I shall restrict myself to commenting upon two points.

First, it must not be forgotten that the criterion of humanisation is a *formal* one. It does not imply that it is a *sine qua non* for an acceptable view of life that it contains the value that all other views of life are as good as itself. It is only required that it contains the value that it is better that a person adheres to another view of life by free choice than in an unreflected manner to itself. This also presupposes some kind of appreciation of pluralism and a readiness to exist alongside other views of life in a pluralistic and democratic society. But it is still possible to say that one's own view of life, from its own particular standpoint, is the best one. Christians thus do not have to deny that Jesus is the way, the truth and the life (Jn 14:6a).

Weber's view does not expect views of life to live side by side without conflict. Rather, he assumes that value conflict will be one of the central features of modern society. It is a natural consequence of the freedom of humans to confront the world that they will do that in different ways. Views of life can therefore be in conflict with each other. Indeed one might say in some sense that they *ought* to be in conflict. The question is not conflict as such, but the means with which it is fought. As long as it is fought in a democratic fashion and accepts the other views' right to existence, conflict is even a good thing, since it promotes social dynamics, not least in the political sphere.

Second, a fundamental questioning of Christianity's capacity to promote the autonomy of individuals has been presented by the post-Christian theologian Daphne Hampson. Hampson claims that Christianity, as a religion which finds revelation in history, promotes heteronomy. In her eyes, it is heteronomous to look to history for guidance about what one should think. For women, according to Hampson, this is especially problematic since the history to which Christians look back is patriarchal.[54]

Hampson seems to have a strong case. If one looks back to the history of Christianity and to the historical Jesus for guidance, one looses some of one's autonomy. As Weber points out, charisma is a form of authority. Therefore one can say that Jesus exercises authority or even dominion over Christians. It thus seems as if the concept of revelation itself risks to set Christian theology in conflict with the criterion of humanisation. The question is if this can be avoided. My contention is that it can,

---

[54] Hampson, Daphne: "On Autonomy and Heteronomy", pp. 6-7.

if Weber's views on fragmentation and the democratisation of charisma in modern society is taken into account.

In modern culture, the grounds for acceptance of charismatic authority shifts from the *ex sese* legitimacy of the charismatic leader to the fact that her or his leadership is accepted by the followers. In the political sphere, Weber says, this can be seen in the fact that both charismatic party-leaders in democracies and charismatically founded dictatorships often are legitimated by elections or referendums. Even Napoleon's seizure of power had to be legitimated by a referendum, for example.[55] The same was, *mutatis mutandis,* the case when Hitler came to power in Germany. Weber does not discuss democratic charisma within the religious sphere, but I want to suggest that it can be used there as well.

In modern society, people can pick and choose between views of life. If Christianity in its diversity does not fit you, you can choose to become a Marxist, a Buddhist or something of the sort. Therefore, any claim to revelational authority, whether it comes from Jesus, Mohammed or the Buddha, will be subject to criticism and be compared with other options. The authority of Jesus will, thus, be more dependent than ever on the free acceptance of his followers. Perhaps people living in Europe during the 17th century did not have much of a choice other than to follow Jesus, at least nominally. They were in a sense bereft of their autonomy. But we are not. Jesus can have revelatory authority for people, but only as long as they really can feel that Christian faith is a true revelation also for them. If they no longer find anything revelatory in the message of Jesus, they are free to turn away from him. Daphne Hampson's challenge can thus be met if the social conditions of modernity is taken into full account. It makes, after all, a difference if one freely has chosen a Christian way of life, or if one is compelled to follow it.

Historically, Christian faith has contained both liberating and oppressive views on humanity. The stress on the importance of individual commitment to God contains a seed of individualism and autonomy. But at the same time Christianity has developed into a triumphalist religion, showing very little appreciation of other ways of life and thought. The seed for that strand of the tradition can also be found within the New Testament, as when Jesus in the Gospel of John (14:6b) declares that "No one comes to the Father except through me". A Christian theology that wants to be relevant in modernity as understood by Weber has to focus on the parts of Christian tradition that points to the value of the

---

[55] Weber, Max: *Wirtschaft und Gesellschaft,* pp. 155-156.

individual and her or his free choice, since modernity, in his conception, is inherently pluralistic and fragmented. There can be no return to Christendom, and anyone who tries will inevitably get in the way of the juggernaut of modernity, which crushes anyone who tries to resist it.

The Kingdom of God

An apt summary of the message of Jesus can be found in the Gospel of Mark: "The time is fulfilled, and the kingdom of God has come near; repent, and believe in the good news" (Mk 1:15). The central element in Jesus' teachings was undoubtedly the kingdom of God, or 'the kingdom of heaven' as it is called in the gospel of Matthew.[56] For the sake of convenience, I shall write 'kingdom of God' throughout my text, even if the reference is to Matthew.

In the liberal theology of the nineteenth century, not least in the thought of Albrecht Ritschl, the concept of the kingdom of God was central. Ritschl, it might be recalled from chapter two, conceived of the idea of the kingdom of God as one of two focal points in the ellipse of Christian theology. It was conceived as an ethical concept, understood as a "harmonious, peaceful, and just order on earth", as Walter E. Wyman Jr. has summarised Ritschl's teaching.[57] Albeit with some different accents from Ritschl, the liberal theologians continued to use the idea of the kingdom of God as a moral concept, meaning God's sovereignty over the individual human soul. It was thus a thoroughly noneschatological notion.[58]

Several New Testament scholars around the turn of the century challenged this view of the concept of the kingdom of God and claimed that Jesus thereby meant something eschatological and apocalyptic. Johannes Weiß, for example, contended that the concept of the kingdom in Jesus' teaching was referring to a sudden and destructive worldwide happening, brought about by God.[59] Albert Schweitzer concluded his famous book on the history of Life-of-Jesus research *Von Reimarus zu Wrede* by saying that the historical Jesus would be a total stranger to modern people. If we try to bring him into our theologies we will be disappointed,

---

[56] Sanders, *op.cit.*, p. 169. That the preaching of the coming of God's kingdom was at the centre of Jesus' mission was recognised also by Weiß, *op.cit.*, p. 12.

[57] Wyman, *op.cit.*, p. 259.

[58] Wyman, *op.cit.*, p. 270.

[59] Weiß, *op.cit.*, pp. 61-63.

according to Schweitzer, since his world and our world are totally different. The liberal theology of Ritschl and his contemporaries had tried to modernise Jesus as an ethical teacher and make him alive in the 19th century, but, Schweitzer writes, "he did not stay, but passed by our time and returned to his own".[60]

It has often been claimed that the rediscovery of Jesus as an apocalyptic and eschatological prophet caused a final blow to liberal theology. In his article *The Kingdom of God in Germany,* Walter E. Wyman Jr. shows in a convincing way that such was not the case. One can say that when the liberal theologians met the charismatic eschatological prophet Jesus from Nazareth, they wrestled with him like Jacob wrestled with God at Jabbok, and, like Jacob, they refused to let go of him unless he blessed them (Gen. 32:26). Harnack, for example, was well aware of the eschatological and apocalyptic character of Jesus' teachings about the coming of the kingdom. In his *Das Wesen des Christentums* he distinguished between two poles in the concept of the kingdom of God. The kingdom is, according to Harnack, both an eschatological concept and a moral one. When it comes to modern theology, he concludes that it is only the moral aspect which is of value. But he was fully aware of the fact that Jesus' teaching had also contained an eschatological perspective.[61]

E. P. Sanders has claimed that the idea of the kingdom of God is multilayered within the New Testament. Basically, according to Sanders, there are two meanings of the concept, which could exist side by side in Jewish thought in Jesus' lifetime. On the one hand, the kingdom was believed to exist in heaven, where God reigns completely. On the other hand, the kingdom of God could be thought of as coming in the future of human history. Sanders writes:

> the kingdom of God always exists *there;* in the *future* it will exist *here.* These two meanings are perfectly compatible with each other. Anyone could maintain both at the same time, and in fact millions still do.[62]

Sanders identifies six different categories of sayings about the concept of the kingdom of God within the synoptic gospels. 1) *The kingdom of God is in heaven.* In many of the gospel sayings it is evident that the

---

[60] Schweitzer, Albert: *Von Reimarus zu Wrede,* p. 397: *"...er blieb nicht stehen, sondern ging an unserer Zeit vorüber und kehrte in die seinige zurück".*
[61] Wyman, *op.cit,* pp. 268-269; Harnack, *op.cit.,* pp. 34-35.
[62] Sanders, *op.cit.,* p. 169.

kingdom is seen as something in which people enter after death, provided that they have led an acceptable life in the eyes of the heavenly
judge (Mk 10:17-25, Mt 7:21-23, Lk 18:17-25). 2) *The kingdom of God
is now in heaven, but will be on earth in the future.* God will, when the
time is ripe, bring about a fundamental change in the world's political,
social and economic conditions. 3) *The future coming of the kingdom
will be accompanied by apocalyptic cosmic events.* 4) *Unspecific sayings about the future kingdom.* There are, according to Sanders, many
sayings in the gospels which point out the future character of the kingdom, without thereby specifying what it will mean and how it will come
about. 5) *The kingdom of God is a special realm on earth, consisting of
people dedicated to a godly life.* Sanders acknowledges that there are no
passages within the gospels which specifically talk about two realms,
but he holds it probable that Jesus' sayings about the kingdom being like
a leaven, which leavens the whole loaf (Mt 13:33, Lk 13:20-21) should
be interpreted in that way. Sanders also categorises one passage which
seems to define the kingdom as something existing within the human
soul under this heading, namely: "The kingdom of God is not coming
with things that can be observed; nor will they say, 'Look, here it is!' or
'There it is!' For, in fact, the kingdom of God is among [*or* within] you"
(Lk 17:20b-21). 6) *The kingdom is present here and now, but only in
Jesus' own ministry.*[63]

From Sanders's analysis it is obvious that the kingdom of God is an
elusive concept in Jesus' teaching as presented by the New Testament.
Some traits in it are difficult to reconcile with each other, as for example the saying on the inward character of the kingdom in the gospel of
Luke and the saying about the apocalyptic tribulations which will
accompany the return of the Son of Man in Mark (13:24-27). There
seems to be no way to avoid the conclusion that the gospels as we have
them do not give us a precise picture of what should be meant by the
notion of the kingdom of God, even if it might safely be said that the
preaching of the kingdom was at the centre of Jesus' ministry.

In the popular image, Jesus is often seen as a very fine human being,
who taught a superior ethics. Even if it is a simplification, it might be
said that many liberal theologians of Weber's time shared that view.
New Testament scholarship has shown that Jesus was not at all like that.
He was an eschatological prophet and a miracle worker. This does not,
however, exclude that he had a view on ethical matters.

---

[63] Sanders, *op.cit.*, pp. 171-175.

One interesting trait, which I have already touched upon, is Jesus' high evaluation of each individual. If one takes into account the eschatological perspective which Jesus undoubtedly had, it is striking that he bothered so much with individuals and their relation to God. Sanders points out that one would have expected much more of black and white-judgements from an eschatological prophet. But Jesus cared about the welfare of every human being.[64] In such a perspective, I think Harnack's point that one of the main traits in Jesus' teachings was to stress the infinite value of the human soul is quite reasonable.[65]

For Jesus, the kingdom of God would bring about a radical reversal of values in human life: the last will be first and the first last. On Sanders's interpretation, Jesus demanded extremely high moral standards of his disciples. He advocated ideals corresponding to an ideal world in which Adam and Eve lived before the fall. Jesus pointed to values like love, compassion for all human beings, and solidarity with the poor. The strong stress on solidarity with the lowly is almost painfully felt in the judgement scene in Mt 25:

> "Come, you that are blessed by my Father, inherit the kingdom prepared for you from the foundation of the world; for I was hungry and you gave me food, I was thirsty and you gave me something to drink, I was a stranger and you welcomed me, I was naked and you gave me clothing, I was sick and you took care of me, I was in prison and you visited me." Then the righteous will answer him, "Lord, when was it that we saw you hungry and gave you food, or thirsty and gave you something to drink? And when was it that we saw you a stranger and welcomed you, or naked and gave you clothing? And when was it that we saw you sick or in prison and visited you?" And the king will answer them, "Truly I tell you, just as you did it to one of the least of these who are members of my family, you did it to me." (Mt 25:34b-40)

Despite his ethical rigorism, Jesus understood that people are weak and cannot always live up to such high standards. His yoke is easy and his burden is light, as Sanders reminds us. It is one thing to set up high moral standards, and quite another to believe that everyone should be able to always live up to them. Jesus seems to have been able to discriminate between these two attitudes.[66]

How could modern Christian theology make use of the concept of the kingdom of God? From what I have previously said, it cannot take over

---

[64] Sanders, *op.cit.*, pp. 193-194.
[65] Harnack, *op.cit.*, p. 43-45.
[66] Sanders, *op.cit.*, pp. 196-204.

the crude apocalyptic ideas of Jesus and his contemporaries. Similarly, it cannot indulge in metaphysical speculations about what will happen after death. I think that the liberal theologians saw something important when they used the idea of the kingdom of God as a kind of ethical notion. But theology ignores at its own peril the warning put forth by Weiß: in using the concept 'kingdom of God' it is imperative to be clear about what the historical Jesus reasonably can be assumed to have said and done, and what is novel theological constructions.

If one, with Weber, holds that human beings need utopian visions in order to orient their action in the world, and wants to find a name for a Christian utopia, the notion 'kingdom of God' seems to be the best at hand, just as 'the classless communist society' can be one name for the Marxist utopia. In the New Testament, and in most subsequent Christian theology, the notion 'kingdom of God' represents a future absolutely good state of affairs, even if different theological traditions have understood very different things to be good. When Christians try to unite the values contained in their faith under one umbrella-concept for their utopian vision, 'kingdom of God' seems very apt to fulfil this function. Expressed a bit differently: the 'kingdom of God' can be seen as a symbol for everything that Christians hold to be a valuable state of affairs.

The discovery of the eschatological character of the kingdom in the New Testament provides Christian theology with an important insight. The kingdom might be here in a hidden way, in the hearts of the followers of Jesus. But it has not been realised in history, nor can it ever be. It is a utopia, a vision of a future order, in which life will be at its very best. If the kingdom of God is seen as a symbol for all values that are contained in the Christian vision of a good life, both its moral and its eschatological character can be preserved. The realisation of the kingdom is postponed to the day when God grants it. But in the meantime, Christians can relate to the symbol and derive practical values from it, values which can guide their action in the world and be at least partly realised.

The eschatological character of the kingdom is a guard against the destructive character of many utopian visions. Paul Tillich argues that utopias acquire destructive character when they are conjoined with a progressivism which thinks that the utopian state of life will more or less inevitably be the end-point of history. Utopianism of this character risks to end up in tyranny, as the history of the twentieth century shows us.[67]

---

[67] Tillich, *Systematic Theology III*, p. 354.

If Christian theology holds on to its insight that the kingdom of God cannot be brought about by human action alone, it can stay clear of fanaticism and tyranny.

How does the Christian utopia, symbolised as the kingdom of God, look like? Of course, it is not up to me to prescribe what Christians ought to believe or hope for. But any Christian theology which wants to be anchored in the historical teachings of Jesus would have to reckon with his emphasis on solidarity with the outcast of society. In some way or another, most Christians have done that, I believe, at least in their better moments. The kingdom of God is, in the words of the apostle Paul, "righteousness and peace and joy in the Holy Spirit" (Rom 14:17b). It can be a vision of the just order of things. But it is not here, nor will it ever come within history.

The full realisation of the kingdom can only be brought about by God. God, as a limiting idea, puts a definite end to human over-ambition. This also implies that Christians can be of very different political convictions. They can disagree upon exactly what the symbol of the kingdom of God implies. This must not be seen as a problem, though. Rather it underlines the eschatological character of the kingdom. But they can also disagree on the adequate means for realising the utopian vision. Both a Christian socialist and a Christian liberal can agree upon the same transcendent end: a just order in which human life would be at its best. They sharply disagree on what means are adequate to reach such an end, however. Such disputes can to a certain degree be settled by science, at least when it comes to short-term means-end calculation.

It seems, on Weber's account, imperative to distinguish between vision and political reality. A vision of a perfectly just order will inevitably "encounter the barriers of social logic", as the sociologist David Martin has recently said.[68] If Christians aspire to change the world by political action, and not only by prayer, they have to act within the conditions set up by political and social reality. This implies that they have to act in ways which might seem contrary to their ideals. They might have to advocate military actions in order to restore peace, or to tell half-truths to the media for party-political tactical reasons, even if non-violence and absolute truthfulness are seen as utopian ideals contained in the symbol of the kingdom of God.

Does not this social logic, to use Martin's term, cast the Christian view of life into serious trouble? Christians seem to stand between two

[68] Martin, *op.cit.*, p. 156.

laws – the law of unconditional love and the harsh law of politics –, as Weber's polarised account of the situation in his *Zwischen zwei Gesetzen* might be formulated.[69] The only way to escape from this dilemma seems to be to allow for a proper distinction between utopian visions and practical values, or, to allude on the terminology of Reformation theology, to allow for a distinction between two realms. Seen in this perspective, the role of the Christian churches as organisations cannot be to take part in the day-to-day political activity of the society in which they exist, but to uphold, develop and present a vision of the good life, which can provide the basis for the political acting of Christian individuals. David Martin has pointed out that it is risky for Christian churches to engage in day-to-day politics, since the unavoidable logic of such activities tend to be contrary to the ideals present in the Christian vision. On certain points, when the world's injustice cries out to heaven, it can be politically wise for the churches to engage in concrete political activity – as for example in the battle against apartheid in South Africa – but Christianity contributes best to the political life of society if it "infiltrates visionary images into the everyday accepted reality".[70]

---

[69] Weber, Max: "Zwischen zwei Gesetzen", *MWG I/15*, p. 97.
[70] Martin, *op.cit.*, p. 160.

BIBLIOGRAPHY

Weber's Texts

Das antike Judentum, GARS III. Tübingen: J.C.B. Mohr (Paul Siebeck), 1921.
"Einleitung", *MWG I/19*. Tübingen: J.C.B. Mohr (Paul Siebeck), 1989,
pp. 83-127.
Jugendbriefe. Tübingen: J.C.B. Mohr (Paul Siebeck), 1926.
"'Kirchen' und 'Sekten' in Nordamerika – Eine kirchen- und sozialpolitische
Skizze", *Christliche Welt 20* (1906), pp. 558-562, 577-583.
"Kritische Studien auf dem Gebiet der kulturwissenschaftlichen Logik", *GAW*
(7. Aufl.). Tübingen: J.C.B. Mohr (Paul Siebeck), 1988, pp. 215-290.
Die Lage der Landarbeiter im ostelbischen Deutschland, MWG I/3. Tübingen:
J.C.B. Mohr (Paul Siebeck), 1984.
Letter to Adolf Harnack 5/2 1906, *MWG II/5*. Tübingen: J.C.B. Mohr (Paul
Siebeck), 1990, pp. 32-33.
Letter to Ferdinand Tönnies 19/2 1909, *MWG II/6*. Tübingen: J.C.B. Mohr
(Paul Siebeck), 1994, pp. 63-66.
Letter to Hans Ehrenberg 16/4 1917, *GPS* (1. Aufl.). pp. 469-470.
"Der Nationalstaat und die Volkswirtschaftspolitik" *MWG I/4*. Tübingen:
J.C.B. Mohr (Paul Siebeck), 1993, pp. 543-574.
"Die 'Objektivität' sozialwissenschaftlicher und sozialpolitischer Erkenntnis",
GAW (7. Aufl). Tübingen: J.C.B. Mohr (Paul Siebeck), 1988, pp. 146-214.
"Parlament und Regierung im neugeordneten Deutschland", *MWG I/15*. Tübin-
gen: J.C.B. Mohr (Paul Siebeck), 1984, pp. 432-596.
"Politik als Beruf", *MWG I/17*. Tübingen: J.C.B. Mohr (Paul Siebeck), 1994,
pp. 157-252.
"Die protestantische Ethik und der Geist des Kapitalismus", *GARS I* (2. Aufl).
Tübingen: J.C.B. Mohr (Paul Siebeck), 1922, pp. 17-206.
"Der Reichspräsident", *MWG I/16*. Tübingen: J.C.B. Mohr (Paul Siebeck),
1988, pp. 220-224.
"R. Stammlers 'Überwindung' der materialistischen Geschichtsauffassung",
GAW (7. Aufl.). Tübingen: J.C.B. Mohr (Paul Siebeck), 1988, pp. 291-359.
*Die Römische Agrargeschichte in ihrer Bedeutung für das Staats- und Privat-
recht*, MWG I/2. Tübingen: J.C.B. Mohr (Paul Siebeck), 1986.
"Roscher und Knies und die logischen Probleme der historischen National-
ökonomie", *GAW* (7. Aufl). Tübingen: J.C.B. Mohr (Paul Siebeck), 1988,
pp. 1-145.
"Der Sinn der 'Wertfreiheit' der soziologischen und ökonomischen Wissenschaften", *GAW* (7. Aufl.). Tübingen: J.C.B. Mohr (Paul Siebeck), 1988,
pp. 489-540.
"Der Sozialismus", *MWG I/15*. Tübingen: J.C.B. Mohr (Paul Siebeck), 1984,
pp. 599-633.

"Wahlrecht und Demokratie in Deutschland", *MWG I/15.* Tübingen: J.C.B. Mohr (Paul Siebeck), 1984, pp. 347-396.
Wirtschaft und Gesellschaft (5. Aufl.). Tübingen: J.C.B. Mohr (Paul Siebeck), 1976.
"Wissenschaft als Beruf", *MWG I/17.* Tübingen: J.C.B. Mohr (Paul Siebeck), 1994, pp. 71-111.
"Deutschlands künftige Staatsform", *MWG I/16.* Tübingen: J.C.B. Mohr (Paul Siebeck), 1988, pp. 98-146.
"Zwischenbetrachtung", *MWG I/19.* Tübingen: J.C.B. Mohr (Paul Siebeck), 1989, pp. 479-522.
"Zwischen zwei Gesetzen", *MWG I/15.* Tübingen: J.C.B. Mohr (Paul Siebeck), 1984, pp. 95-98.

Translations of Weber's Texts

Ancient Judaism, eds. Gerth, Hans H. & Martindale, Don. London: Allen & Unwin, 1952.
Ekonomi och samhälle, vol II. Lund: Argos, 1985.
From Max Weber. Essays in Sociology (2nd ed.), eds. Gerth, Hans H. & Mills, C. Wright. London: Routledge, 1991.
The Methodology of the Social Sciences, eds. Shils, Edward A. and Finch, Henry A. New York: The Free Press, 1949.
Political Writings, eds. Lassman, Peter and Speirs, Ronald. Cambridge: Cambridge University Press, 1994.
The Protestant Ethic and the Spirit of Capitalism. London and New York: Routledge, 1992.
Roscher and Knies: The Logical Problems of Historical Economics. New York: The Free Press, 1975.

Literature

AGEVALL, Ola: *A Science of Unique Events. Max Weber's Methodology of the Cultural Sciences.* Uppsala: Uppsala University, Department of Sociology, 1999. *Diss.*
ALDENHOFF, Rita: "Max Weber and the Evangelical-Social Congress", *Max Weber and His Contemporaries,* eds. Mommsen, Wolfgang & Osterhammel, Jürgen. London: Allen & Unwin, 1987, pp. 193-202.
ALSTON, William: "Biblical Criticism and the Resurrection", *The Resurrection. An Interdisciplinary Symposium on the Resurrection of Jesus,* eds. Davis, Stephen T. *et al.* Oxford: Oxford University Press, 1997, pp. 148-183.
– *Perceiving God. The Epistemology of Religious Experience.* Ithaca, New York: Cornell University Press, 1991.
ANDERSSON, Lars: *Alienation. En genomgående linje i Karl Marx' tänkande.* Nora: Nya Doxa, 1997. *Diss.*
BARKER, Martin: "Kant as a Problem for Weber", *British Journal of Sociology 31* (1980), pp. 224-245.

BARR, James: *Fundamentalism* (2ⁿᵈ ed.). London: SCM Press Ltd., 1981.

BATSON, Daniel *et al.*: *Religion and the Individual. A Social-Psychological Perspective*. New York and Oxford: Oxford University Press, 1993.

BAUMGARTEN, Otto: *Meine Lebensgeschichte*. Tübingen: J.C.B. Mohr (Paul Siebeck), 1929.

– *Neue Bahnen. Der Unterricht in der christlichen Religion im Geist der modernen Theologie*. Tübingen und Leipzig: J.C.B. Mohr (Paul Siebeck), 1903.

– *Politik und Moral*. Tübingen: J.C.B. Mohr (Paul Siebeck), 1916.

BEETHAM, David: *Max Weber and the Theory of Modern Politics* (2ⁿᵈ ed.). Cambridge: Polity Press, 1985.

BELLAH, Robert *et al.*: *The Good Society*. New York: Alfred A. Knopf, 1991.

– *Habits of the Heart. Individualism and Commitment in American Life*. Berkeley, Los Angeles and London: University of California Press, 1985.

BENDIX, Reinhard: *Max Weber. An Intellectual Portrait*. London: Methuen & Co. Ltd., 1966.

BENDIX, Reinhard & Roth, Günther: *Scholarship and Partisanship. Essays on Max Weber*. Berkeley, Los Angeles and London: University of California Press, 1971.

BERGER, Alan L.: "Hasidism and Moonism. Charisma in the Counterculture", *Sociological Analysis 41* (1981), pp. 375-390.

BERGER, Peter: "Charisma and Religious Innovation. The Social Location of Israelite Prophecy", *American Sociological Review 28* (1963), pp. 940-950.

BERGSTRÖM, Lars: *Grundbok i värdeteori*. Stockholm: Thales, 1990.

BOLOGH, Roslyn: *Love or Greatness. Max Weber and Masculine Thinking. A Feminist Inquiry*. London: Unwin Hyman, 1990.

BOWKER, John: *Problems of Suffering in Religions of the World*. Cambridge: Cambridge University Press, 1970.

BRUBAKER, Rogers: *The Limits of Rationality. An Essay on the Social and Moral Thought of Max Weber*. London: George Allen & Unwin, 1984.

BRUUN, Hans Henrik: *Science, Values and Politics in Max Weber's Methodology*. Copenhagen: Munksgaard, 1972.

BURGER, Thomas: *Max Weber's Theory of Concept Formation. History, Laws and Ideal Types*. Durham, North Carolina: Duke University Press, 1976.

COAKLEY, Sarah: "Response", *The Resurrection. An Interdisciplinary Symposium on the Resurrection of Jesus,* eds. Davis, Stephen T. *et al.* Oxford: Oxford University Press, 1997, pp. 184-190.

COLLINS, Randall: *Max Weber. A Skeleton Key,* Masters of Social Theory 3. Beverly Hills, London and New Dehli: SAGE Publications, 1986.

CUNEO, Michael: "Values and Meaning: Max Weber's Approach to the Idea of Ultimate Reality and Meaning", *Ultimate Reality and Meaning. Inter-disciplinary Studies in the Philosophy of Understanding* 13/1990, pp. 84-95.

CUPITT, Don: *Taking Leave of God*. London: XPRESS REPRINTS, 1993. Originally published by SCM Press, 1980.

DAVANEY, Sheila Greeve: "Mapping Theologies. An Historicist Guide to Contemporary Theology", *Changing Conversations. Religious Reflection and Cultural Analysis,* eds. Hopkins, Dwight N. & Davaney, Sheila Greeve. New York: Routledge, 1996, pp. 25-41.

DREES, Willem B.: "The Significance of Scientific Images: A Naturalist Stance", *Rethinking Theology and Science. Six Models for the Current Dialogue*, eds. Gregersen, Niels Henrik & van Huyssteen, J. Wentzel. Grand Rapids, Michigan and Cambridge: Eerdmans Publishing Company, 1998, pp. 87-120.

DRESCHER, Hans-Georg: *Ernst Troeltsch. His Life and Work*. Minneapolis: Fortress Press, 1993. Original ed.: *Ernst Troeltsch. Leben und Werk*. Göttingen: Vandenhoeck & Ruprecht, 1991.

DUNN, James: *Christology in the Making. A New Testament Inquiry into the Origins of the Doctrine of the Incarnation*. London: SCM Press Ltd., 1980.

DULLES, Avery: *Models of Revelation* (2nd ed). Maryknoll, New York: Orbis Books, 1992.

ELIAESON, Sven: *Bilden av Max Weber. En studie i samhällsvetenskapens sekularisering*. Stockholm: Norstedts, 1982. *Diss.*

– "Influences on Max Weber's Methodology", *Acta Sociologica 33* (1990), pp. 15-30.

ESPOSITO, John L.: *Islam. The Straight Path* (3rd ed). New York: Oxford University Press, 1998.

EVANS, Craig A.: "Life-of-Jesus Research and the Eclipse of Mythology", *Theological Studies 54* (1993), pp. 3-36.

FIORENZA, Elisabeth Schüssler: *Jesus – Miriam's Child, Sophia's Prophet. Critical Issues in Feminist Christology*. London: SCM Press Ltd., 1995.

FROMM, Erich: *Escape from Freedom*. New York and Toronto: Rinehart & Company, Inc., 1941.

GERMER, Andrea: *Wissenschaft und Leben. Max Webers Antwort auf eine Frage Friedrich Nietzsches*, Kritische Studien zur Geschichtswissenschaft 105. Göttingen: Vandenhoeck & Ruprecht, 1994.

GIDDENS, Anthony: *Capitalism and Modern Social Theory. An Analysis of the Writings of Marx, Durkheim and Max Weber*. Cambridge: Cambridge University Press, 1971.

– *The Consequences of Modernity*. Cambridge: Polity Press, 1990.

– *Politics and Sociology in the Thought of Max Weber*. London: Macmillan Press, 1972.

GLEBE-MØLLER, Jens: *Politisk dogmatik*. Århus: FK-TRYK, 1982.

– *Den teologiske ellipse*. København: Akademisk forlag, 1989.

GOLDMAN, Harvey: *Max Weber and Thomas Mann. Calling and the Shaping of the Self*. Berkeley, Los Angeles and Oxford: University of California Press, 1988.

GOULDNER, Alvin: "Anti-Minotaur: The Myth of a Value-Free Sociology", *The New Sociology. Essays in Social Science and Social Theory in Honor of C. Wright Mills,* ed. Horowitz, Irwing Louis. New York: Oxford University Press, 1964, pp. 196-217.

GRAF, Friedrich Wilhelm: "Einleitung", *Der deutsche Protestantismus um 1900*, eds. Graf, Friedrich Wilhelm and Müller, Hans Martin, Veröffentlichungen der Wissenschaftlichen Gesellschaft für Theologie 9. Gütersloh: Chr. Kaiser/Gütersloher Verlagshaus, 1996, pp. 9-16.

– "The German Theological Sources and Protestant Church Politics", *Weber's Protestant Ethic: Origins, Evidence, Contexts*, eds. Lehmann, Hartmut & Roth, Guenther. Cambridge: Cambridge University Press, 1993, pp. 27-49.

– "Die 'kompetentesten' Gesprächspartner? Implizite theologische Werturteile in Max Webers 'Protestantische Ethik'", *Religionssoziologie um 1900,* eds. Krech, Volkhard and Tyrell, Hartmann, Religion in der Gesellschaft No. 1. Würzburg: Ergon Verlag, 1995, pp. 209-248.

– "Max Weber und die protestantische Theologie seiner Zeit", *Zeitschrift für Religions- und Geistesgeschichte 39* (1987), pp. 122-147.

GRAHAM, Loren R.: *Between Science and Values.* New York: Columbia University Press, 1981.

GRENHOLM, Carl-Henric: *Protestant Work Ethics. A Study of Work Ethical Theories in Contemporary Protestant Theology,* Acta Universitatis Upsaliensis, Uppsala Studies in Social Ethics 15. Uppsala: Almqvist & Wiksell International, 1993.

GRENHOLM, Cristina: *The Old Testament, Christianity and Pluralism,* Beiträge zur Geschichte der biblischen Exegese 33. Tübingen: J.C.B. Mohr (Paul Siebeck), 1996.

– *Romans Interpreted. A Comparative Analysis of the Commentaries of Barth, Nygren, Cranfield and Wilckens on Paul's Epistle to the Romans,* Acta Universitatis Upsaliensis, Studia Doctrinae Christianae Upsaliensia 30. Stockholm: Almqvist & Wiksell International, 1990. *Diss.*

GROSS, Paul, *et al.* (eds.): *The Flight from Science and Reason,* Annals of the New York Academy of Sciences 775. New York, New York: The New York Academy of Sciences, 1996.

GUNKEL, Hermann: *Israel und Babylonien. Der Einfluss Babyloniens auf die israelitische Religion.* Göttingen: Vandenhoeck & Ruprecht, 1903.

– *Die Propheten.* Göttingen: Vandenhoeck & Ruprecht, 1917.

– *Die Religionsgeschichte und die alttestamentliche Wissenschaft.* Berlin-Schöneberg: Protestantischer Schriftenvertrieb, 1910.

– *Was bleibt vom Alten Testament?* Göttingen: Vandenhoeck & Ruprecht, 1916.

GUTIERREZ, Gustavo: *A Theology of Liberation. History, Politics and Salvation.* London: SCM, 1974. Original ed.: *Teologiá de la liberación, Perspectivas.* Lima: CEP, 1971.

HABICHLER, Alfred: *Reich Gottes als Thema des Denkens bei Kant. Entwicklungsgeschichtliche und systematische Studie zur kantischen Reich-Gottes-Idee,* Tübinger Studien zur Theologie und Philosophie 2. Mainz: Mattias Grünewald Verlag, 1991. *Diss.*

HALEY, Peter: "Rudolph Sohm on Charisma", *Journal of Religion 60* (1980), pp. 185-197.

HAMMER, Olav: *På spaning efter helheten. New Age – en ny folktro?* Stockholm: Wahlström & Widstrand, 1998.

HAMPSON, Daphne: *After Christianity.* Valley Forge, PA: Trinity Press, 1996.

– "On Autonomy and Heteronomy", *Swallowing a Fishbone? Feminist Theologians Debate Christianity,* ed. Hampson, Daphne. London: SPCK, 1996.

HANEGRAAF, Wouter J.: *New Age Religion and Western Culture. Esotericism in the Mirror of Secular Thought.* Leiden: E. J. Brill, 1996.

HARE, Richard: *Freedom and Reason.* Oxford: Clarendon Press, 1963.

HARNACK, Adolf: *Das Wesen des Christentums.* Leipzig: J. C. Hinrichs'sche Buchhandlung, 1902.

HECHT, Martin: *Modernität und Bürgerlichkeit. Max Webers Freiheitslehre im Vergleich mit den politischen Ideen von Alexis de Tocqueville und Jean-Jacques Rousseau,* Beiträge zur Politischen Wissenschaft 103. Berlin: Duncker & Humblot, 1998. *Diss.* Freiburg im Breisgau, 1997.

HEELAS, David: *The New Age Movement. The Celebration of the Self and the Sacralization of Modernity.* Oxford: Blackwell, 1996.

HELD, David: *Models of Democracy.* Cambridge: Polity Press, 1987.

HELL, Leonard: *Reich Gottes als Systemidee der Theologie. Historisch-systematische Untersuchungen zum theologischen Werk B. Galuras und F. Brenners,* Tübinger Studien zur Theologie und Philosophie 6. Mainz: Grünewald, 1993.

HEMBERG, Jarl *et al.*: *Människan och Gud. En kristen teologi.* Malmö: Liber förlag, 1982.

HENNIS, Wilhelm: "Personality and Life Orders: Max Weber's Theme", *Max Weber, Rationality and Modernity,* eds. Lash, Scott & Whimster, Sam. London: Allen & Unwin, 1987, pp. 52-74.

HENRIKSEN, Jan-Olav: "Guds rike og etikken – uten sammenheng? Linjer til en systematisk-teologisk rekonstruksjon", *Tidskrift for Teologi og Kirke 69* (1998), pp. 47-63.

HERRMANN, Eberhard: *Erkenntnisansprüche. Eine orientierende erkenntnistheoretische Untersuchung über Fragen zum Verhältnis zwischen Religion und Wissenschaft,* Studia philosophiae religionis 12. Malmö: CWK Gleerup, 1984.

– "Gud, verklighet och den religionsfilosofiska debatten om realism och antirealism", *Svensk teologisk kvartalskrift 75* (1999), pp. 50-63.

– *Meaning and Truth in Religion,* Utrechtse Theologische Reeks 32. Utrecht: Universiteit Utrecht, Faculteit der Godgeleerdheid, 1996.

– "A Pragmatic Approach to Religion and Science", *Rethinking Theology and Science. Six Models for the Current Dialogue,* eds. Gregersen, Niels Henrik and van Huyssteen, J. Wentzel. Grand Rapids, Michigan and Cambridge: Eerdmans Publishing Company, 1998, pp. 121-156.

– *Scientific Theory and Religious Belief. An Essay on the Rationality of Views of Life.* Kampen: Kok Pharos, 1995.

– "The Trouble with Religious Realism", *Studia Theologica 50* (1996), pp. 31-50.

HERRMANN, Wilhelm: "Der Glaube an Gott und die Wissenschaft unserer Zeit", *Gesammelte Aufsätze.* Tübingen: J.C.B. Mohr (Paul Siebeck), 1923, pp. 189-213.

HICK, John: *The Metaphor of God Incarnate.* London: SCM, 1993.

HOLMBERG, Bengt: "Den historiske Jesus. Nutida diskussionsläge och bedömning", *Jesustolkningar i dag,* ed. Hartman, Lars. Stockholm: Verbum, 1995, pp. 23-54.

HOLTE, Ragnar: *Människa, livstolkning, gudstro. Teorier och metoder inom tros- och livsåskådningsvetenskapen.* Bodafors: Doxa, 1984.

HOLSTEIN, Jay A.: "Max Weber and Biblical Scholarship", *Hebrew Union College Annual 46* (1975), pp. 159-179.

HOMAN, Harald: *Gesetz und Wirklichkeit in der Sozialwissenschaften. Vom Methodenstreit zum Positivismusstreit.* Tübingen, 1989. *Diss.*

HONIGSHEIM, Paul: "Max Weber: His Religious and Ethical Background and Development", *Church History 19* (1950), pp. 219-239.

HOPKINS, Julie: *Towards a Feminist Christology. Jesus of Nazareth, European Women and the Christological Crisis.* Kampen: Kok Pharos, 1994.

HUFF, Toby E.: *Max Weber and the Methodology of the Social Sciences.* New Brunswick and London: Transaction Books, 1984.

JASPERS, Karl: *Max Weber. Politiker, Forscher, Philosoph* (2 Aufl.). Bremen: Johs. Storm Verlag, 1946.

JEANROND, Werner: *Call and Response. The Challenge of Christian Life.* Dublin: Gill & Macmillan, 1995.

JEFFNER, Anders: "Att studera livsåskådningar", *Aktuella livsåskådningar I. Existentialism och marxism,* eds. Bråkenhielm, Carl-Reinhold, *et al.*, Lund: Doxa, 1982. pp. 11-21.

– *Att studera människosyn,* Tema T Rapport 21. Linköping: Universitetet i Linköping, 1989.

– *Biology and Religion as Interpreting Patterns of Human Life.* Oxford: Harris Manchester College, 1999.

– *Kriterien christlicher Glaubenslehre. Eine prinzipielle Untersuchung heutiger protestantischer Dogmatik im deutschen Sprachbereich,* Acta Universitatis Upsaliensis, Studia Doctrinae Christianae Upsaliensia 15. Uppsala: Almqvist & Wiksell International, 1976.

– *Theology and Integration. Four Essays in Philosophical Theology,* Acta Universitatis Upsaliensis, Studia Doctrinae Christianae Upsaliensia 28. Stockholm: Almqvist & Wiksell International, 1987.

– *Vägar till teologi* (2 uppl.). Stockholm: Verbum, 1981.

JONSSON, Kjell: *Vid vetandets gräns. Om skiljelinjen mellan naturvetenskap och metafysik i svensk kulturdebatt 1870-1920,* Arkiv Avhandlingsserie 26. Lund, 1987. *Diss.*

JOHANSSON, Sten: "Max Weber", *Sociologiska teorier. Studier i sociologins historia,* ed. Asplund, Johan. Stockholm: Almqvist & Wiksell, 1967, pp. 46-72.

JUNUS, Petra: *Den levande gudinnan. Kvinnoidentitet och religiositet som förändringsprocess.* Nora: Nya Doxa, 1995. *Diss.*, Uppsala.

KANT, Immanuel: *Religion within the Boundaries of Mere Reason and other Writings.* Cambridge: Cambridge University Press, 1998. Originally published in German with the title *Religion innerhalb der Grenzen der bloßen Vernunft,* Königsberg, 1793.

KÄSLER, Dirk: *Max Weber. An Introduction to His Life and Work.* Cambridge: Polity Press, 1988. Original ed.: *Einführung in das Studium Max Webers.* München: C. H. Beck'sche Verlagsbuchhandlung, 1979.

KALLENBERG, Kjell *et al.*: *Tro och värderingar i 90-talets Sverige. Om samspelet livsåskådning, moral och hälsa.* Örebro: Libris, 1996.

KAUFMAN, Gordon: "The Epic of Evolution as a Framework For Human Orientation in Life", *Zygon 32* (1997), pp. 175-188.

– *An Essay on Theological Method* (2nd ed.), American Academy of Religion, Studies in Religion 11. Missoula, Montana: Scholars Press, 1979.

– *In Face of Mystery. A Constructive Theology.* Cambridge, Mass. and London: Harvard University Press, 1993.

– *God – Mystery – Diversity. Christian Theology in a Pluralistic World.* Minneapolis: Fortress Press, 1996.

– "Reconstructing the Concept of God: De-reifying the Anthropomorphisms", *The Making and Remaking of Christian Doctrine. Essays in Honour of*

Maurice Wiles, eds. Coakley, Sarah & Pailin, David. Oxford: Clarendon Press, 1993, pp. 95-115.

KRECH, Volkhard & Wagner, Gerhard: "Wissenschaft als Dämon im Pantheon der Moderne. Eine Notiz zu Max Webers zeitdiagnostischer Verhältnisbestimmung von Wissenschaft und Religion", *Max Webers Wissenschaftslehre. Interpretation und Kritik,* eds. Wagner Gerhard & Zipprian, Heinz. Frankfurt am Main: Suhrkamp, 1994, pp. 755-779.

KYMLICKA, Will: *Contemporary Political Philosophy. An Introduction.* Oxford: Clarendon Press, 1990.

LIEBERSOHN, Harry: *Religion and Industrial Society. The Protestant Social Congress in Wilhelmine Germany,* Transactions of the American Philosophical Society 76. Philadelphia: The American Philosophical Society, 1986.

LINDBECK, George: *The Nature of Doctrine. Religion and Theology in a Postliberal Age.* London: SPCK, 1984.

LINDSKOUG, Kerstin: *Hänförelse och förnuft. Om karisma och rationalitet i Max Webers sociologi.* Lund: Dialog, 1979.

LINTON, Magnus: "Gudsförnekarnas innerliga tro", *Arbetaren 14-15* (1998), pp. 19-23.

LÖWITH, Karl: *Max Weber and Karl Marx,* Controversies in Sociology 12. London: George Allen & Unwin, 1982. Original ed.: "Max Weber und Karl Marx" *Gesammelte Abhandlungen. Zur Kritik der geschichtlichen Existenz.* Stuttgart: Kohlhammer, 1960, pp. 1-67.

LYNN, Jonathan & Jay, Anthony: *Yes Minister.* New York: Harper & Row, 1981.

– *Yes Prime Minister.* London: BBC Books, 1989. First published in two volumes, 1986 and 1987.

MACCULLOCH, John A.: *The Religion of The Ancient Celts.* London: Constable 1991 (1911).

MACINTYRE, Alisdair: *After Virtue. A Study in Moral Theory* (2nd ed.). London: Duckworth, 1985.

MACQUARRIE, John: *In Search of Deity. An Essay in Dialectical Theism.* London: XPRESS REPRINTS, 1993. Originally published by SCM Press, 1984.

– *In Search of Humanity. A Theological and Philosophical Approach.* London: SCM Press, 1982.

– *Jesus Christ in Modern Thought.* London: SCM Press, 1990.

MARTIN, David: *Reflections on Sociology and Theology.* Oxford: Clarendon Press, 1997.

MCFAGUE, Sallie: *Models of God. Theology for an Ecological Nuclear Age.* London: SCM Press,1987.

MCGUIRE, Meredith: *Religion: The Social Context* (2nd ed.). Belmont, California: Wadsworth Publishing Company, 1987.

MARSHALL, Gordon: *Presbyteries and Profits. Calvinism and the Development of Capitalism in Scotland, 1560-1707.* Oxford: Clarendon Press, 1980.

MARX, Karl: *A Contribution to the Critique of Political Economy.* Moscow: Progress Publishers, 1970.

-*Marx/Engels Gesamtausgabe* II:2 (MEGA). Berlin: Dietz Verlag, 1980.

MILBANK, John: *Theology and Social Theory. Beyond Secular Reason.* Oxford: Blackwell, 1990.

MÖLLER, Göran: *Etikens landskap. Etik och kristen livstolkning.* Stockholm: Arena, 1995.

MOMMSEN, Wolfgang: *The Age of Bureaucracy. Perspectives on the Political Sociology of Max Weber.* Oxford: Blackwell, 1974.

– *Max Weber and German Politics 1890-1920.* Chicago and London: The University of Chicago Press, 1984. Original ed.: *Max Weber und die deutsche Politik 1890-1920* (2. Aufl.). Tübingen: J.C.B. Mohr (Paul Siebeck), 1974.

– *The Political and Social Theory of Max Weber.* Cambridge: Polity Press, 1989.

NEVILLE, Robert Cummings: *The Truth of Broken Symbols.* Albany, New York: State University of New York Press, 1996.

NIAL, Tore: *Heinrich Rickerts kunskapsteori med hänsyn till närbesläktade fichteanska tänkesätt.* Göteborg: Elanders Boktryckeri, 1939.

NIETZSCHE, Friedrich: *Ecce Homo. How One Becomes What One Is.* London, Penguin Books, 1992.

NUSSER, Karl-Heinz: *Kausale Prozesse und sinnerfassende Vernunft. Max Webers philosophische Fundierung der Soziologie und der Kulturwissenschaften.* Freiburg & München: Verlag Karl Alber, 1986.

NYGREN, Anders: *Religiöst apriori. Dess filosofiska förutsättningar och teologiska konsekvenser.* Lund: Gleerupska universitetsbokhandeln, 1921.

OAKES, Guy: *Weber and Rickert. Concept Formation in the Cultural Sciences.* Cambridge, Mass. and London: The MIT Press, 1988.

OLLIG, Hans-Ludwig: "Die Religionsphilosophie der Südwestdeutschen Schule", *Materialien zur Neukantianismusdiskussion,* ed. Ollig, Hans-Ludwig. Darmstadt: Wissenschaftliche Buchgesellschaft, 1987, pp. 428-457.

OWEN, David: *Maturity and Modernity. Nietzsche, Weber, Foucault and the Ambivalence of Reason.* London and New York: Routledge, 1994.

PAGE, Edward: *Political Authority and Bureaucratic Power. A Comparative Analysis.* Brighton, Sussex: Wheatsheaf Books Ltd., 1985.

PERSSON, Per Erik: *Kyrkornas bekännelser. Kort handbok i symbolik.* Lund: LiberFörlag, 1970.

REPSTAD, Pål: "Between Idealism and Reductionism. Some Sociological Perspectives on Making Theology", *Religion and Modernity. Modes of Co-existence,* ed. Repstad, Pål. Oslo: Scandinavian University Press, 1996, pp. 91-117.

– "Introduction", *Religion and Modernity. Modes of Co-existence,* ed. Repstad, Pål. Oslo: Scandinavian University Books, 1996, pp. 1-9.

RICHMOND, James: *Ritschl. A Reappraisal. A Study in Systematic Theology.* London: Collins, 1978.

RITSCHL, Albrecht: *Die christliche Lehre von der Rechtfertigung und Versöhnung III* (3. Aufl). Bonn: Adolph Marcus, 1888.

RICKERT, Heinrich: *Der Gegenstand der Erkenntniss. Ein Beitrag zum Problem der philosophischen Transcendenz.* Freiburg im Breisgau: C. A. Wagner, 1892.

– *Die Grenzen der naturwissenschaftlichen Begriffsbildung. Eine logische Einleitung in die historischen Wissenschaften.* Tübingen und Leipzig: J.C.B. Mohr (Paul Siebeck), 1902.

RINGER, Fritz: *The Decline of the German Mandarins. The German Academic Community, 1890-1933.* Cambridge, Mass.: Harvard University Press, 1969.

– *Max Weber's Methodology. The Unification of the Cultural and Social Sciences.* Cambridge, Mass. and London: Harvard University Press, 1997.

RÖSSLER, Dietrich: "Der Subjektivität der Religion", *Otto Baumgarten. Studien zu Leben und Werk,* ed. Steck, Wolfgang. Neumünster: Karl Wacholtz Verlag, 1986, pp. 11-23.

ROWE, William L: "The Problem of Evil and Some Varieties of Atheism", *American Philosophical Quarterly 16* (1979), pp. 335-41.

RUETHER, Rosemary Radford: *Sexism and God-Talk. Toward a Feminist Theology.* Boston: Beacon Press, 1983.

SAMUELSSON, Kurt: *Religion and Economic Action.* London: Heinemann, 1961.

SANDERS, Ed Parish: *The Historical Figure of Jesus.* London: The Penguin Press, 1993.

SCAFF, Lawrence: *Fleeing the Iron Cage. Culture, Politics and Modernity in the Thought of Max Weber.* Berkeley, Los Angeles and London: University of California Press, 1989.

SCHÄFER, Peter & Kippenberg, Hans (eds.): *Envisioning Magic. A Princeton Seminar and Symposium.* Leiden, New York and Köln: Brill, 1997.

SCHALK, Peter: "Twisted Cross. The Religious Nationalism of the German Christians", *Studia Theologica 52* (1998), pp. 69-79.

von SCHELTING, Alexander: *Max Webers Wissenschaftslehre. Das logische Problem der historischen Kulturerkenntnis. Die Grenzen der Soziologie des Wissens.* Tübingen: J.C.B. Mohr (Paul Siebeck), 1934.

SCHLEIERMACHER, Friedrich: *Der christliche Glaube nach den Grundsäzen der evangelischen Kirche im Zusammenhange dargestellt* (2 Aufl.). Halle: Verlag von Otto Hendel, [year of publication missing].

– *On Religion. Speeches to its Cultured Despisers.* Cambridge: Cambridge University Press, 1988. Original ed: *Über die Religion. Reden an die Gebildeten unter ihren Verächtern,* 1799.

– *Über die Religion. Reden an die Gebildeten unter ihren Verächtern.* Berlin: Walter de Gruyter, 1999.

SCHLUCHTER, Wolfgang: *Paradoxes of Modernity. Culture and Conduct in the Theory of Max Weber.* Stanford, California: Stanford University Press, 1996.

– *Rationalism, Religion and Domination. A Weberian Perspective.* Berkeley, Los Angeles and Oxford: University of California Press, 1989. Original eds: *Religion und Lebensführung* (chapters 1-2, 4-8, 11-14). Suhrkamp Verlag, 1988; *Aspekte bürokratischer Herrschaft* (chapters 2-3) 2nd ed. Suhrkamp Verlag, 1985, *Rationalismus der Weltbeherrschung* (chapter 4). Suhrkamp Verlag, 1980.

SCHNÄDELBACH, Herbert: *Philosophy in Germany 1831-1933.* Cambridge: Cambridge University Press, 1984. Original ed.: *Philosophie in Deutschland 1831-1933.* Frankfurt am Main: Suhrkamp, 1983.

SCHROEDER, Ralph: *Max Weber and the Sociology of Culture.* London, Newbury Park, New Dehli: SAGE Publications, 1992.

SCHWEITZER, Albert: *Von Reimarus zu Wrede. Eine Geschichte der Leben-Jesu-Forschung.* Tübingen: J.C.B. Mohr (Paul Siebeck), 1906.

SCHWEITZER, Arthur: "Hitler's Dictatorial Charisma", *Charisma, History and Social Structure,* eds. Glassman, Ronald M. & Swatos, William H. Jr.,

Contributions in Sociology 58. New York, Westport, Connecticut, London: Greenwood Press, 1986, pp. 147-162.

SCHWENTGER, Wolfgang: "Western Impact and Asian Values in Japan's Modernization: A Weberian Critique", *Max Weber, Democracy and Modernization*, ed. Schroeder, Ralph. Houndmills, Basingstoke and London: Macmillan Press Ltd., 1998, pp. 166-181.

SEGADY, Thomas: *Values, Neo-Kantianism and the Development of Weberian Methodology*. New York: Peter Lang, 1987.

SIGURDSON, Ola: *Karl Barth som den andre. En studie i den svenska teologins Barthreception*. Eslöv: Symposion, 1996. *Diss.*

SKOGAR, Björn: "Teologins språk – och livets. Några dominerande teologiska profiler under svenskt 1900-tal", *Modern svensk teologi. Strömningar och perspektivskiften under 1900-talet*, eds. Lindberg, Lars & Nilsson, Gert. Stockholm: Verbum, 1999, pp. 17-68.

– *Viva vox och den akademiska religionen. Ett bidrag till tidiga 1900-talets svenska teologihistoria*. Stockholm: Symposion Graduale, 1993. *Diss.*

SOCKNESS, Brent: *Against False Apologetics. Wilhelm Herrmann and Ernst Troeltsch in Conflict,* Beiträge zur historischen Theologie 105. Tübingen: J.C.B. Mohr (Paul Siebeck), 1998.

SLAGSTAD, Rune: "Liberal Constitutionalism and Its Critics: Carl Schmitt and Max Weber", *Constitutionalism and Democracy,* eds. Elster, Jon and Slagstad, Rune. Cambridge: Cambridge University Press, 1988, pp. 103-129.

SÖDERBLOM, Nathan: *The Nature of Revelation*. New York: Oxford University Press, 1933. Original ed.: *Uppenbarelsereligion* (2 uppl.), 1930.

SOHM, Rudolph: *Kirchenrecht,* Bd 1: *Die geschichtlichen Grundlagen.* München und Leipzig: Duncker & Humblot, 1923 (1892).

STENMARK, Mikael: "Science and Ideology", *Ideology in Science and Economics,* Studies in Ethics and Economics 6, eds. Grenholm, Carl-Henric & Helgesson, Gert. Uppsala: Uppsala University, Department of Theology, 1999, pp. 11-36.

– *Rationality in Science, Religion and Everyday Life. A Critical Evaluation of Four Models of Rationality*. Notre Dame, Indiana: University of Notre Dame Press, 1995.

STRAUSS, Leo: *Natural Right and History*. Chicago: The University of Chicago Press, 1953.

SUNDMAN, Per: "The Good Manager – A Moral Manager?", *Ethics, Economics and Feminism,* Studies in Ethics and Economics 3, eds. Grenholm, Carl-Henric & Helgesson, Gert. Uppsala: Uppsala University, Department of Theology, 1998, pp. 41-50.

– *Human Rights, Justification and Christian Ethics,* Acta Universitatis Upsaliensis, Uppsala Studies in Social Ethics 18. Uppsala: Almqvist & Wiksell, 1996. Diss.

SUTHERLAND, Stewart: *God, Jesus and Belief. The Legacy of Theism*. Oxford: Blackwell, 1984.

SWEDBERG, Richard: *Max Weber and the Idea of Economic Sociology*. Princeton, New Jersey: Princeton University Press, 1998.

– *Max Weber's Handbook in Economics: Grundriss der Sozialöknomik,* Work – Organization – Economy, Working Paper Series No. 51. Stockholm: Stockholm University, Department of Sociology, 1997.

TENBRUCK, Friedrich: "The Problem of Thematic Unity in the Works of Max Weber", *Max Weber. Critical Assessments*, ed. Hamilton, Peter. London and New York: Routledge, 1991, pp. 232-263. Originally published in *British Journal of Sociology 31* (1980).

TILLICH, Paul: *Systematic Theology* (vols. 1-3). London: XPRESS REPRINTS, 1997. Originally published 1951, 1957, 1963, respectively.

THEOBALD, Robin: "The Role of Charisma in the Development of Social Movements", *Archives de Sciences Sociales des Religions 49* (1980), pp. 83-100.

THERBORN, Göran: *European Modernity and Beyond. The Trajectory of European Societies 1945-2000*. London, Thousand Oaks, New Dehli: SAGE Publications, 1995.

TROELTSCH, Ernst: "Zur Frage des Religiösen Apriori", *Gesammelte Schriften II*. Tübingen: J.C.B. Mohr (Paul Siebeck), 1913, pp. 754-768.

– "Ueber historische und dogmatische Methode in der Theologie", *Gesammelte Schriften II*. Tübingen: J.C.B. Mohr (Paul Siebeck), 1913, pp. 729-753.

– *The Social Teaching of the Christian Churches*. Louisville, Kentucky: Westminster/John Knox Press, 1992 (1931). Original ed: *Die Soziallehren der christlichen Kirchen und Gruppen,* Gesammelte Schriften I. Tübingen: J.C.B. Mohr (Paul Siebeck), 1912.

– *Die Soziallehren der christlichen Kirchen und Gruppen,* Gesammelte Schriften I. Tübingen: J.C.B. Mohr (Paul Siebeck), 1912.

– "Das Wesen des Modernen Geistes", *Gesammelte Schriften IV*. Tübingen: J.C.B. Mohr (Paul Siebeck), 1925, pp. 297-338.

TURNER, Bryan: *Max Weber. From History to Modernity*. London and New York: Routledge, 1992.

TURNER, Stephen: "A Weber for the Right-Thinking", *International Journal of Politics, Culture and Society 12* (1998), pp. 253-275.

TYRELL, Hartmann: "Religion und 'intellektuelle' Redlichkeit: zur Tragödie der Religion bei Max Weber und Friedrich Nietzsche", *Sociologia Internationalis 29* (1991), pp. 159-177.

– "'Das Religiöse' in Max Webers Religionssoziologie", *Saeculum 43* (1992), pp. 172-230.

WAGNER, Gerhard & Zipprian, Heinz: "Methodologie und Ontologie: Zum Problem kausaler Erklärung bei Max Weber", *Zeitschrift für Soziologie 14* (1985), pp. 115-130.

WALLIS, Roy: "The Social Construction of Charisma", *Social Compass 29* (1982), pp. 25-39.

WARREN, Mark: "Max Weber's Liberalism for a Nietzschean World", *American Political Science Review 82* (1988), pp. 31-50.

WEBER, Marianne: *Max Weber. A Biography*. New Brunswick and London: Transaction Publishers, 1988. Original ed: *Max Weber. Ein Lebensbild.* Tübingen: J.C.B. Mohr (Paul Siebeck), 1926.

WEDBERG, Anders: *Filosofins historia. Antiken och medeltiden* (2nd revised ed.). Stockholm: Bonniers, 1968.

WEHLER, Hans-Ulrich: *The German Empire 1871-1918*. Oxford: Berg Publishers Ltd., 1985. Original ed.: *Das deutsche Kaiserreich 1871-1918*. Göttingen: Vandenhoek & Ruprecht, 1973.

WEIß, Johannes: *Die Predigt Jesu vom Reiche Gottes*. Göttingen: Vandenhoeck & Ruprecht, 1892.

WILES, Maurice: *The Remaking of Christian Doctrine*. London: SCM Press Ltd., 1974.
– *What is Theology?* London, Oxford, New York: Oxford University Press, 1976.
WILLEY, Thomas E.: *Back to Kant. The Revival of Kantianism in German Social and Historical Thought, 1860-1914*. Detroit: Wayne State University Press, 1978.
WINDELBAND, Wilhelm: *Präludien, Bd 2. Aufsätze und Reden zur Philosophie und ihrer Geschichte* (9. Aufl). Tübingen: J.C.B. Mohr (Paul Siebeck), 1924.
von WRIGHT, Georg Henrik: *Explanation and Understanding*. London: Routledge, 1971.
WYKSTRA, Stephen J.: "The Humean Obstacle to Evidential Arguments from Suffering. On Avoiding the Evils of Appearance", *International Journal for Philosophy of Religion 16* (1984), pp. 73-93.
WYMAN, Walter E. Jr.: "The Kingdom of God in Germany. From Ritschl to Troeltsch", *Revisioning the Past. Prospects in Historical Theology*, eds. Engel, Mary Potter & Wyman, Walter E. Jr. Minneapolis: Fortress, 1992, pp. 257-277.
YOUNG, Iris Marion: *Justice and the Politics of Difference*. Princeton, New Yersey: Princeton University Press, 1990.
ZINGERLE, Arnold: *Max Webers historische Soziologie. Aspekte und Materialien zur Wirkungsgeschichte*. Darmstadt: Wissenschaftliche Buchgesellschaft, 1981.

Biblical quotations are taken from *The New Revised Standard Version* (Anglicized edition). Oxford: Oxford University Press, 1995.

DATE DUE

#45220 Highsmith Inc. 1-800-558-2110

PRINTED ON PERMANENT PAPER • IMPRIME SUR PAPIER PERMANENT • GEDRUKT OP DUURZAAM PAPIER - ISO 9706

ORIENTALISTE, KLEIN DALENSTRAAT 42, B-3020 HERENT